KU-036-119

INVISIBLE WALLS

A Journalist in Search of Her Life

HELLA PICK

W&N

WEIDENFELD & NICOLSON

First published in Great Britain in 2021 by Weidenfeld & Nicolson
This paperback edition published in 2022 by Weidenfeld & Nicolson
an imprint of The Orion Publishing Group Ltd
Carmelite House, 50 Victoria Embankment
London EC4Y 0DZ

An Hachette UK Company

1 3 5 7 9 10 8 6 4 2

Copyright © Hella Pick 2021

Extracts published courtesy of the *Guardian*

All rights reserved. No part of this publication may be
reproduced, stored in a retrieval system, or transmitted, in
any form or by any means, electronic, mechanical,
photocopying, recording or otherwise, without the prior
permission of both the copyright owner and the above publisher.

The right of Hella Pick to be identified as the author of
this work has been asserted in accordance with the
Copyright, Designs and Patents Act 1988.

A CIP catalogue record for this book
is available from the British Library.

ISBN (Mass Market Paperback) 978 1 4746 1375 0
ISBN (eBook) 9781474613767
ISBN (Audio) 978 1 4746 1894 6

Typeset by Input Data Services Ltd, Somerset

Printed in Great Britain by Clays Ltd, Elcograf S.p.A.

www.orionbooks.co.uk
www.weidenfeldandnicolson.co.uk

CONTENTS

For

George Weidenfeld - *In Memoriam*

and

Matthew & Jemima - *The Future Generation*

ACKNOWLEDGEMENTS

This book has a large international cast of characters: family, friends, lovers, colleagues, politicians, diplomats, the well-known and the lesser-known. They owe their appearance in this chronicle of my life to two people: Felicity Bryan, my agent who sadly has not lived to see the book she encouraged me to write; and Alan Samson, Chairman of Weidenfeld & Nicolson, who has supported this enterprise and acted as my editor with extraordinary vigour and friendship. I am deeply indebted to both and cannot thank them enough.

I had long been urged to write a memoir. But it was only after my longstanding friend Jim Naughtie had introduced me to Felicity Bryan that the project took shape. I soon learned that when Felicity believed in an author, she would offer support with wisdom and unquenchable enthusiasm. I became a fortunate beneficiary. Alan Samson has been generous with his commitment, has given constant encouragement, and helped to keep up my morale even after a serious accident that threatened to derail the writing of this memoir.

A circle of close friends surrounded me and gave me the strength to fight my way back to full recovery and resume the writing of this book. They included Martin and Mori Woollacott, David Nissan, Gwyn Williams, Cate Haste, Nicola Glucksmann, Diana Frankel, Helena Kennedy, Iain Hutchison, Linda Christmas, Simon May, Barbara Spitz, Michael Maclay, Charlie Lansdowne, Jim and Ellie Naughtie, Pauline Neville-Jones, Geraldine Sharpe-Newton, Gaby, Matthew and Jemima Fyjis-Walker, Anne Chorley, Anne Corcoran, Andy and Joanna Kerman, Hans and Paivie von Ploetz, Wolfgang and Jutta Fischer, Audrey, Edward and Crispin Glover, Christopher and Pascal Mallaby, Mike Shipley, Jonathan and Ruth Steele, Mimi Lipton, Sepp Fegerl, Alina and Clara Bennett, Jonathan and Teresa Sumption, Frances Cairncross, Brian and Ann Lapping, Jeremy Bilder, Thomas and Debora Harding, Bertie and Clare Goodwin, Robert and Emma Chorley, Nicholas Chorley, Julian and Linda Heaton Cooper and Michael Zimmermann. I am eternally grateful to my friends for their love and support as well as to the doctors and nurses who cared for me. I thank them all individually and collectively.

Nicola Glucksmann, Christa von Richthofen, Linda Christmas, Simon May and Michael Maclay were asked to read a few selected chapters. I am grateful for the penetrating insights they gave me – and I apologise if I have not always followed their advice.

The contents of this book rely mostly on my own, somewhat patchy memory, on a sparse collection of documents and letters, my published work in the *Guardian* and elsewhere, and on conference reports written while working for George Weidenfeld's Institute for Strategic Dialogue. I am deeply grateful to Katherine Viner, Editor of the *Guardian*, for allowing me to quote from some of my articles, and thank the paper's Richard Nelsson for giving me access to the digitalised version of the *Guardian* archive.

After the loss of Felicity Bryan in June 2020, I was fortunate that her colleague, Carrie Plitt, ably looked after me for an interim period. I am now in the good hands of my friend, Caroline Michel, the CEO of PFD and am grateful to her and her staff for looking after my interests.

I am also grateful to Nicholas Jones for gently guiding me through the audio recording of *Invisible Walls*.

Due to Covid-19, I have not met all the staff at Weidenfeld & Nicolson who have worked on my book. So it is all the more important to thank them for their roles and their advice in bringing this book to completion. Celia Hayley combed through my overlong manuscript and suggested judicious cuts; Lucinda McNeile has overseen the detailed editing and Simon Fox copy-edited the book with incredible attention to detail and smoothed out rough edges. The end product of course is my responsibility alone.

15 March 1939 – London, Liverpool Street Station: an arrival hall, bewildered children. Among them stands *Kindertransport* child Number 4,672. An 11-year-old girl from Vienna hears her name called up. She says 'Goodbye', the only English phrase she knows, to the foster parents who have volunteered to take care of her. The child does not know whether she will ever be reunited with either of her divorced parents. Just over five months later the Second World War will begin, which will trigger the Holocaust.

3 December 1989 – Malta, the Soviet ship *Maxim Gorky*: a spacious lounge, the scene is set for a summit meeting with President Bush. The Diplomatic Correspondent of the *Guardian* is having coffee with Mikhail and Raisa Gorbachev, Soviet Foreign Minister Shevardnadze and assorted members of the Soviet military command. The Soviet leadership is relaxed while they wait for the US President. But heavy storms leave Mr Bush marooned out at sea on a US destroyer. He fails to materialise on the *Maxim Gorky* and the summit has to be called off. A day later the two leaders meet on dry ground in Malta and promise an end to the Cold War.

9 May 1996 – London, the *Guardian*'s boardroom: a farewell party for the long-serving Diplomatic Editor, an occasion for fond home truths and mockery. A self-declared poet laureate has composed the 'Ella Elegy'. It includes a clarion call:

Congregate a cast list stellar
Drawn from Hella's vast umbrella,

Moguls rich as Rockefeller,
Glittering beauties out of Kneller,
David Mellor, Yuri Geller,
Not (because he is dead) Ben Bella,
Possibly Perez de Cuellar?

Plus all those who could not come
Here are messages from some:
'Retirement, Hella? That's absurd.
'Love and kisses' – Douglas Hurd
'What's all this about your going?
'I forbid it' – David Owen
'Times are tight; we have reined our belts in,
Can't be with you' – Boris Yeltsin
'Hella. Sorry to be vague. An opera
Singer?' – Ronald Reagan
'You must stay till 90, silly,
See you soon' – Love Bill and Hilly
Plus billets doux from Denis Healey,
Some in Polish, some Swahili.

Mandarin and Guardian dweller,
Raise the roof and drain the cellar,
Charge your glasses now 'to Hella'.

Number 4,672 and the *Guardian* journalist were one and the same.
I had travelled a long way during those 57 years. But this was not
the end of the journey. For the next two decades I diverted into
a new career, working for George Weidenfeld and his Institute for
Strategic Dialogue, and found new worlds. An American colleague
once dubbed me the 'eternal traveller', even though much of my life
has been with home firmly established in London. The journey of my
working life, however, has been far from stationary, and the search
for escape from a refugee's feelings of insecurity has continued.

A journalist's life is often seen as very glamorous. And yes, I
have met and interviewed many prominent people in the world of

politics and diplomacy, and the arts. But of course most of it is about commitment, hard work and, crucially, the ability to win the trust of one's contacts, editors and readers. A handful of leaders, including the first Prime Minister of Nigeria, Abubakar Tafawa Balewa, the former German Chancellor, Willy Brandt, and Mieczyslaw Rakowski, the former Polish Prime Minister, became firm friends. I was in St Brigidy's, the Solidarnosc Church, in Gdansk with Lech Walesa on the day he was awarded the Nobel Peace Prize. I was travelling with the then Foreign Secretary, Sir Geoffrey Howe, when we sat on plush settees on the highest vantage point of the Khyber Pass and were briefed by the Gurkhas on the war in Afghanistan, with the fighting clearly visible in the valleys below our vantage point. I interviewed President Ceausescu of Romania and lunched with him and Prime Minister, Jim Callaghan at No. 10. I was given a bunch of red roses by Poland's President Jaruzelski and was told by Bulgaria's President Zhivkov how he liked to cheat the Soviet Union by supplying faulty goods. I accidentally fell into President Kennedy's arms at a party at his holiday retreat in Hyannisport. I was at the St Leger in the company of the Aga Khan to watch Shergar win the race, the last time this famous horse was seen in public before his mysterious disappearance.

As a school child I never harboured the ambition to become a journalist. Even as a student at the London School of Economics, my writing was limited to my essays. As a recent graduate on a job hunt it was pure accident when I unexpectedly landed a job as 'Commercial Editor' on a magazine called *West Africa*.

This was in 1957. Information technology had not even reached the cusp of revolutionary change. My articles were mainly composed on old-fashioned, often clunking typewriters, but when I was abroad they generally had to be written by hand, or simply made up from notes and off-the-cuff remarks dictated over a telephone to 'copytakers', a now extinct group of newspaper employees. Telephone lines were often bad or non-existent, and the only means of communication with the London office was 'Telex', a form of telegram that now belongs to the history of communication. I had to learn my craft without the internet, without smart phones, without Google,

Twitter, Facebook or 24-hour rolling news. However, there was none of the competition from social media and the citizen journalist that confronts today's professional journalists. The concept of instant news dissemination was almost alien. I once had to sit for several days on a scoop, a story about a political murder in the newly minted Republic of Congo, because I had no means of getting it through to London.

Without the World Wide Web, newspapers could only be read in hard copy, printing had to be adjusted to fixed times and journalists had to work to fixed deadlines. Membership of the National Union of Journalists was obligatory on most national newspapers, with salaries largely negotiated by the union. News organisations used business models that seem mind-bogglingly antique today.

During my early years in journalism a woman writing about foreign affairs was a rare species. The small handfuls of women in the media were by and large confined to covering domestic and social issues written for 'women's pages' – a category slow to be dropped even by progressive news media. Women covering foreign affairs were generally considered an exotic and far-from-welcome intrusion into an entrenched breed of males enjoying their well-tried mix of camaraderie and fierce competition.

I was very lucky during my three years with *West Africa*. There was a small, outstanding group of journalists writing about the political and constitutional transition in West Africa. They included the *Observer*'s Colin Legum, Basil Davidson, and *le Monde*'s Andre Blanchet and Philippe Decraene. They were all secure in their deep knowledge of the West African scene. When the inexperienced Hella Pick turned up, they not only made me welcome, but were also genuinely helpful, often sharing both contacts and information. And as I became more experienced, they also came to respect the information I was able to pool with them. At the time, I did not see myself as a trailblazer, let alone a role model for women journalists. And later, as more women entered the profession, I will always carry my blame that I failed to join them as they campaigned to open the media to women comprehensively and on equal terms. I remained a one-person 'show', preferring to write about interesting women and showing by my example that women in the media – or, for that matter, elsewhere – are the equals, and often more, of men.

The period with *West Africa* was in many ways one of the happiest, most unburdened times of my life. I had found a measure of escape from a loving, but all too possessive mother reluctant to let me go. I had found challenging but deeply satisfying work. I was meeting remarkable African leaders and joining the debates about different forms of independence that were sometimes as fierce and divisive as the Brexit debate. Above all, it was a period where I was remarkably free of self-doubt. I had not yet fully understood that I was in the company of countless refugees who, irrespective of their achievements, carried throughout their lives a sense of insecurity that would never truly evaporate.

That realisation gradually grew on me after I had left behind the rarefied world of *West Africa* and settled for much wider horizons as the *Guardian*'s correspondent at the United Nations. My career progressed. Yet my life was driven by an unending need for recognition that my work was first-class; and in love affairs, by constant reassurances that my commitment was fully returned. Insecurity is not the best recipe for fulfilment. While it did not help, I gradually came to understand that I was not alone with my insecurities. I have yet to meet a refugee who does not to some degree share similar feelings – though their ways of dealing with them may be very different to mine. This insecurity has not prevented full integration into British life but has everything to do with the fact of having been uprooted from one's origins.

Awareness of the problem fortunately did not drive me to brood or sorrow about the past but instead always to look and to march forward. During more than three decades at the *Guardian* I worked in the US and in Europe. I wrote about the Cuban Missile Crisis and the Kennedy assassination, about the Selma march and the civil rights movement, about NATO and arms-control negotiations. I travelled with President Nixon to Moscow and later witnessed his resignation. I switched from the US to Europe, covered Britain's Common Market Entry negotiations, the Helsinki Declaration and spent the closing years of the Cold War as East European

Correspondent, witnessing the erosion of the Soviet Union's empire. During my last ten years at the *Guardian* I was Diplomatic Editor, a job that took me to high-level meetings around much of the world.

In 1996 the Editor, Alan Rusbridger, declared that the *Guardian*'s readers were all younger than most of his senior journalists. I was a key target. Many thanks for your services, but it is time to make way. A profound surge of insecurity and inadequacy followed. I was not prepared for retirement. Rescue was at hand in the form of the publisher, (Lord) George Weidenfeld. We had long been friends. Now he commissioned a book – a biography of Simon Wiesenthal. That focused my mind on issues I had long pushed aside about being Jewish, about anti-Semitism and Zionism, about guilt and punishment and justice.

I am a secular Jew, who rarely associated with Jewish causes or Jewish institutions and long hesitated even to acknowledge publicly that I belonged to the tribe – even though I knew that everybody who knew me knew. Simon Wiesenthal in a small way and George Weidenfeld in a big way finally made me understand the import- ance of taking pride in being Jewish, and that this was part of my make-up as a human being. George was a crusader for the security of Israel and a committed, notable fighter against anti-Semitism. I could not remain disengaged and my values took a turn for the better. I involved myself closely in the German–Jewish Studies Centre at Sussex University, and after the university decided to establish the Weidenfeld Institute of Jewish Studies, I became an active fund-raiser and advocate for the institution.

When the Wiesenthal biography was finished George Weidenfeld had another idea for me. I could help organise one of his 'Club of Three' conferences, where high-level diplomats, politicians and business leaders from the UK, France and Germany met behind closed doors to discuss matters of European interest. It turned into a new career involving Club of Three events and later I became Director of Arts and Culture programmes in his new Institute for Strategic Dialogue. This widened my horizons with an exciting new layer of interesting experiences and personalities. George himself was one of the most remarkable people I have ever been able to count as a friend, and working with him produced a constant feast of ideas and challenges.

Lord Norman Foster feted George's 90th birthday with an unforgettable party in Switzerland that was a roll-call of the great and the good from the world of politics, business and the arts – and there was I, *Kindertransport* child number 4672, able to count many in this extraordinary gathering as friends or acquaintances. Surely my 'Weidenfeld era' should have been enough to finally overcome my insecurities. And yet it was not. I cannot free myself from the need for reassurance, even when I am receiving public praise. It is an open prison from which I have not found the key to escape. I am confined by invisible walls.

CHAPTER I

GOODBYE, AUSTRIA – HELLO, UK

'I had a good journey. Passport control was straightforward. They only demanded to know whether we had typewriters. I couldn't sleep during the first night on the train. On the second night we were on the boat. Most of us were sick, I was not. Next morning we were examined by doctors; but I didn't even have to undress. Then we were put into a train to London. There we were taken to a reception room and handed over to our guarantors. I was met by Gladys, the daughter of my hosts, the Infields. She is a charming girl . . .'

I posted this brief unemotional account of my *Kindertransport* journey to my mother in Vienna the day after my arrival in London on 16 March 1939. I was 11 years old. The significance of what had happened to me and its impact on my identity and character, my relationships and my work, have taken much longer to understand – it is taking a lifetime.

Some refugees have perfect recall and a plethora of documents and letters of their pre-Hitler lives in Germany or Austria to reconstruct their background and tell their stories. I envy them. I only have shattered scraps of memory to underpin the odd heaps of letters and documents that have survived, to build a picture of my childhood in Vienna and my arrival in London. There is a handful of small fading photos of a seemingly carefree, stable pre-Hitler existence: a picture of a handsome young couple – my parents; another of a happy-looking grandmother holding a baby – me; little children romping in a park; a solidly built little girl, topless, muscles flexed, standing on the edge of a swimming pool and ready to show off her swimming prowess. I have a schoolchild's birthday book filled with messages of eternal friendship and little illustrations to mark the birthday of an eight year old, or could it be a nine year old? There are scatterings of letters and postcards and the occasional document evidently hoarded by my mother, who was fortunate enough to get out of Austria some three weeks after my own arrival in the UK. She must have stuffed them into one of the smallish suitcases refugees were allowed to take on their journey. Though this trophy only fills in a few gaps in my memory, it also reveals some buried truths that shatter long-held versions of my mother's love life after her divorce. I have a blurred image, forever implanted in the mind, of an arrivals hall at Liverpool Street Station merging into a second-floor bedroom of a house in Brondesbury Road in London's West Hampstead. Almost 80 years later I am taken to the archive of World Jewish Relief and discover two files – one on me, the other on my mother – and I learn that I was number 4,672 of the 10,000-strong *Kindertransport* contingent brought to Britain from Germany and Austria in response to *Kristallnacht*, the anti-Jewish atrocities committed in November 1938.

Like countless other small children growing up in comfortable middle-class families, I must have led a largely untroubled life in pre-Hitler Vienna. True, one element was missing – my father. My parents divorced when I was only three years old and I rarely saw him. But I had my loving grandparents and mother, and I had plenty of friends; first as playmates in the park and later when I became a pupil in my local primary school. It was a mixed school, boys and girls, and, judging by the names, with a fair number of Jewish children and teachers. My surviving birthday book plays witness to ecumenical friendships. Everybody called me Helli, a version of my name that continued for many years. The book was given to me for my seventh birthday in 1935 by one of my classmates, Peter Bergel, and was inscribed with a little poem:

Zu deinem heutigen Wiegenfest
Will ich dies Buch Dir
Schenken

Ich wünsche Dir das
Allerbest
Du sollsts stets an mich
Denken
[On today's birthday
I want to give you this book
And wish you the very best
You should always think of me]

I have to confess that I don't remember him at all. The book has entries that continue until June 1938 – three months after the *Anschluss*. For my birthday that year, Dorli Kessler wrote: '*Im Glück sei niemals stolz, im Unglück edelmütig; dem Freund stehts getreu, und gegen Feinde gütig. Erinnere Dich an deine Mitschülerin.*' [In happiness never show pride; in unhappiness be generous; stay true to friends and be generous with enemies. Remember your school friends.] The book has many drawings and poems from my friends, but also several messages from my teachers. '*Sei stehts stolz auf dein Volk und deinen Glauben, und Du wirst immer den richtigen Weg finden*' [Remain proud of your people and your beliefs, and you will always find the right way], wrote Viktor Rosenfeld, who taught religion in my school, in 1937, a year when the storm clouds in Austria were already mounting. Three months after the *Anschluss*, in May 1938, another teacher, Dr Wilfred Holländer, wrote one of the last entries in my little book. It hints that the good times had ended: '*In Not sei geduldig, im Glück sei gütig, Frisch vorwärts in Gefahr*' [In need be patient; in happiness be kind; in danger go forward with determination]. My memory has a complete blank about my schooling for the remainder of my time in Vienna.

I was obviously a happy child – happy in my surroundings, industrious and learning well at school, popular among friends, and deeply – perhaps even too deeply – attached to my mother. I was too young when my parents divorced to know my father or understand the circumstances surrounding the break-up of the marriage. The problem had been my father's orthodox Jewish family, my mother always told me later. Having been brought up in a secular

Jewish household and falling in love with my father Ernst, who was similarly secular, she had not anticipated that there would be interference from his orthodox background. I have always suspected there was far more to the break-up. But as in many other matters, I failed to press my mother for a deeper explanation, and I never had the chance to question my father when I was old enough to need an explanation. I never saw him again after he emigrated to the United States in 1938, and I only have a single impersonal letter from him, written in 1957, shortly before he died. It reads like a stranger's letter.

For intermittent periods after 1935 or 1936 there was another father figure in my life. My mother had fallen in love with a Russian émigré, Maxim Kaplan. He was a struggling businessman, living between Vienna and Paris. I adored him, and I have found letters that show his deep affection for me. If there were love letters to my mother, she does not appear to have preserved them. She always spoke of him as the great love of her life and for some years she and Kapi – as we all called him – were happy together. She frequently spent time with him in Paris, leaving me with the grandparents. But by 1938 the affair had evidently begun to sour. Kapi was in Paris, unable to find a firm foothold in business and dependent on a more affluent brother who had emigrated to Britain. Kapi had a gift for drawing and was trying to make a living out of animated postcards that made bird or animal or human noises to accompany the drawings. He sent me an illustrated letter to explain them. Sadly, the enterprise went nowhere. My mother seems to have written incessant complaints about being neglected and being discouraged from resuming the Paris visits. Kapi's replies, which my mother preserved, continuously stressed that she failed to understand the difficulties in which he found himself – his lack of means, his poor accommodation and ill-health – but also included lengthy descriptions of his business endeavours.

At one point I must have written to him to ask why my mother had not received any letters. Treating me as a responsible adult, he explained that he had told her about his difficulties and how depressed he was. But she had stopped showing any understanding or kindness and so it was better, for the time being, to remain silent.

Throughout the turmoil between Kapi and my mother, the trusting correspondence between Kapi and me seems to have continued. In one of the last letters, written a couple of months after the *Anschluss*, he demonstrates his concern for my well-being and asks whether I am still allowed to go to school, and also whether my non-Jewish school friends had remained in touch with me.

I never asked how Kapi fitted into my mother's social circle, or even if she introduced him to her friends and her few cousins. But he certainly knew my grandmother, who seems to have liked him but rightly feared that the relationship with my mother could not last.

By the middle of 1938, when Austria's Jews were battling in search of asylum, Kapi and my mother again clung to each other – by post. However, I have found no trace of letters from Kapi after my mother and I reached Britain. Then war broke out, and Kapi disappeared in the maelstrom. In 1946, my mother tried to trace Kapi's brother in the forlorn hope that Kapi himself had survived. She even engaged a small-time detective for what was then the princely sum of £2.50 (I have found the receipt). He tracked the brother down to Hampton Hill in Richmond where he apparently had a small toy factory. Once again I am frustrated: I do not know whether she followed this lead. Kapi remains a blurred but happy memory.

Never really having had an enduring father figure in my life, it is hard to judge how much I have missed. But what I have learned all too well is that the relationship between a single mother and a single daughter is always complex, and in our case was not made any easier by dint of becoming refugees. In Vienna it was still a relatively straightforward mother–child love. I adored my mother as a child. I must have been about six years old when I gave her a love letter. On a small page bordered with simple drawings I wrote:

Mutter
Und bin ich einmal erwachsen
Und wäre ich noch so reich
Nie käm ein Schatz auf Erden
Dir liebe Mutter gleich
[Mother

And when I am grown up
And were I ever so rich
There could never be on earth any valuable
That approaches you]

My mother – Mitzi, as she was called during her Austrian life and
Hanna in her British life – returned these sentiments with equal
force and showered her love on me. But in Vienna she also had her
outside interests, her circle of friends, plenty of admirers, and first
my father and later Kapi. But as a newcomer in Britain her world
inevitably shrank. It didn't take long for her to master the English
language. People liked her and she slowly built up a few friendships
both with other refugees and more gradually with British acquaintances. No significant men ever again emerged in her life. Inevitably
her main focus was on me.

In Vienna my mother moved mostly among comfortably off
Jewish families who considered themselves fully assimilated into
the Austrian middle class – and failed, perhaps deliberately, to
see how much of it was illusory. She gave herself to a world that
was seemingly blind to the break-up of the old structures and the
unstoppable spread of National Socialism, a world that was clinging
to the age-old Viennese motto of never a care in the world: 'Es kann
Dir nichts g'schehen' [Nothing (bad) will happen to you]. Mitzi was
well educated, a lover of music who as a young woman went almost
daily to the opera or the theatre. I can still remember going for
long walks with her where she would sing long excerpts from The
Marriage of Figaro or one of the other Mozart operas. She also knew
her operettas, and sometimes hummed tunes from Das Weisse Rössl
am Wolfgangsee, telling me that I was conceived in the real White
Horse Inn in Wolfgang.

My mother did not go to university. But she did go to a cooking
school – something that stood her in good stead after she ended up
as a refugee in Britain, having to work as a cook from 1939 until the
end of the war. In Vienna she still belonged to a generation where
relatively few women had professional ambitions, and my mother
never held a paid job during the Austrian part of her life. However,

more as a hobby than out of any desire to do paid work, she spent time in a friend's millinery business and learned how to make hats, and as a side interest, how to treat leather and make gloves. This was a godsend after the war in Britain, when she could finally break away from domestic employment and make a modest living as a milliner.

My mother's parents, Olga and Alfred, came from Iglava in Slovakia. They spent most of their lives peacefully in Vienna, comfortable in their skin as secular Jews and keeping their distance from any form of political involvement during Austria's bitter, strife-ridden 1930s, the erosion of democracy and the unstoppable spread of the Nazi party. Like so many other Viennese Jews, they seem to have kept their eyes closed and clung to the belief – or was it wishful thinking? – that somehow their quiet lives would remain undisturbed. Alfred was a civil servant. Olga had two daughters. The first-born died only a few months old, and neither my grandmother nor anyone else was ever prepared to tell me more. My mother, born in 1900, was named Johanna Marie and was brought up as an only child. Alfred died in 1934. But my grandmother was still a lively woman in her mid-60s during those sinister March days in 1938 when Austria's semi-dictatorship, the Second Republic, was in its death throes, more than ready to fall into Hitler's gripping arms. All the old certitudes died on 15 March 1938 when the *Führer* stood on Vienna's Heldenplatz and told 200,000 cheering Austrians that their country, 'the oldest eastern province of the German people, will now be the newest bastion of the German Reich'. Any illusions that Austria's turn towards National Socialism, and its commitment to persecution of the Jews, could be stemmed were finally shattered. Hitler's peroration and call to arms had sealed the fate of Austria's Jewish population. They had become an endangered species.

Jews were targeted immediately. Shops were plundered, men and women were forced to perform menial tasks, academics were removed from their posts, and the Dachau concentration camp in Bavaria received its first consignment of Austrian Jews. The persecution of the Jews intensified to its horrific climax, *Kristallnacht* on 9 November 1938, when Vienna's synagogues were sacked, Jewish shops looted, and Jews were demeaned and demoralised to utter despair.

I write these words, and yet I have to confess that I cannot claim to have any personal memory of these events. It is deeply shaming to confess this profound hole in my memory. After all, I was ten years old and was clearly bright and thoughtful. Yet I cannot recall how I felt about or reacted to the dreadful scenes around me. All I have are letters that my mother kept which reflect her constant concern for me and for Olga, and her hopes for getting away from Austria – and if at all possible, getting out with at least some of their possessions. A few families had had the foresight to emigrate before the *Anschluss*, when it was still relatively easy to leave with their assets and find a new home, preferably in the United States. Now that Austria's Jews understood beyond doubt that they had become an endangered species in their home country, the vast majority wanted to emigrate. The Nazis were far from opposed to this. They wanted to empty the country of its Jews. They had not yet considered the Final Solution and encouraged emigration. But only the individuals could leave. Their possessions, bank accounts, stocks and shares would remain behind and would be confiscated. Exit visas would be granted but only for one-way journeys. All passports marked with the tell-tale 'J' would expire soon after the journey and could not be renewed. I still have my mother's passport, together with the Nazi documents that confirm the confiscation of her bank accounts, and that all taxes had been duly paid.

Agonising discussions about where to go and what to do began immediately after the *Anschluss*. Olga and my mother both applied for visas to the United States, her first choice, but also to the UK. My name was included in my mother's visa applications. But they also took two fateful decisions and fell into a trap. They agreed that Olga would be safer in Prague while my mother would remain in Vienna, each of them waiting and living in hope of visas and asylum abroad. Olga left for Prague. Mother and daughter wrote to each other almost every day, full of anxiety about what would become of them, and whether Olga's health would stand up to all the stress. A close friend who was still able to travel freely between Prague and Vienna regularly visited her, and his letters show that he helped her financially, as her scarce resources were running out.

The other bad calculation was to entrust all my mother's and Olga's stocks and shares to a Swiss courier, a man by the name of Hans Allenbach, who undertook to deposit them in Swiss banks. They were far from alone in using intermediaries to try and salvage some of their wealth before the Nazis could seize it. Maybe other couriers were trustworthy. Allenbach was not. He disappeared and the money disappeared with him. My mother grew suspicious soon after the handover. But to no effect. The Zurich address he had provided proved to be fictitious. All efforts to find him failed, both while my mother was still in Vienna, and again after the end of the war. I have a list of the booty Hans Allenbach effectively stole. While he had enriched himself, we had now become impoverished. Lack of money remained a constant worry for many years – in fact until I was earning enough to supplement my mother's resources.

At some point in 1937 or 1938 a new man had appeared in my mother's life. His name was Rudolf Anzenhofer. He was in his 40s, was single with a prosperous business, was not Jewish and was securely rooted in Vienna without the slightest need or inclination to emigrate. I never learned how he met my mother. What is certain is that they had an affair and that he took great risks to help her after the *Anschluss*. There are some remarks that my mother made many years later, as well as hints in letters that she received from 'Rudi', that suggest she had a secret abortion, either shortly before she left Vienna or very soon, and most mysteriously, after her arrival in the UK. Whatever the truth, I do know that she somehow kept alive a belief that if he survived the war, he would marry her – and she could return to Austria. Close to the end of the war, she even launched a Red Cross search for him, describing him as her 'fiancé'. Yet his first post-war letter was to tell her that he had married and had two 'lovely' children. But even if the prospect of marriage had been a delusion, Rudi proved to be a true friend both before the war and again after its end.

After the *Anschluss* my mother no longer felt it was safe for us to be living in our flat in Döbling and wanted to be in the inner city. Rudi found her a safer flat that belonged to an acquaintance, Hilde Glesinger, who shared it with us. I do not seem to have appreciated the risks that Hilde took for me. Deeply buried, I have a vague recollection of Gestapo knocks at the door. I must have been old enough to sense the danger. I have no idea how I felt. But being so close to my mother, I must have been hugely terrified. Many years later – in 1964 – my mother wrote to me that

> If you would try to remember our last months in Vienna during our stay with Hilde . . . After the Gestapo knock on the door I always said 'goodbye' to you and to her, not knowing whether I would ever see you again. It happened perhaps five times that I was 'invited' to see the Gestapo to tell them about mother's and my money and about other things. To my absolute amazement I always came back. It was Mrs Glesinger who helped me through that ghastly time and it was her I had to trust to look after you in case I did not come back. And believe me, as I think back I still cannot understand how my then, still perfectly working brains and nerves made me stand up to Them and even be quite liked, or let's say not hated, by my German Nazi interrogators. When I needed Hilde she was like a brick, absolutely wonderful to you and to me, and I am sorry I never told her in as many words. One took it then as quite natural to be in great danger all the time. But to keep somebody like me in her flat, who was repeatedly taken away by the Gestapo, was very brave. Fortunately she was a happy-go-lucky person who never reflected much about the situation and thought that nothing could ever happen to her.

This was the sinister background to my mother's efforts to get me and herself out of Austria and to find asylum for her mother. On the waiting list for American visas, our names were low down and there was little prospect of success. My father was of no help. He had obviously seen the warning lights of the impending Nazi take-over and had applied early enough to be among the relatively small quota of refugees that the US was prepared to welcome. He had left Austria early in 1938, a few months before the *Anschluss*. He took no further interest in my well-being, and indeed ignored efforts early on during the war to make him meet his alimony obligations towards my upkeep.

British visas were only issued to individuals who would not be a liability to the British taxpayer and could provide a guarantor to take care of them. In practical terms there were only two options: have someone in the UK wealthy and generous enough to provide accommodation and steady financial help, or to enter domestic service. No other form of employment would be allowed. For the majority, and certainly in my mother's case, domestic service was her only avenue to safety. There was a considerable shortage of domestic workers in Britain, and so visas were relatively easy to obtain. However, the visas did not include children, and there were a few heartbreaking cases where the mother had gone ahead, leaving a child behind in Austria in the hope that the child would be included on the *Kindertransport*. In the advertisement columns of *The Times* a special section was set up for 'Refugee advertisements'. A typical advertisement read:

LL.D. of Vienna, Jew, musical, versed in literature, bridge player, very adaptable, in distressful circumstances appeals urgently to kind-hearted persons for guest permits for himself and wife (excellent cook, housekeeper and knitting modellist).

I have been unable to trace the advertisement where my mother offered her services as a cook or housemaid. But I do have a yellowed copy of a newspaper cutting with the plea my mother placed to find a sponsor that would allow my grandmother to get away from Prague. It read: 'Guarantor urgently needed. Lady (61) must leave Czechoslovakia. Danger.' A guarantor was eventually found. But Olga's visa only came through three weeks before the war broke out, too late to secure her exit permit.

Grete Marmorek, one of my mother's close friends, and a distant relative of my father, managed to secure a British visa for herself before the end of 1938, and once in London set out to find guarantors both for my mother and for Olga. But in constant fear of the Gestapo and uncertain that she would obtain a British visa or even be allowed an exit permit from Austria, my mother was agonising about what to do to ensure that at least her child would be able to reach safety. The only sure way out was the *Kindertransport* children's rescue scheme established by the British government in 1938 as part of its response to *Kristallnacht* in November 1938. The mission, as it is always described, was primarily to rescue Jewish children whose father or both parents had been thrown into concentration camps or were no longer in a position to look after them. Each child was required to be sponsored by individuals or organisations in the UK prepared to take care of the child, provide a home and cover their education. 10,000 German and Austrian children were rescued during that short period until the outbreak of war. Though it was a great achievement, more than twice that number, often destitute children, had to be left behind.

It is not widely known that the *Kindertransport* children were only given temporary British visas, and that there was a very strict and highly controversial selection process. Researchers are still working to establish all the facts. In 1938, Vienna's Jews consisted of two groups: the long-settled bourgeois middle class, and the more recent influx of orthodox East European *Stetl* Jews who had fled to Austria to escape the pogroms in their former countries. After *Kristallnacht* there were thousands of destitute, often orphaned, *Stetl* children in Vienna. The *Kultusgemeinde* (the Jewish Community organisation), already only barely able to function, lacked the funds to help them. The Nazis had given the *Kultusgemeinde* the responsibility for drawing up the *Kindertransport* list. So they put the Stetl children high on the list. However, their pleas were ignored, not just by the British authorities but also by the ad hoc group of volunteers, initially known as the Movement for the Care of Children from Germany and Austria, who had been instrumental in persuading a reluctant Neville Chamberlain to recognise the humanitarian crisis and allow the *Kindertransport* scheme to be set up. Chamberlain did not want to increase the number of Jews in Britain, and insisted that the visas had to be temporary.

The leading figure among the volunteers overseeing the scheme, still fondly remembered by many *Kindertransport* children, was Lola Hahn Warburg, a member of the prominent banking family. She was a Zionist. Her priority was to select *Kinder* who would eventually move on to Palestine and help in building up the state. So she wanted *Kinder* who were certified to be in perfect physical and mental health and with good educational attainment. Photographs had to be submitted. Apparently Mrs Warburg was looking for intelligent and not particularly Jewish-looking children who were 100 per cent physically and mentally fit. *Kinder* were given a final fitness examination on the boat bringing them to Harwich. Children are known to have been rejected as failing to meet the mental fitness test on the grounds that their mothers had committed suicide. The *Kinder* also had to have a profile that would enable them to fit reasonably smoothly into British society. Given the tough criteria set for the selection process, it is not surprising that virtually all the *Kinder* were well-brought-up children from middle-class families. Only an insignificant number came from an orthodox background, and the *Stetl* children stood little chance. Very large numbers of them perished and it has taken decades for research to be undertaken into this hugely damaging blemish on the *Kindertransport* scheme.

My mother would not have known of these discriminatory practices when she decided to place me on the *Kindertransport* list. Fortunately my profile conformed with British requirements. I have no documents to show exactly when my mother put my name on the list drawn up by Vienna's *Kultusgemeinde*, which handled the *Kindertransport* applications. But I have no doubt she felt torn apart and helpless at the prospect of separation and sending me off alone into the unknown, far from certain that we would be reunited. I am sure the decision could only have been triggered by her summons to the Gestapo, and her fears that she would not be able to save herself, let alone be allowed to leave Austria.

I have the documentation and passport with all the entries essential to enable her to travel and enter Britain. It reflects a tale of hard choices and conflicting loyalties that should never have had to be put to the test. On 11 January 1939, my mother received a letter from 'The Coordinating Committee for Refugees' that included a Home Office work permit as a domestic. The letter instructed her that on arrival in the UK she had to go straight to Leeds, where she would be placed 'in a suitable position'. Why Leeds? There was no explanation. My mother's travel document was a German Reich passport issued on 16 February 1939. It had a prominent 'J' printed in bright red on its title page. It confirmed that the passport was only valid for one year and could not be renewed. The passport showed that a British visa was granted on 27 February 1939. It was for 'A Single Journey only', and stipulated that it was only valid for 'domestic' employment. Confirmation that all tax liabilities had been met and that permission to leave had been granted was stamped into the passport on 14 March 1939. But even though my mother was now free to come to the UK, still she hesitated. Ignoring my entreaties to come to London sooner, she did not leave until 27 March. This is where the story becomes even more dramatic: the passport also had a Czech visa issued on 3 March 1939 – just under two weeks before Hitler's invasion of the Czechoslovak Republic, in defiance of the Munich Declaration. She was torn between coming straight to the UK – and reunion with me – or instead going to Prague to help her mother. She must have thought she could secure a British visa for Olga so that they could together come to Britain. Had she gone to Prague, I would probably never have seen her again.

Once my *Kindertransport* permit had been secured and a date had been set for my departure, my future guardians were put in touch with my mother. She kept the letters that Ethel Infield (who would become my 'Aunt Ethel'; her husband would be my 'Daddy') wrote to reassure her. In January 1939, Mrs Infield wrote:

> We are all looking forward so much to Hella's coming. You may be sure we shall do all we can to make her happy so that she can quickly forget all her recent sorrows. As to yourself, I do not know of a post [This was when my mother was still in search of a domestic job, which would enable her to secure a visa] and shall let you know if I hear of anything. It really is so difficult here; more than you imagine . . . I don't know if you know much about my family. I have a pair of twins, son and daughter, aged 17; also a younger son of 13. Hella will be under the special charge of my daughter who will really mother her and care for her. She is anxiously awaiting the moment when her new duties will begin.

Another letter was sent on 28 February. My journey had evidently been delayed: 'I am so sorry that there has been this long delay in Hella's arrival. We are all looking forward to her coming and hope it will be soon now.' The delay seems to have been caused because, for some reason, the Infields had been required to resubmit their guarantee to take over responsibility for me. Mrs Infield added that she had not yet received my clothes. These had to be sent, as the *Kinder* themselves were only allowed a small overnight case. The last letter to my mother while she was still in Vienna was sent on 16 March, the day after my arrival, when I also wrote my own account. My new 'Aunt Ethel' wrote:

> Helli has arrived quite safely. She seems quite well and happy. She is a dear little girl and we all like her very much. I am sure she will quickly settle to life over here. I hope you will soon be able to come over here. I think it is advisable to do so as quickly as possible.

My mother already had a British visa. But she still had no exit permit, and she was still torn between going to see her mother in Prague and coming to England: she seems to have thought she could do both. That was wishful thinking. A day after my own safe arrival in London, she wrote that before leaving Austria she still wanted to see Olga, who was 'now in great danger'.

After sending my short matter-of-fact account of the journey from Vienna and my arrival in the Infields' home, I wrote daily letters and postcards to my mother chronicling how the days passed. Reading these letters now, I am surprised by the self-possessed, half-adult tone and steady handwriting. I was certainly trying to adapt to my new surroundings – as long as I could keep up the hope that the separation from my mother would soon be over. The enormity of what had happened to me had not yet registered. On my first day I wrote: 'For breakfast I had an egg, white bread and coffee – that is what the English have. Then Gladys took me with her to do some shopping and the money just came pouring out of her purse . . .' I went on to describe what we had for lunch and later for tea, and added: 'I need nothing else to be happy except to have you, my beloved mother, with me.' I signed the letter with millions and millions (in figures) of kisses. But this is followed by a telling sentence: 'Please don't go to Prague.'

A couple of days later, my anxiety about my mother's plans became more evident. I sent what I described as a 'short but important postcard. I demand that you leave no later than Saturday and come direct to London. I understand the situation better than you do. Please do what I say.' The messages became more insistent by the day. The last one I have found, which must have been sent shortly before my mother actually arrived in London, 'orders' her 'to come to me at the latest by 28 March. I need you and you must get to safety. Nothing else is as important, not even my grandmother.'

My letters and cards were, of course, all written in German. But I told my mother that all the Infields had a smattering of German and that there was a German maid in the house. It also seems that almost immediately after my arrival, I started going to intensive English teaching classes and absorbed English speedily. The Infields felt I was ready for school, and I spent the summer term at the Brondesbury and Kilburn High School, not far from their home. I have my end-of-term report with the headmaster's comment that 'Hella has made a good beginning. Conduct good.'

Life at the Infields', however, seems to have been turning sour. In letters to my mother I complained that all my letters were opened and my phone calls were overheard. I had no privacy. I told her that I was constantly watched. But although my mother had now arrived in the UK, there was no question that we could live together. During those months in London I was floating in a twilight zone. I was in limbo. My life was with my 'Daddy' and 'Aunt Ethel' and their children, Gladys, Brian and Gerald. My heart was with my mother, now a domestic servant and cook in a household in Godalming. We could meet, at the most, once every two weeks, occasionally a little more often. But it was not possible for me to spend a night staying in my mother's employer's house, and the Infields did not encourage overnight visits in their home. My mother was occasionally invited for lunch, but never to stay. Godalming was at least close enough to London for day visits.

It would have been even worse had my mother acted on the terms of her work permit and reported on arrival to Leeds. Fortunately Grete Marmorek had managed to find my mother the Godalming job. She had to cook for a large family in a house where her place was definitely 'downstairs'. The mistress of the house would descend into the nether world each morning to decide menus, and that was most of the contact my mother had with the upstairs world. It was, of course, a novel experience, and it was certainly not the best way to adapt to a new world. She tried to break free and get a job in a hat-manufacturing business owned by an acquaintance from Vienna. But there was no way of changing the terms of her work permit. The only other way of escape was to find a better, friendlier domestic job.

And then my mother struck gold. An academic at the London School of Economics, Professor Theodore Chorley, loved *Apfelstrudel* and other Viennese specialities. The family was in need of a cook. Somebody — nobody remembers who — suggested Hanna (as she now called herself) Pick. She got the job — and gained a new family for herself, and soon also for me. Everybody could also eat *Apfelstrudel* to their heart's content.

The Chorleys had two sons, Roger and Patrick, and a daughter, Gillian, who was my age. They lived in the Rookery, a spacious house set in a large garden in Stanmore on the northern outskirts of London. Soon I was invited to spend my spare time at the Rookery, and we all became friends and happily played together. Friendships that lasted a lifetime were formed. Meals were taken together. My mother was at last more relaxed, though concern to get Olga away from Prague was a never-ending worry.

During those summer months, all hopes that war could be avoided had faded. But the Chorleys decided to spend August, as was their habit, in the Lake District. They had a second home there, called Randapike, not far from Hawkshead and close to Lake Windermere. It was taken as a matter of course that my mother would go with them. But they also invited me to join them. The Infields agreed to let me go – though they still expected me back in time for the autumn term at my London school.

On 30 August Rudi posted a letter to my mother advising her not to be nervous about the political situation. In Vienna, he wrote, 'everybody is relaxed because we feel our demands are just. We simply cannot believe that England will not see that war cannot resolve them.'

At Randapike such views would have been considered unrealistic and dismissed. War was seen as almost inevitable. My mother, helpless to get her to Britain, became more anxious by the day about Olga. But the adults made sure that we children had a happy, carefree time. We swam in the lake and clambered over the fells. My mother cooked us great food, and we chatted and played. In that blissful month I crossed a line: I ceased to be a visitor in Britain. I discovered that Britain could also be home.

CHAPTER 2

A PEACEFUL WARTIME: GROWING UP IN THE LAKE DISTRICT

As the clever hopes expire
Of a low dishonest decade:
Waves of anger and fear
Circulate over the bright
And darkened lands of the earth,
Obsessing our private lives;
The unmentionable odour of death
Offends the September night.

W. H. Auden, 'September 1, 1939'

On 29 August 1939 the *Daily Telegraph* carried a blaring headline: '1,000 Tanks massed on the Polish Frontier – Ten divisions ready for swift stroke'. Just like Auden's poem, the futility of appeasement was about to be exposed in an explosion of war and millions of lost lives. Two days later the same journalist who had broken the story that war was imminent was in the Polish border city of Katowice watching from her window as the first German tanks were rolling mercilessly into Poland. Those breaking news stories were written by 25-year-old Clare Hollingworth, the pioneering journalist who became my mentor, colleague and generous friend many years later when I had reached roughly the same age as she was in 1939.

While Clare secured scoop of imminent war thanks to a sudden gust of wind that briefly lifted camouflage tarpaulins to reveal the German troops and their armaments on the border with Poland, ready to go to war, I was scrambling on the fells in the Lake District, absorbing its timeless, peaceful beauty, clinging to the Chorley family and learning to grasp that Britain very likely would become my permanent home. I doubt that we children fully recognised the dark warning clouds that the prospect of war had cast over our summer idyll. But the adults necessarily planned ahead. Theo and Katharine would go back to London and do war work. (Theo held senior jobs throughout the war, first at the Home Office, then at the Ministry of Security and, for the last two years of the war, back in his beloved North-West as Deputy Commissioner for Civil Defence for the region.) Roger and Patrick, their two sons, went back to their boarding school, and Gillian would be a boarder at Rydal Hall School in the Lake District.

There was also the awkward question of what to do about my mother and about me. The Chorleys would not need her services while they were busy with war work. But they had grown fond of her, understood her fears and loneliness, certainly felt a degree of responsibility for her, and wanted to ensure that she found another understanding employer. As for me, logically I should go back to the Infields in London, who had, after all, only 'lent me out' for the summer holidays and remained responsible for my schooling and upkeep. But logic does not necessarily take account of feelings. My mother was adamant: she did not want to be parted from me again. And I did not want to be parted from her. Displacement and loneliness: it was inevitable that we would cling to each other. It was our good fortune that the Chorleys not only understood but decided to help. They agreed that we should stay together and should remain in the Lake District. The Infields reluctantly agreed and decided to stand by their commitment and provide a small financial contribution for my upkeep and schooling.

The Chorleys went into action. Local friends were asked to find a family who might be in need of domestic help, willing to employ a refugee and also willing to take in her daughter. A private boarding school in Ambleside called Fairfield was approached and agreed to offer me a free place for the first few months. Within days we moved into Wood Close in Grasmere, the welcoming home of an elderly lady, Mrs Delmar Banner. When the autumn term opened I would take the bus to Ambleside and start what turned out to be five years of schooling at Fairfield.

The parameters of wartime life appeared to have been settled. In one way, of course they had. We were fortunate enough to be in a part of Britain that was spared air raids and had no direct experience of the war. Yes, we had the same food rationing as the rest of the country, and yes, we saw soldiers on leave or recovering from wounds. But everyday life felt normal, undisturbed and, dare I say, peaceful. I have a stack of letters from school friends and the Chorley family and am amazed that there is not a single sentence that refers to the war. My school friends simply wrote about their school holidays, described tennis parties, visitors, discussed plans for post-school life. Occasionally there would be a reference to a brother coming home on leave. The war was not foremost in our young minds. The only jolt came with the news that Gerald, one of the Infields' sons, had been badly wounded. Fortunately he survived to live a long and happy life – and became my lifelong friend.

But of course there was nothing quite 'normal' for my mother or for me during this peaceful Lakeland version of the war. We were now nominally stateless, having been deprived by the Nazis of our Austrian nationality. With the beginning of the war, the British government now classed us as 'enemy aliens', living on temporary visas – borrowed time – in the UK. We regularly had to report to the local police. My mother was finding it very difficult to adjust. It was hard for her to accept our poverty, our need for charity and the inevitable inroads on our independence. She longed for escape from her lowly status as a domestic. She missed Vienna, missed her friends, was still groping for news of Kapi, and at the same time hoped for some means of securing reassurance of Rudi Anzenhofer's loyalty. To add to the mix, there was her greatest anxiety: she was agonising about Olga's survival now that all hope of getting her away from Czechoslovakia had to be abandoned. During the first few months of the war postal services were still, mysteriously, functioning. We were still receiving densely written postcards from her, and my mother, without knowing for certain that they would be delivered, was sending lengthy letters in return. If all this was not enough, there was, to crown it all, her preoccupation over my future. What would become of me? How would I adjust and develop in this new environment? What chances would this new life give me?

All this gnawed on her. Yet outwardly she managed to present a cheerful, pleasant persona. Everybody she met liked her. But I knew better. I was living with a loving but deeply unhappy woman.

I find it easier to analyse what my mother's feelings were at that time than to map my own feelings. I was probably floundering on an incoherent search for identity, futilely seeking to deny my roots while trying to find firm ground for an implant. My main aim seems to have been to blend in, to appear as English as possible; in my school uniform, to look like any ordinary English schoolgirl and not to stand out in a crowd. My English had to become perfect. My accent should disappear. While I condescended to speak the odd word in German at home – less and less so as the months progressed – German would be utterly and completely banned outside the home. Even on an empty footpath without a single other human being in sight, if my mother so much as dared to express one sentence in German, I would hiss at her to 'shut up' and run away to disassociate myself from her. However, a year or two into the war, I developed a schoolgirl's 'pash' on one of the teachers, who urged me to remember that German was my mother tongue, and this persuaded me to recover the language. But by then English had become the norm at home and almost all communication with my mother was in English. From then, I never again wrote to her in German. Even she tended to write most of her letters to me in English.

If hiding my Austrian roots was an obsession, hiding my Jewishness went even deeper. I could not bring myself to speak of it, or even acknowledge it for many years. Unlike the teacher who restored me to the German language, there was nobody during those school years, or later during my LSE times, to make me understand that I was now living in an environment where it was safe to declare myself Jewish. My mother was a confirmed agnostic and made no attempt to change her Jewish-refusenik daughter's mind. Only when I made my first trip to New York and saw that this was a city full of Jews leading normal lives as an integral part of American society did I finally understand that Jewishness did not have to spell danger and need not be a handicap. But even then it took decades more before I really felt comfortable – and secure – as a Jew.

Back in September 1939, Wood Close was a soft landing for my mother and for me. Mrs Delmar Banner, an elderly widow whose son was one of the Lakeland's best-known artists, was welcoming, pleased to gain both an intelligent woman and a good cook (that is, after my mother had mastered what was to her an alien beast, the Aga cooker). Mrs Banner treated me warmly, evidently happy to have a helpful young girl under her roof. She intended to be more than a mere employer. She wanted to give us a home. The large house was set on a slight incline near the top end of a lane that led from the head of Grasmere Lake past Wordsworth's Dove Cottage. Behind Wood Close was the path that led up to Alcock Tarn, a walk that became a favourite in all seasons, but especially a great place for swimming on hot summer days. Grasmere village itself was a ten-minute walk away and all around us were more fells, more walks, and of course the lake itself. It was love at first sight. However long the absence, Grasmere is a love that has remained with me.

I will never know how life would have developed if we had been able to stay at Wood Close. But after we had lived there for a few months Mrs Banner fell ill and died. Her son and his wife, the sculptor Josephina de Vasconcellos, closed the house. Once again we had to be on the move. Though in a beautiful setting, this time it was a tough landing. Mrs Gillian Anderson and her husband at Bowns Wood, a sprawling contemporary white-painted house set in extensive gardens on the shore of Lake Windermere, required a cook. My mother fitted the bill, and they agreed that I could join her. The house had a servants' wing with a small flat for us. It had its own back entrance. Just as in her first placement in Godalming, my mother was once again the servant, never to be considered a friend or worthy of special attention as a refugee in need of reassurance. I was tolerated as the servant's daughter. I cannot remember ever having any conversation with my mother's employers, or indeed being invited into the main house. I was allowed to go down the garden to the lake to swim and even occasionally to use the rowing boat – but I always had to make sure the Andersons were not in the garden. It was a deeply confusing – and disturbing – situation for a schoolgirl whose fellow pupils, almost without exception, came from affluent homes, in most cases with domestic staff. I could not bring myself to explain my circumstances, and only my two best friends, both of whom happened to be day pupils, were ever invited to Bowns Wood. And of course Gillian Chorley was always welcome during school holidays. She and I bonded gradually and deeply, and became the best of friends.

When we were still in Grasmere I took the bus to school, driving along Grasmere Lake and Rydal Water into Ambleside. But once we were at Bowns Wood, I managed to acquire a hefty second-hand bicycle, and biked the three or four miles past Waterhead and through Ambleside to the school, which lay at the far end. Fairfield comprised four detached houses on the main road towards Rydal and beyond. At the back there was a large garden with views of Lough-rigg and the hills beyond. On the other side of the road, standing in the substantial grounds of Scale How, was a teachers' training institution, the Charlotte Mason College. Fairfield served as an ancillary 'practising' school for Charlotte Mason students. The College, founded in 1892, was the 'mothership' of The Parents' National Educational Union (PNEU), a teaching concept originally intended as a method for home teaching which gradually also spawned schools in many parts of the world. Charlotte Mason, a contemporary of Coleridge and Wordsworth (who often visited Scale How), was an educator who translated a liberal-arts philosophy into a curriculum designed to stimulate and broaden children's (in fact, girls were her only target) minds, ideas and ambitions, and at the same time instil in them a strong code of morals and ethics. But her mindset stopped short of seeing education as a pathfinder to meaningful careers for her 'girls'. She was looking to turn out well-educated, above-the-average, marriageable women. But beyond support for women in the teaching profession, there was no belief that the girls should be prepared for universities and given a wider career concept. In her generation Charlotte Mason's ideas were to a degree ahead of her time. But even during the war, the unbalanced curriculum was already looking tired. The absence of any but the most basic teaching of science and maths made her curriculum dangerously lopsided. My education certainly suffered from this, and has made it much harder for me to fully understand the massive impact of the scientific and technological advances of my time.

Fairfield was a girls' school with around 200 boarders and a small number of day pupils. There were no boys' schools nearby, and my life throughout the Lakeland years was spent in largely female company – not the best preparation for the transition to adult life. The school's motto was: 'I am, I can, I ought, I will'. Our badge had a skylark rising high into the sky. It was supposed to symbolise the ability of all of us to rise to great heights – and to stay there. The staff was a mix of highly qualified teachers – most of them products of the Charlotte Mason College – and some of the senior students from the College working at Fairfield as part of their training. I can only remember one male teacher. It was he who helped me to overcome my refusal to speak or read, or even think in German.

I must have settled down in the school fairly easily. The teachers, sensibly, made no effort to explain to the pupils the circumstances of my arrival in England or how I had come to be at Fairfield. No mention was made of the fact that I was Jewish and I certainly did not refer to it. My school reports gave me consistently good marks for Bible Studies. The teaching was ecumenical and covered both the New and the Old Testaments.

The head mistress, Ida Moffatt, seems to have taken a special interest in me from the outset, and supported me to an extraordinary degree throughout my years at the school. After my first six months at Fairfield, Miss Moffatt wrote in my school report: 'Hella is a satisfactory pupil. She works well and with intelligence. She is inclined to be impatient when met with a difficulty and likes to be helped immediately before really trying to help herself.' In 1941, when my mother had so little money that she had no means to buy the next term's school books, Miss Moffatt paid for them. She wrote to my mother:

> Hella is now going into Form V where she will need many new books. They are a fairly heavy item and I shall be grateful if you will accept this cheque for the payment of them . . . I ask that you say nothing of this to anyone, but I am anxious that Hella should have the books so that she can make the most of her studies. I know that you have made and are making many sacrifices for her. It is too much to ask of you to get these books for her.

Fairfield had its own company of Girl Guides, and I became an enthusiastic member, rising to a Pathfinder's status. Among my outstanding memories was the occasion when the troop went camping in a field near Beatrix Potter's house. After a night of heavy rain and emerging from our tents wet, certainly the worse for wear, the portly figure of the real, live Beatrix Potter appeared and invited us to come and dry up in her house. Of course we had all read, and in my case certainly loved, her books. Suddenly to be spending time in her presence was heaven on earth.

Exaltation of a very different kind was part of a play that the Guides performed one year in the local church hall. The plot centred on the conversion of a tribal chief to Christianity. I was growing fast, and thanks to a sturdy appearance, I was given the dubious honour of playing the chief. I wore a colourful, voluminous garment.

Even though this was no more than enjoyable play-acting, I had in fact become interested in the Church of England – or rather, St Oswald's Church in Grasmere. A Gothic-style church dating back to the 14th century, St Oswald's was the parish church of the Wordsworth family, where William's grave has become a tourist attraction. I cannot remember why I first dragged my mother to the Sunday services. But I loved the ritual, learning, and soon singing the hymns and avidly listening to the vicar's sermons. It never gave me a genuine sense of true Christian belief and I certainly had no desire to become a church member. But at the time, those hours spent at church services in Grasmere were a respite from tension and gave me a sense of peace, a sense of belonging.

However, there was something more important that drew me constantly back to Grasmere. That something consisted of living human beings who befriended me. It was a couple, Ophelia and William Heaton Cooper. Ophelia was a well-established sculptor, working under her maiden name, Ophelia Gordon Bell, and Heaton was one of the Lakeland's leading landscape painters. They lived in the centre of the compact village in a small house grafted onto the side of the studio where Heaton exhibited and sold both his originals and prints of his own and his late father's paintings. I met them through Marion Lederer, a German refugee who had become my mother's friend and was working as a sales help in the studio. I became a fixture there, spending as much of my spare time there as I could. They were my rocks. To me, they were a magic family who steadied me and tried to help me address some of my insecurities.

Heaton and Ophelia were both trusting members of Moral Re-Armament (MRA), a Christian-based interfaith movement, now largely forgotten, formed by Frank Buchman in 1938 as a successor to his Oxford Movement. Both during the war and in the early post-war period, it was a prominent force, with followers among the great and the good. But it eventually became mired in controversy and lost much of its following. Heaton, a committed Christian, and Ophelia both felt that MRA brought them fulfilment and helped to guide their relationship and the upbringing of their young children, and even their work. Every morning after breakfast they would sit in silence for ten minutes or so, 'listening to God'. Then they would share the guidance they believed they had received, and the day proper would commence. I was allowed to join the Listening Time. They never tried to convert me or suggest I should join MRA. I cannot pretend that I ever felt that God was speaking to me. If I recall these sessions now, they certainly do not lose the sincerity of their intent and yet seem almost absurd. But at the time it all felt meaningful. I sensed the faith that guided Heaton and Ophelia. It helped to establish an enduring moral reference for my way of life.

Heaton always spoke of his conviction that life was a long search for 'absolute honesty, absolute purity, absolute unselfishness and absolute love'. In my teens I was still too young to understand that these were only distant, unattainable goals. Naively I probably thought that Heaton had acquired those absolutes and was practising them. But realism was not entirely absent. I dimly perceived that Ophelia had greater difficulties in coping with those high ideals. In a letter to me she wrote of her own struggles to find a safe middle ground, and urged me to get 'my own purpose and standards simple and clear enough for them to be infectious to others morally, emotionally and intellectually. In life, we must build bridges between persons, classes, nations.' It was advice that resonated with me. After all, journalism is about bridge-building, and, in later life, working with George Weidenfeld meant working with the ultimate model of a cultural bridge-builder.

As a teenager in the Lakes I was aching and groping to establish a secure identity. Perhaps I hoped that I would somehow be able to rise to what I saw as Heaton's moral heights. I wanted to find a way of getting my daily messages from God. I dreamed of an adult life that would give me, like the Heaton Coopers, a triangle of husband, self and God – and children thrown in as a bonus. I declared that I would never want to be married anywhere except in Grasmere Church. What a dreamer I was! I never found those invisible doors opening the way to such a stable heaven on earth.

Ophelia died of a brain tumour in 1975 and Heaton died in 1995. But they have never quite left me. I live with one of Ophelia's small sculptures and one of Heaton's paintings, and I collect the paintings of my close friend, their son Julian, an artist of the first rank.

Marion Lederer and her husband Frank were among a small group of refugees who had gravitated to the Lake District. Hans Keller, the notable musician and outstanding music critic, was another refugee who landed there – in his case, in 1941 – after being released from detention on the Isle of Man. His sister had married an Englishman who was serving in the armed forces and had taken a house in Windermere to keep their family safe. Hans, who was 23 at the time, found himself lodging nearby. His first teacher in Vienna, the violinist and physician Oscar Adler, had also found refuge in the Lake District. Soon the two musicians teamed up, found a few more and played chamber music. I well remember the small private concerts they organised. Sometimes Hans played the cello, sometimes the violin. It was a fluid ensemble; improvisation inevitably reigned. It was my first introduction to live chamber music and I revelled in it. Half a life later I found myself living in the same London neighbourhood as Hans, and we met again and became friends. By then Hans had made a great name for himself in the music world, had become Controller of BBC Radio Three and was married to the artist Milein Cosman. I never shared Hans's fascination with contemporary music. But that was no bar to occasional enjoyable evenings round my table.

It was only in 2019, at one of the concerts to celebrate the centenary of Hans Keller's birth, that I discovered more about the circumstances that had brought him to the Lake District – and indeed to Britain. Sitting next to me was a stranger. She overheard a friend calling me 'Hella' and instantly asked whether I was Hella Pick. It turned out she was Hans Keller's aunt and remembered me visiting their Windermere house. Eno Blythe believed she even had photographs of me. Of course, I soon visited her and was looking at an image of my 13-year-old self standing in the third row, smiling broadly in a small group photograph of refugees that also included Dr Adler and his wife, but no Hans Keller. This set off a renewed search among my own photographs and led to the discovery that I too had a copy. Eno then told me that her father, who was a man of means and generosity, had given the necessary financial guarantees to secure UK visas for all seven close members of his wife's family, including Hans Keller. And it was not only family. He had also brought out Dr Adler and provided for his stay in the Lakes.

Sadly, my grandmother had no benefactor to rescue her from Prague in time to reach Britain before the outbreak of war. In July 1939, the British Committee for Refugees from Czechoslovakia told my mother that they had applied to the Home Office for a visa for Olga. Nothing was said about timing, and my mother was asked not to make further enquiries but simply to wait. On 4 August 1939,

Olga sent a postcard suggesting that the visa had been granted. She quoted a communication from the Home Office telling her to 'apply for a visa to the British Passport Control Office at the British Consulate in Prague'. She applied immediately. Now, she wrote, she was waiting, running around Prague rather aimlessly. On a card sent a week later she complained about endless forms having to be filled in and sounded despondent, overwhelmed by her problems. I have two more letters from her, a short note sent to me in October 1939 and a long one dated 17 January 1940, sent to my mother. My little letter wishing me well in my new school included a photo, so 'that you will not forget me'. There was no danger of that. The long letter is barely legible, but appears to talk of some of the friends in Prague and also contains many questions about other friends who had managed to emigrate.

That was the end of direct communication with Olga. From then on the only messages that could be exchanged went via the International Red Cross. They had to be limited to around 30 words and could only be sent very infrequently. In July 1940, I sent a message: 'Endless greetings. Kisses for your birthday. Hope you are well. Here everything quiet and beautiful. I swim, I wander, am cheerful.' Olga's reply: 'You brave girl, dearly loved. Paper kisses from your grandmother. God gave you to me. Time has taken you away. Wander on – into my arms – be cheerful.'

On 16 August 1940 my mother and I sent 'Kisses and love. Be well and at peace. Here [the Lake District] all remains beautiful.' On the reverse side of the Red Cross form is the reply which appears to have been sent later in the year: 'Do not worry, can work, have help from Helena [a friend], am doing nursing, have pauses to rest. Happy Christmas and New Year. With burning love.' No indication of where she was, or whether she was still free.

There were no more Red Cross messages. It was impossible not to fear that she had perished. Fast forward to the end of the war. On 8 March 1945 a letter arrived addressed to me, not my mother, from Marina Pauliny, vice-chair of the Czechoslovak Red Cross. Written in Czech, it confirms that Olga was taken to the Theresienstadt concentration camp. Next day a further letter from Mrs Pauliny was delivered, this time in English, and without reference to the earlier communication. It informed me that a Mrs Olga Spitz was in a camp, Les Avants, in Zurich. For a brief moment there was hope. But it transpired that the survivor in Switzerland was not my grandmother. There could be no other conclusion than that Olga had died. But we still did not know where or when. It could have been in Theresienstadt, or worse, in another concentration camp, where she might have been gassed.

It was only many years later, long after my own mother had died, that cousins in America found documentation about an Olga Spitz who was deported to Minsk in November 1941. It is not recorded whether she died in the Minsk ghetto, where Jews were held prisoner, or was taken to the nearby extermination camp, Trostinets, which the Germans set up in 1942, and where many Czechs and Hungarians were killed. In any event, the dates attached to that documentation did not tally with my grandmother's birth or marriage, and I concluded this must have been a different Olga Spitz.

We concluded that my grandmother had met her end in the Czech concentration camp, Theresienstadt. We were wrong. Her end was far worse. It was only after this book was first published in 2021 that the Wiener Library offered to research Olga's fate. They established that she had indeed been forcibly taken to Theresienstadt in 1942. But after five weeks there she was put on a cattle truck transport destined for a Polish 'transit' ghetto at Izbica. There was no further trace of her. She could have perished in the train or at Izbica. And if she survived these she would have been gassed at a nearby concentration camp. Even though many years after Olga perished, the information unearthed by the Wiener Library came as a deep shock. It is a small relief that my mother never knew.

In 1946, my mother, though reconciled to the fact that Olga could no longer be alive, sent a desperately sad letter to acquaintances in Prague, asking whether there was any way of finding out what had happened. She went on to ask whether Olga had left any message for her, or had left anything behind that she could have – 'even a handkerchief or some other little memento they could send'.

The contrast between the tranquil Lake District and the horrors of the concentration camps and the Final Solution, and of the war itself, could not have been greater. But daily life was far from worry-free. Though wartime shortages made frugality inevitable, our poverty added an extra layer. We had a comfortable roof over our heads. But lack of money was ever present. I learned to cut patterns and sew my own dresses and blouses. I learned to knit my own sweaters. I minimised my bus travel and used the bicycle as much as I could. My mother's pay was not enough to cover even the most basic expenses. For much of the basics we had to rely on the charity of the refugee organisations. It was shaming.

There was never enough to cover the school bills. During my first term at Fairfield I had a free place. But it was not renewed and fees had to be paid. For two years, 1940–41 and 1941–2, the fees were covered by my London foster parents, the Infields. But in the autumn of 1942 'Daddy' Infield sent a letter to inform the Refugee Children's Movement (which later became World Jewish Relief) that his payments would end the following year, 1943, after the Easter term. That would roughly coincide with my 16th birthday, when I could be considered to have reached working age. The Refugee Children's Movement had overall responsibility for the welfare of the *Kindertransport* children. Prompted by the Infields' decision, the Manchester-based Regional Director of the organisation asked my mother if she had 'any plans for Hella's future? Is there any special kind of training you would like her to have, or is she specially gifted in any way? . . . If we are to arrange for her to take a practical course when she leaves school it is necessary to make plans well in advance.' Though the writer appeared to assume that I would leave school when I reached 16, she added, 'I understand Hella has worked extremely well at school, and we would like to help her in any way possible.' The only help I wanted was to continue at Fairfield, and in April 1943 the Refugee Children's Movement finally agreed to cover my school fees for a further year.

The cost of each term, together with incidentals and bus fares, was six guineas! Even by the value of sterling then, my debt to the Refugee Children's Movement is far greater. By enabling me to remain at school, their financial help fundamentally changed the course of my life. The Infields' decision to stop supporting me had been no arbitrary decision, and probably had little to do with financial problems. It simply reflected the family's view that it was time for me to start earning my own living. After my 16th birthday, they felt my formal education should end. They envisaged a short secretarial course and then an office job. I revolted. I was doing well at school academically and making good progress with French (but showing less prowess at sport!). My end-of-term reports were consistently good, and I was so proud when the teachers concluded in the summer of 1941 that 'Hella has the ability to grasp ideas as well as master facts'.

Then came the Infield thunderbolt – the withdrawal of financial help with my schooling. The shock of being advised that the time had come to end my formal education was great. I was desperate to remain at school until my matriculation. Even before the Refugee Children's Movement had decided to support me, Ida Moffatt, the headmistress who befriended me, took my case to the Principal of Charlotte Mason College, the formidable Joyce van Straubenzee. She agreed that I was suitable teacher material and offered to let me have a free place at Fairfield, if no other source was available, to conclude my education with two years in the Sixth Form. The idea was that I would then move on smoothly to the teacher-training course at Charlotte Mason College.

This attracted me no more than secretarial work. A letter from 'Daddy' Infield showed the kind of pressure being put on me:

> I have discussed with Auntie Ethel the pro's and con's of the College and the Secretarial course, and we have today written to Miss van Straubenzee accepting (or rather advising you to accept) her kind and generous offer of free education in Class VI to be followed by a two-year residential course at the College. I think it is a wonderful offer and you are to be heartily congratulated on having earned it.

I had no vocation to teach. I felt trapped. I wanted to stay at school, pass my matriculation and go on, not to a teacher-training college, but to university. I turned to Katharine Chorley. Initially she too advised that I should take up the Charlotte Mason offer, arguing that it was very important for me 'to gain a niche in English life so that you feel you are a real working part of the English community'. That remark really hurt: it showed that all my efforts to integrate had not taken me very far. I was still seen as an outsider, even by a wise friend who knew me well. But I was not prepared to give up. I had the good sense not to reject Miss Straubenzee's offer, as that would have meant leaving school, but also not to confirm my acceptance. I had my mother's support: wanting to keep me close, she did not relish the prospect of me spending two years as a residential student at Scale How.

In 1943, I passed my School Certificate with three Distinctions, good enough to give me exemption from matriculation, and gaining me warm praise from Ida Moffatt: 'I am delighted that you have done so well and that all your hard labours are rewarded.' This only reinforced my determination to secure a university education.

I was pressing Theo Chorley to help me get to the London School of Economics. Shortly before my 17th birthday in 1944, I was offered an interview for admission to LSE. The School had been evacuated to Cambridge for the duration of the war. I had no money for my fare to Cambridge but secured it from the Refugee Children's Movement. Now I also had to make clear that I did not intend to take up the teacher-training course at Charlotte Mason College. This produced a withering letter from Miss van Straubenzee. She told my mother that my choice was 'not very sensible. Hella will be no nearer getting a job at the end of her course [at LSE]. It is extremely doubtful that girls like Hella will be taken for reconstruction work after the war.' Once again I was seen as the outsider. The formidable teacher had also decided to revise her view of my suitability as a teacher: 'Hella now does not seem to me nearly as suitable for this training and it might be difficult in that case to post her afterwards.' Offer withdrawn!

My LSE interview went well and I was accepted. But a cold shower came with the good news. Accepted? Yes. For the 1944–45 academic year? No. The School's Secretary explained that the Ministry of

Labour had dictated that LSE could not admit a larger number of women students than it had admitted in the year before the war – in other words, an instruction to keep down the quota of women students! A large number of well-qualified women had already applied. LSE could not take them all and had decided on an age bar. Only girls over 18 would be admitted for 1944–45. As I was only 17, I was automatically excluded under this ruling. I would have to wait another year. I was devastated – devastated too soon, as I had failed to take on board that I had also been put on a waiting list. Within a month I received the news that I would after all be able to start my studies in the autumn of 1944.

All the years at Fairfield I had kept a 'Nature Notebook'. Each pupil had to record the flowers and the birds they saw on their walks during the changing seasons. Mine has many drawings and closely observed descriptions of the flora. But my last entry, in July 1944, is on a different, incoherent note: 'Today we break up for the last time after 5 years. I don't feel half as sad as I ought to feel. Still – It's pretty sad. Now there isn't even school anymore. Only a home that isn't a home.' Stability was not in sight.

CHAPTER 3

THE WAR ENDS –
ADULT LIFE BEGINS

Autumn 1944. The Allied forces were in Europe and slowly advancing on Germany. The Russian front was also painfully moving forward. Amid all the suffering and destruction, hopes were rising that the war was tortuously gearing up to its bitter end. Liberation of the concentration camps and their few survivors could at last be envisaged. Hitler's dominion would be over. But for the survivors among his victims, there could be no roll-back to life in pre-Hitler Europe. For me, a radical new beginning lay ahead.

I was not all of 17 years young. I was installed in Cambridge, enrolled at the London School of Economics. The security of the self-contained Lakeland world had been left behind. My school years were over. My undergraduate years were beginning. I had experienced none of the horrors of war and spent the school years in a predominantly female society. The culture shock was considerable. Could I take it in my stride?

To secure my LSE interview, it must have helped to have had an introduction from Professor Theo Chorley, who, though absent on wartime duties, was the School's Cassel Professor of Commercial Law. I sent his wife, Katharine Chorley, a disconsolate note when I learned that I would have to wait until my 18th birthday before entry to LSE. She tried to console me with this advice: 'it is often better to have a year of practical life before going to the university, and you are so young, you can afford the time'. She may well have been right. But I never had the chance to find out, since LSE relented and admitted me without further ado. Now, when I try to reconstruct that period of my life between leaving childhood behind and my beginnings as a journalist, it surprises me still that LSE should have accepted a barely 17-year-old on the strength of school records and one interview. Instead of enforcing their rule against women students below the age of 18, an exception was made for me. It was my first score as a woman pioneer!

And then there was another mystery. The Chorleys must have mentioned my name to Professor Harold Laski, one of LSE's most famous teachers. Laski had a record of helping refugees. He may have seen a potential in me of which I was certainly unaware. Whatever the motive, he decided that I was LSE material, and aware that I was impecunious, he decided to help with my LSE fees – £60 per annum! – and covered them for two years. It was a 'private' arrangement, and he insisted that there should be no reference to his gift in any official correspondence. The best way to thank him for this singular generosity was to justify his confidence in me by working – and, as it turned out, succeeding – to earn a good degree in Politics and Government.

To be at LSE and at the same time to be in Cambridge, living in College accommodation, was a very special experience – very different to life on the non-residential home campus after LSE moved back to London in 1945. But before I could even begin to appreciate university life, there was the upheaval of leaving the Lake District and settling into a new, very different world which was much more in touch with the war that continued to rage. It was a given that my mother would not be left behind. The idea of separation was never even contemplated. Lack of money alone made rebellion impossible. She was still bound by the Home Office order restricting her to domestic work. Once again the Chorley network went into action. And that is how she found herself working in the household of one of Britain's intellectual elites, the Cornford family. At first neither of us fully appreciated that Frances Cornford and her husband Francis were Cambridge aristocracy; or that the Darwins were close family and Gwen Raverat, Frances's cousin, was a near neighbour and frequent visitor; or that Vanessa Bell and the Bloomsbury set were friends. They made both of us welcome, treated us as new friends and made it easier to settle into this novel landscape. Though I was housed in a university hostel and only stayed in the Cornford house during the winter break, it was a perch that stimulated my intellectual curiosity, opened new cultural horizons and certainly provided a challenging impetus to my studies.

I had a special rapport with Gwen Raverat, whose charm and quiet grace impressed me as much as learning about the entanglements of Darwin family life in Edwardian Cambridge, so vividly portrayed in her book *Period Piece*. She had partied with Rupert Brooke. She had been on the fringes of the Bloomsbury circle, and Virginia Woolf had been a good friend. What marked her out for me was that this remarkable woman had kept her individuality and independence and yet was able to define herself as part of a close-knit, if often difficult, web of family and friends. How I longed for that kind of security.

LSE had been in Cambridge, hosted by Peterhouse College, since the beginning of the academic year in autumn 1939. Though its Director, Sir Alexander Carr-Saunders, chafed at the move, it had been forced on the School by the decision of the Ministry of Works that it required the School's premises for war work. During my year in Cambridge, LSE had fewer than 1,000 students, with women unsurprisingly in the majority. Though the staff had also been reduced, with many seconded on war work, students received a great deal more personal attention than is possible today, when the LSE student body has multiplied more than tenfold. In Cambridge I could sit at the feet of Professor Laski, benefit from his lectures and participate in seminars that he led. He took a close interest in my progress, but of course he was a hard taskmaster who critically scrutinised the essays I produced. The degree subjects included economic analysis and policy, constitutional and economic history. My special subject was political and social theory and institutions, which I studied under his guidance.

Even in my second and third years, when LSE was back on its London campus and student numbers had doubled, it remained possible to maintain a close teacher–student relationship with Harold

Laski. But I was also lucky enough to have K. B. Smellie, Professor of Political Science, as my immediate supervisor. Humorous, quizzical, with a brilliant mind, he was less remote than Harold Laski and excelled in drawing his students into a world of politics and government, theory and practice. He reinforced my growing – and, as it turned out, career-defining – interest in politics and world affairs.

In Cambridge social life was pleasant but undramatic. From time to time I met Brian Infield, the younger son of my foster parents, who had been too young to be called up for national service and had become a King's College student. I moved in a mixed group, remained a virgin and was content. I have come across a letter I wrote in January 1945 but apparently failed to post. The handwriting still has the marks of an adolescent. Addressed to Paul – I have no idea who he was – the letter starts by complaining about the lack of heating and the bitter cold:

I have never been so cold before. We only have heating in the Common Room and the Study and even here we only have a little gas fire where one first has to warm one's front, then one's back and then start the manoeuvre all over again. Our bedrooms are quite indescribable. I wear sweaters and socks in bed . . . Under these conditions it is hard to concentrate on work. Still, I managed to huddle in a corner with a warm water bottle and wade through some really stiff books. I feel very righteous today. I have also begun my essay on antisemitism, and much to my surprise find that I can manage tolerably well, even in German. However as soon as I finish this I have to write another 10 essays; this time for Prof Laski on British constitution issues.

The letter finishes with a naively written paragraph:

I am going to be a psychologist's guinea pig tomorrow. I am to be tested for an experiment. I am curious what characteristics it will reveal. I don't know whether to look forward or be afraid. The experimenter doesn't know me – I wonder whether he will want to know me after this experiment.

Reading this many years later, I wonder what all this was about, what conclusions were drawn from this intelligence(?) test.

By the end of 1944 it was becoming obvious that LSE would return to London in time for the 1945–46 academic year. Once again we – my mother and I – would have to be on the move. This time she was determined to avoid yet another spell of domestic work and to secure a Home Office permit enabling her to become self-employed and establish herself as a milliner. Twice in 1944 she had applied to change the terms of her permit. Twice she was told she could only have a six-month permit for alterations to clothes, with millinery specifically excluded. Finally, early in 1945, with the help of the Cambridge branch of the Central Committee for Refugees, she was granted a one-year permit for 'alterations and repairs to clothes, household linen and hats at home for private customers and provided you do not employ other labour'. She was obliged to provide a detailed account of her earnings, and the permit would have to be renewed on an annual basis.

The next hurdle was to find affordable accommodation in London. I would lose the independence of living out. We would again be living together. This mutual dependence was a constant strain. At the end of the summer term in 1945 the Cambridge interlude ended, and with the war finally over, we were installed in a small rented flat in Ealing in West London. For my mother, the next hurdle was to find customers before her tiny savings were exhausted.

For me, the immediate challenge after the end of the academic year was to earn some money during the long vacation before the move to London. The Cambridge Refugee Committee had described me as a 'very pleasant and happy young lady', and this convinced the Youth Service Volunteers (organisers of holiday camps for young people) that I was capable of running their girls' camp at Thornthwaite near Keswick in the Lake District. I spent the summer there looking after successive batches of around 30 girls. My duties were extensive. Under the supervision of the warden, I had to arrange their work, excursions and organised activities. I had to keep a diary of what took place each day and a record of each girl's activities. I also had to arrange lectures, and get the girls to undertake some work for the local community. Somehow there was also supposed to be time for the girls to make curtains, cushions, lampshades and 'other things that would improve the appearance of the Village Institute' where the girls were housed. As if all this was not enough, I was told there had to be strict supervision to ensure 'the girls kept reasonable hours'. For the first time, I had responsibility over the lives of others. And another first: my small earnings were at a level where I had to pay a few shillings of income tax!

As usual, I kept up a steady flow of letters to my mother, and as usual, she saved several. They make a fascinating read. At first I felt overwhelmed by my tasks and declared that I was miserable. But that changed rapidly. I discovered that I was quite enterprising in planning the girls' activities. As I was on familiar Lakeland territory, I made use of local friends for advice and also persuaded Heaton Cooper to give lectures to my charges.

> I have to arrange their [the girls'] whole life – excursions, climbs, lectures, socials, dances, their work, their free time, chaperone their dances and accompany them on all organised activities. I am in charge when the warden is away, and on top of that I have a copious correspondence with the Director of Education, petrol officers and various other officials.

Taking the girls out to swim always worried me:

> It's such a responsibility making sure that they don't drown and keeping them all together and are home at the right time; and then to draw up a programme for the following week, making sure there is a plan for each day . . . I do hope I will get a helper. This week I have got a 19-year-old teacher who has helped a lot . . .

Evidently she had no problem working with me, an 18-year-old. Somehow, in spite of the work load, I found time to relax, for sun-bathing or visiting a friendly local resident who allowed me the use of her bathroom. Gillian Chorley and sometimes her brother Roger, who were staying at Randapike, came to see me.

One night I had to decide whether to expel two girls who had been out until 1.30 a.m., well after the 11 p.m. curfew time. Another night my authority was challenged when three of 'my' girls were caught in the nude swimming with boys. 'I have found out now that I can manage people and arrange things well,' I told my mother. And I was 'even going to be quite a famous person – reporters from *Picture Post* [then Britain's leading news magazine] are coming to spend a whole week for interviews and photographs, and the *News Chronicle* are also coming!' For the first time I was pictured in print. Fame indeed!

The 1945 election was held while I was at Thornthwaite. Theo Chorley, who had run as a Labour candidate, lost by a handful of votes. His disappointment was deep but was soon mitigated when the new Prime Minister, Clement Attlee, awarded him what was to be the last hereditary peerage. Since then only life peerages have been given out.

I was supremely happy with the election result, but like most people, I was also surprised by Labour's victory. I told my mother: 'I just cannot get over it. It seems absolutely incredible. With Laski and his ideas once more influential with the government, things will be much easier for refugees – for us!'

The return to London was a return to largely unfamiliar territory for my mother and me. During the few pre-war months we had spent in London, neither of us had gained more than a superficial knowledge of the city. Now, in the autumn of 1945, we found ourselves in a city massively disfigured by Hitler's bombs. I had a daily commute to LSE on the venerable Central Line and did not take long to find my way around and adjust to big-city life.

My two remaining years at LSE passed in a whirl of study and social life. I had to work my way through long reading lists. One essay led to the next. Lectures and seminars were good for the thinking buds and encouraged debate. Existentialism began to occupy my mind, and turned me into an amateur philosopher questioning many of the concepts of right and wrong that my schooling, together with my Grasmere friends, the Heaton Coopers, had instilled in me. As well as philosophy there was activism: I was urged to join 'Young Austria', a movement started by a group of young refugees to support their fellow refugees, keep alive the roots that had bound refugees to Austria, and also to promote understanding of Austria's history and culture. I became a reluctant member and learned, to my lasting regret, that my nature is not well suited to organised campaigning.

I did not see it as a contradiction that I nevertheless became an enthusiastic member of the Fabian Society. For me, it was a great way of getting to know like-minded people, exchanging ideas and enjoying social occasions. I always relished our organised country walks and engaged in earnest political discussion with fellow Fabians that usually ended in good-humoured banter in a village pub. It was during this period that I made friends with Ralph Miliband (later I came to know David and Ed) and also met Ernst Wohlgemuth, a fellow student whose future wife, Evi, would become my very closest friend.

The money problem was never far away, even though I was the lucky recipient of one of LSE's Special Free Place Awards in two successive years, which enabled me to complete my studies. The International Student Service also came to my rescue in my final year after Professor Laski's financial help came to an end. A cousin, Egon Oesterreicher, gave me money to cover the fee for my final exams at LSE. I found holiday jobs to earn a little extra. But of course, none of this addressed my mother's financial situation, which cast a big shadow over my life. She had great taste and was dexterous with her hands and really was an excellent milliner. She was unwell and suffered from varicose veins. It was not easy to find customers. An appeal to the Ealing Synagogue produced a rebuff. Acquaintances from Cambridge recommended her to some London friends and a few got in touch. Slowly she built up a small client base. But it was always a hand-to-mouth situation. I hated being a beggar. Financial insecurity began to haunt me. Long after my mother's death, I still woke up in a sweat from a dream in which I had not given her sufficient financial support.

Money was not the only worry. During the war she had lived in a bubble of suspense. Now the reality of what she had lost, what she was missing, was hitting her hard. There was no longer any doubt that her mother had died in a concentration camp. There were no signs of life from Kapi. Her hopes were further shattered when she learned that Rudi Anzenhofer had married. Her furniture had been auctioned off cheaply by the Nazis, and it gradually became crystal-clear that it was impossible to retrieve the funds that had been entrusted to the courier after the *Anschluss* to bank in Switzerland. For a while she became very depressed and asserted that she had 'always hated London' and wanted to get away. Though she now had a small circle of friends, and gradually became more positive and cheerful, she still felt that I was the only treasure left to her – quite a responsibility for me to bear.

I took my final exams in June 1947. The same cousin who covered the exam fees now gave me a wonderful present: he paid for a summer course at Lausanne University to improve my French. I found a room in the Pension Cuenoud and covered my keep by providing household help. Without the warm-hearted but also cleanliness-fixated owner, Mlle Cuenoud, I might never have learned that it is important to clean the outside of saucepans just as immaculately as the inside. That lesson was a parable for life, and it's also been useful for the condition of my kitchenware!

I enjoyed the pension and its kaleidoscope of guests. I enjoyed the university work, and I enjoyed afternoon trips to a lakeside bathing hut that Mlle Cuenoud allowed me to use to go swimming. It was a romantic spot: the still, blue waters of Lac Leman with views across to the Mont Blanc region, and behind me the vineyard-studded Swiss countryside. The neighbouring hut belonged to a handsome physical instructor, Claude Giroud, whom I found unbelievably attractive. My heart beat faster – but in vain – every time he turned up to swim. We talked, we swam together, and I was thrilled when he even took me out for tea and cakes in a grand Lausanne café. But one thing did not lead to another . . . The attraction was evidently not as mutual as I had hoped!

During my first three weeks in Lausanne my heart was also beating faster by the day for a very different reason – in anticipation of my exam results. On 23 July the suspense was over. At 7 p.m. a telegram came from my mother: 'Congratulations Class II Upper division. Supposed to be very good. Am happy for us both.' It was only a few points short of a First. I was now a bona fide Bachelor of Science (BSc Econ.). Congratulations from the Chorleys and from Professor Smellie followed almost immediately. I wrote to my mother:

I can hardly believe it. Is it really true? Are you sure you didn't make a mistake? If it's really true then an Upper Second is so much better than I ever imagined. It's even good enough to satisfy Prof Laski . . . I still can't believe I have done so well.

Laski sent his congratulations. He was satisfied! Mlle Cuenoud and the pension guests celebrated with me – not with champagne but with a specially confected ice cream.

My French was improving rapidly and at the end of my course two friends came from England to join me for a short holiday in the mountains. Unexpectedly, there were soon four of us. Staying in Chateau D'Oex, I heard a voice say, 'Hello.' I recognised him – I'd met him at a party at Trinity College in Cambridge. He was Eli Lauterpacht, a law student who would become one of the UK's most distinguished lawyers of Interrnational Law. He was on his own and somehow attached himself to our little party for the rest of our holiday. The friendship survived. Though we rarely met, we always remained in touch.

University was now behind me. Armed with my BSc, the time had come to find a proper job, to earn money. To my surprise, I had no desire to nail myself to the UK, even though I knew I would soon be given British nationality. I wanted an international job. To be precise, I had an *idée fixe* that my future lay with the United Nations, whose charter I had studied at LSE. I was starry-eyed about the opportunities it offered for international cooperation and conflict prevention. I applied to the UN in New York, and to the UN in Geneva. But all to no avail. The UN had quotas for each country, and what counted was country of origin. Austria only had a small quota. Combined with my inexperience, my Austrian origin counted against me. Much later, when I came to the UN as the *Guardian*'s correspondent and saw something of the UN's bureaucracy, I recognised that I had had a lucky escape. It would not have suited my temperament and might only have brought me disillusionment. But in 1947 I only felt frustration.

Still fixated on an international body as my career destination, I applied to the OEEC (the Organisation for European Economic Co-operation), which emerged from the Marshall Plan and was formed in 1948. But it was rejection all over again. Those uprooted Austrian roots stood in the way of realising my internationalism. I was still not reconciled to settling down to work in Britain. I was restless and did not know where I belonged. My thoughts turned to possibly using my father to get myself to America and look for work there. But I quickly realised that this was foolish thinking. My father had ignored repeated attempts to catch up on alimony payments, and worse, he had made no attempt to contact me after the end of the war. I am tempted to say that his apparent decision to write me out of his life did not touch me. But of course, that cannot be entirely true. It diminished him. But it also had the effect of diminishing me.

While I was figuring out where to turn next in my search for work in an international field, Professor Smellie offered me a stop-gap solution. He would pay me to do research work for him. It was a great help, both financially and also because it left me enough time both to explore job avenues and to explore a little of Western Europe and my affinity to Austria. It also allowed me to help my mother in her efforts to secure restitution from Austria. My mother had never shared the views of many refugees, who considered Austria to be fundamentally anti-Semitic and felt they could never bear to see the country again. I always felt that had she been able to afford it, she would have preferred to join the handfuls of émigrés – like the artist and later my good friend Georg Eisler – who had decided soon after the war to go back to live in Austria. But she sensed that I needed wider horizons and was unlikely to join her. So that was a non-starter, and in 1947 she successfully applied for British nationality for herself, and as I was still a minor, also for me.

Even though she obviously pined for Austria, she was hesitant about a visit to Vienna. She couldn't entertain the thought of meeting the married Rudi in his family context — though they were exchanging letters and she was constantly pressing him to come and see her in London. She eventually made one brief trip to her beloved Vienna, but only saw him briefly and certainly stopped short of meeting his wife. Rudi's love for my mother — if it ever really existed — had gone. But the loyal friendship had not wavered. His letters showed concern for her well-being and her health after she complained of depression and constant problems with her legs. He collected as much information as possible on what had happened to the shipment of her furniture and possessions seized by the Nazis in 1939 and advised her about applying for reparations. If she decided to return to live in Vienna, he even offered to have her stay with him and his family until she could find a permanent home. He also reminded her that he still had a few of her possessions that had been rescued before the war. After much agonising, my mother asked me to make an exploratory visit to Vienna and bring back whatever I could carry.

I did not hesitate. I was keen to reacquaint myself with the city of my birth. It was 1949. Austria was under four-power occupation. Vienna was still in recovery mode, not least from the war-damage and post-war shortages. The old glory was gone. Austria saw itself as one of Hitler's victims and was still far from admitting guilt as a Nazi perpetrator. Democratic institutions had to be refurbished under the beady eye of the Soviet occupation. The country's impatient search for an independent and meaningful stature in post-war Europe was unresolved.

Proudly flourishing my shiny new British passport, I arrived in Vienna wondering how would I respond. Would I see myself as a foreigner or a native? It was something in between. I felt an outsider, but not a foreigner. It took many more visits and several years before I became fully acclimatised to Vienna and began to feel a genuine affinity and stopped questioning whether it was possible to have a sense of belonging to the country which had ejected me. Gradually I concluded that Austria had an acceptable place in the jungle of my identities. The question I continue to pose is where Austria lies in the pecking order of identities.

I stayed with the Anzenhófers during that first reunion with Vienna. They made me welcome, treated me as an instant friend and, to my surprise, I felt at ease with them. After that first stay in the city, Rudi always wrote to me rather than to my mother and used me as the messenger. He had tired of her demands and complaints.

Vienna was by no means my only foreign trip during those post-graduation years. With the money I was earning in London, I went back, mostly with friends, to Austria, to the Tirol and the Salzkammergut. I inspected the Hotel Weisses Rossl in St Wolfgang where my mother spent her honeymoon, and decided that I had been conceived in a satisfactory place! I wrote to her from there that 'I am beginning to see why you always came here. It really is so very lovely.' I had become an avid mountain walker – I stop short of describing myself as a climber, as I have no head for rock climbing – and relished a trip to Zermatt where I joined friends to walk to great heights and do ten-hour-long expeditions. And still I had enough willpower to sit down and write a close account to my mother, before joining the others for boisterous meals!

I came to know and enjoy Paris. I again went knocking on the door of OEEC, and again failed to win an entry. I spent a couple of winter holidays working for a travel agent, taking small groups on skiing holidays to Switzerland. I went to stay with 'Auntie Ethel' and 'Daddy' Infield, who had retired to Jersey. They had followed my progress through LSE and the move to London, and were keen to see me again. I reported to my mother that they had become very boring, had no real curiosity for what I was making of my life and wasted their evenings watching TV. But even so, it felt reassuring to see that the bond, going back to my first days in London, had not been entirely broken.

In London much of my social life revolved around the now long-abandoned Linguists Club. Designed as a meeting place for linguists, language learners and anyone who had an interest in languages, it had an international membership and developed into a club for dancing, watching films, discussions, travel and generally socialising. It suited my temperament and my international outlook. I was never short of boyfriends. But my only serious suitor was Jean, an attractive, very bright Swiss I had met at the Pension Cuenoud in Lausanne. He was a fledgling diplomat and came to London on several occasions to persuade me to marry him. I pushed him away every time. I did not think I was made to be a Swiss diplomat's spouse. On gloomy days when I have longed for family life and children of my own, I have sometimes, but only very cursorily, wondered whether I made a mistake.

All through those exploratory post-LSE years, my mother remained determined to keep a close grip on me. When I was away she expected daily letters and sent daily letters, usually laced with concern for my well-being, and sometimes sending food parcels. She wanted to be informed of every detail of my life and was forever worrying that something might happen to me. Once, when I was in the Tirol and she had not heard from me for three days, she even sent a telegram to Rudi Anzenhofer asking him to find out whether I was OK! Of course, I did not give my mother a blow-by-blow account of everything I was experiencing. But I did willingly make time to write three- or four-page letters at the end of most days telling her enough to satisfy her. Our interdependence was still powerful enough for me to accept and respond to her possessive love. But tensions were begging to surface. Rebellion was inevitable.

In 1949, I finally landed an interesting job with the Colonial Development Corporation (CDC), a public-investment vehicle set up by the Attlee government to promote agricultural development in British colonies. After a short trial period I acquired my first title. I was appointed 'Market Research Assistant' with responsibility for studying the economies of Britain's colonial empire in West Africa. My task was to evaluate marketing prospects for their agricultural products. It was my first brush with West Africa, and I never suspected that this experience would be the bridge to my entry into journalism. My work at CDC also triggered an enduring interest in third-world development issues. But again, I could not have guessed that this would eventually lead me into the Aga Khan's world and a commission to write his biography. I was doing well at CDC and had a good relationship with the department head, Penelope Piercy. In a letter confirming my promotion, I was told that 'Miss Piercy has asked me to tell you that she is very thrilled with the contacts you have made. You have worked a magic spell and got access in all the right places!'

I continued to progress and enjoy the work, and got on well with my colleagues. But I was chafing at the bit. I wanted wider horizons, bigger challenges, more opportunities to prove myself. At CDC it was a desk-bound, nine-to-five job, and I realised that I would never be really comfortable as a cog in a large bureaucratic machine. Even so, I gave market research a second try by accepting an offer to work for British Nylon Spinners, a big ICI–Courtauld-owned company. Founded in 1940 to produce this newly developed artificial fibre, the company had become an innovative enterprise engaged in an ever-wider search for new end-use products. But a couple of years working there only reinforced my conclusion that market research could never be a career for my restless, rootless spirit.

I again started to scan the multitude of job offers (yes, this was the magical time when there was no shortage of opportunities for young graduates), and one day I hit on an advertisement for a Commercial Editor at a periodical called West Africa. I thought to myself that thanks to my experience at CDC I knew a fair amount about the countries of West Africa. The work might open new horizons beyond the UK. So why not apply? The rest is history – at least, my history!

CHAPTER 4

NOVICE IN AFRICA

It is 6 March 1957 in Accra. At the stroke of midnight the Union Jack is lowered and a British colony, the Gold Coast, passes into history. A new story begins. A flag bearing the pan-African colours of red, yellow and green swooshes up the pole. Ghana is born and has already scored a first. It is the first British colony in West Africa to gain independence. A massive crowd is jumping wildly up and down, cheering 'Freedom, Freedom' and waving a myriad of flags. Swaying dangerously on a narrow platform, flanked by two of his stalwart lieutenants, stands their exuberant leader, Kwame Nkrumah. Modest in size but outsize in charisma, this is a leader whose long fight for independence has now been rewarded. His voice is hoarse. But the message is clear: 'Freedom! At long last, the battle has ended! And thus Ghana, your beloved country, is free for ever. Freedom!' But Nkrumah is proclaiming a wider message – only the first battle has been won: 'Our independence is meaningless unless it is linked to the total liberation of Africa. The new Africa is ready to fight its own battles and show that the black man is capable of managing his own affairs. Freedom!'

The British monarchy, in the person of Princess Alexandra of Kent, is there in full panoply to witness the loss of a colony and to welcome a newly independent recruit to the British Commonwealth. In recognition of the significance of the event, the US Vice-President – Richard Nixon at that time – has come, and so have many other luminaries from around the world. Martin Luther King earns an ultra-vociferous welcome when he declaims that 'a new order is coming into being. The universe itself is on the side of freedom and justice.' He can hardly guess that within half a dozen years colonial West Africa will have become a collection of sovereign states. But the proud demeanour, the winning smiles and the emotional embrace of Kwame Nkrumah all demonstrate Martin Luther King's confident instinct that Ghana's achievement of independence will have an impact far beyond the shores of West Africa and will act as a vital spur to America's civil rights movement. Soon the music strikes up. The crowds spread out into the city. All through the night Accra is filled with throngs of cheerful people. Most of the women are draped in colourful traditional Kente cloth. Intoxicated with or even without alcohol, everybody is happily swaying to the rhythms of the country's High Life music.

Absorbing the scene – and readily drawn into the dancing – is the Commercial Editor of the magazine *West Africa*. I am that person. I was 29 years old and, to my surprise, had finally found a fit for my professional abilities and ambitions. At the time it also satisfied my emotional needs. There was nothing routine about the work. I became totally immersed in decolonisation and the African world. I was meeting a kaleidoscope of interesting people and getting a close-up look at the politics of independence. I could make frequent sorties to West Africa and could loosen my mother's grip. Within the small community of common interest and expertise in West African affairs, I was making a name for myself – a very small one, of course. It bolstered my self-confidence. It became part of my quest for personal independence as a working woman. Oh yes, it seemed that I could also write well enough to satisfy a discerning editor and his magazine's readership!

I had brought to the job a modicum of knowledge about the countries of West Africa. But I had no first-hand experience of the region, and I was virtually the only woman – and the only novice – among the handful of experienced Western journalists covering the end of Empire in British and French West Africa. I was lucky. My male colleagues welcomed me to the 'club'. Colin Legum of the *Observer* and André Blanchet and Philip Decreane of *Le Monde* taught me invaluable short-cuts to understanding the intricacies of

African politics and became close companions. Throughout my time in covering African affairs, I cannot recall being subjected to any kind of deliberate discrimination.

Perhaps I wasn't looking? Everything about journalism was still so novel. Everything about Africa was an adventure and a stimulant. I never paused to consider that I was doing a rather unusual assignment at a time when it was hardly common for women journalists to cover politics and current affairs; certainly not on the African scene. I had no pretentions to see myself as a pioneer, let alone a role model. But I did have ambition. I did want to be successful! Oh, and as a footnote: I did have a very foolish pretention to maybe making an impact – a tiny little impact – on the course of West Africa's politics!

The early months with *West Africa* magazine were a crash course in learning about an African world on the road to independence. Initially I was puzzled by the sharp differences of approach between the leaders of British West Africa and and their French African counterparts, but soon came to believe that the clue was to be found in the deep, and very different, cultural impact that Britain and France had made on their West African possessions. Just like Nkrumah, the leaders of Nigeria, Sierra Leone and Gambia demanded full independence. They had few cultural or emotional links to the 'mother country'. On the other hand, most of French Africa's leaders were so deeply immersed in French culture that they were prepared to settle for something less: General de Gaulle was offering full autonomy within a quasi-federal structure – a Franco-African Community – that would preserve a constitutional link with France.

I saw how France had nurtured and subsidised the economies of its West African colonies far more generously than the British had in their region of West Africa. I saw how France had deliberately woven French African leaders into the fabric of French society. But I also observed how the Soviet Union was trying to penetrate West Africa and draw the region into the periphery of the Cold War. I sat in on endless discussions about African unity and the need for pan-African structures. I learned that Africans had their own concepts of democracy and witnessed how they questioned Western-style parliamentary democracy as a model for Africa. This was not a time for preoccupation with the evils of colonialism or of slavery. I also found that deep tribal and religious fissures were all too rarely addressed. In the fever of impending independence, future constitutional arrangements were neglected and social tensions were pushed aside. This was a period of hope and optimism in West Africa, and of confidence in black leadership and a stable, prosperous future. In retrospect it looks like a mirage. At the time it felt real. I was fortunate to experience it.

A riveting cast of characters came into my life. Among my new friends I counted many of the leading political players in West Africa. The most outstanding among them were Kwame Nkrumah in Ghana, Sekou Toure in Guinea, Felix Houphouet-Boigny in Ivory Coast, Leopold Senghor in Senegal and Nnamdi Azikiwe in Nigeria.

Toure and Nkrumah were both radical socialists with few cultural bonds to hold them to the colonial powers. They were wedded to full independence and dreaming of a continent united in its commitment to socialism. Their influence on African affairs went far beyond their own countries.

For many years Houphouet-Boigny, as leader of the Rassemblement Democratique Africain (RDA), a party straddling the countries of French West Africa, was the most conspicuous spokesman for conservative forces in the region. He was a Roman Catholic who eventually built himself a monument in the form of an outsize, bitterly controversial basilica in his birthplace, Yamoussoukrou. He was simultaneously an African nationalist and an ultimate French establishment figure, devoted as much to France as to his own country, a believer in capitalism and convinced that French African states had to gain economic independence before cutting all constitutional links with France.

Leopold Senghor was a cosmopolitan at ease in any society, an intellectual and a poet who invented the term 'negritude' to define black culture. He had close links to France, including a chateau home, and his approach to independence for his country was unique and distinct from those of the other French African leaders.

Nnamdi Azikiwe in Nigeria was, in common with most of the

country's other prominent politicians, too preoccupied with Nigeria's ethnic and economic complexity to embroil himself in the affairs of the others, all of them smaller countries of West Africa. 'Zik' became independent Nigeria's first head of state. Yet even before the Nigerian Federation raised its independence flag in 1960, there were signs that he would become a disruptive force in his country's future and threaten its break-up. Remember the Biafra war!

This was still a remarkably safe world where security measures were virtually unknown. Prominent people moved around freely. These men – and the leaders were almost all men – were freely accessible to journalists prepared to write about them and their ambitions. They were all the more susceptible to the unusual experience of an attractive young woman who could do more than smile, was interested, inquisitive, and with her writing was helping to raise their profile and ambitions to an audience in the outside world. It was a heady time to be let loose among optimistic African leaders convinced that the end of their colonial status would open up vistas of peace, prosperity and African unity. Black power would indeed matter on the geopolitical stage. It was quite mesmerising, realising how easy it was to gain their trust and form warm friendships. The main problem was steering away from the bedroom.

None of this had ever been part of a career plan. Nor had it been part of my mother's plans for her daughter. She had a very simple desire. I should meet the right man – whatever 'right' meant in that context. We should fall in love, marry, produce children and be happy for ever after . . . Trips to Africa were not considered to be the most conducive path to finding a partner. In fact, my sorties to Africa only caused my mother worries about my safety. When I was away I was peppered with missives worrying about the untold dangers I must have been facing in the midst of all 'those black men'. Regular letters and reassurances did not help. Yet, at the same time she was proud of my work, and praised me to high heaven to her friends.

Journalism had not been on my mind when I graduated with an iron determination to work in the United Nations. Market research at the Colonial Development Corporation and with British Nylon

Spinners had not provided an answer to a maiden's prayers. But CDC had given me a glimpse of West Africa and had given me my calling card when I answered an advertisement for an economics graduate to become the Commercial Editor of the London-based weekly magazine *West Africa*, a publication of which I was completely ignorant. To my great surprise the Editor, David Williams, decided take the risk and shape me into a journalist. It sounds self-serving to say that David was a brilliant editor who recognised talent. But I was not the only person whom he took under his wing. David also gave two of my successors, Bridget Bloom and Walter Schwartz, their start to a successful media career. When David offered me my job in 1953, he wrote that he was

> most interested to see the CDC Market report you were kind enough to send me. Preparing these reports is certainly valuable experience for the kind of work the commercial editor does here . . . I cannot pretend that any salary I can offer is adequate for your experience and qualifications. But I do think that here you would have work that is much more interesting than most.

He was right on both counts. The salary (£550) was low, and remained low. In 1958, when I applied for membership of the National Union of Journalists, I was initially turned down because I was still only earning £950 p.a., a figure below the NUJ minimum for someone of my experience. But no matter about poor pay. The work turned out to be gripping and involved assignments way beyond a Commercial Editor's remit.

Initially my task was to fill a weekly page with news items of interest to enterprises trading with West Africa. I had to become knowledgeable about cocoa prices and the diamond trade, about shipping issues and import and export levels. Not, perhaps, the most enthralling task. But I was impressed by David and intrigued by the prospect of observing close-up the end of key parts of the British and French colonial empires. I might be able to put my French studies to good use. I had some inkling that this would not be a dead-end job. I took the plunge.

West Africa was launched in 1917 as a weekly news magazine to serve colonial civil servants and British commercial interests in Nigeria, the Gold Coast, Sierra Leone and Gambia. By the time I joined the paper in 1955, coverage had been significantly broadened. It had become essential reading for its reporting of political developments and independence movements in French as well as British West Africa. Ownership of the magazine had passed to the Daily Mirror Group, which had also acquired a group of daily papers in what were still the British colonies in West Africa. Cecil King, Chairman of the Mirror Group, had built up a remarkable library of books and publications about West Africa, and treated the magazine very much as his personal fiefdom.

The magazine's budget was tight, the staffing was minimal and it soon became clear that my remit would extend way beyond the coverage of commerce. By the mid 1950s the writing was on the wall for colonial rule. Significant steps towards self-government had already been taken in several countries of West Africa. The question now was to determine the terms on which Britain and France would finally withdraw from their possessions. Britain was committed to the principle of full independence and engaged in negotiations with the African leadership. The French position was different. General de Gaulle, back in power in the Fifth Republic, was happy to give full autonomy to French West Africa and treat its leaders as equal partners. But he was set on a confederal structure that would retain political as well as economic links with France. My magazine was closely covering these end-of-empire negotiations. David Williams knew every leader of consequence in British West Africa, and was familiar with the ministers and officials in charge of the British end of the independence negotiations. He often acted as a go-between. Since I spoke French, a language he lacked, he quickly decided that French West Africa should be added to my more pedestrian portfolio. I accepted with pleasure.

My first venture into French Africa actually took place in London, when I was asked to write a review of 'Les Ballets Africains de Guinea', a small troupe of Guinean dancers on a world tour. Not for a moment did I suspect that an evening spent watching joyous

African dances would trigger a chain reaction that propelled me to the inner circles of French Africa's leading politicians. By no stretch of the imagination could I claim to have any expertise on African music or dancing. In my review I must have tried to hide my ignorance by highlighting that the women dancers had covered their breasts with fake oranges to conform with British law prohibiting any kind of female nudity. The music, with its haunting mix of African rhythms and traditional tunes, made a far more enduring impact. I have never tired of listening to the recording given to me by Keita Fodeba, the founder of the troupe.

Fodeba turned out to be a close friend and comrade of Sekou Toure, French Africa's most radical leader and future President of Guinea. After my evening at the ballet, Fodeba kept in touch. I still have letters where he mapped out future tours for his troupe and unsurprisingly asked me to write about his plans in *West Africa*. I don't think I did. But he bore no grudge and instead urged me to come to Guinea. When I let him know that my editor had authorised a visit, Fodeba wrote to apologise that he was too busy 'to look after me full-time', adding that he nevertheless hoped to see a great deal of me. Thanks to that friendship, I met Sekou Toure, a connection that gave me entry to the wider circle of French Africa's leadership.

Not many months after my start at *West Africa* I discovered, to my relief and delight, that I was not desk-bound at the office in London. David wanted me to get out into the field and get to know my parish at first hand. Nigeria was first on the list, and rather than fly straight to Lagos, I made footfall in Kano, the chief city of Northern Nigeria. Kano's ramshackle, noisy rabbit warren of streets and tiny cavernous shops, its pervading smells of dried fish and curry powders, the colourful clothes – it all went beyond anything I had imagined. My first African meal also taught me my first African lesson: an African curry is powerful. 'If it doesn't make you sweat, you haven't eaten a proper meal,' my African host informed me. Sweat or no sweat, I needed quantities of water before I found my voice again.

But I recall my first evening in Kano most notably for my naivety. Invited by the British representative in Kano to a welcome dinner,

I enthusiastically offered to accompany some of the men when they rose from the table and said they were going into the garden to admire the moonlight. I received dark looks from white faces and from black faces and was held back by my hostess, who discreetly explained the real meaning of this outdoor activity. The mistake was not repeated.

The first letter I received from my mother after my arrival in Nigeria told me how much she worried about the risks of infection from dirty lavatories. 'There is a polio epidemic in West Africa. Please always make sure you put piles[!] of clean paper on the seat, or better still do your business standing.' She clearly thought I should opt for the moonlight method.

That first visit to Nigeria was more of a courtesy call. The stirrings of independence were there, of course. But it would take until 1960 to achieve it. Meanwhile the Gold Coast under Kwame Nkrumah's leadership was already on the fast-forward track. Britain had devolved some powers to the local administration and Nkrumah was Prime Minister. Reporting on the situation there had priority. I made it my business to get to know him. It was absurdly easy. Once a week Pan-Am brought a planeload of passengers to Accra. This was considered an important social event, and many notables would come to the airport for afternoon tea and to provide an informal welcoming party for the arrivals. Nkrumah was a regular and I introduced myself. I knew his history as a pioneer in the independence movement and had been told of his powers of rhetoric. On that first encounter, I was surprised by his warm, deceptively unpretentious demeanour. Soon I had ready access to him – though our exchanges were as much about cocoa prices and a controversial Volta River hydro-electric project vital to the country's economy as about independence and African unity. Nkrumah had a British secretary who was very close to him and made sure that the relationship did not stray into forbidden territory. That suited me fine. I think it suited him less! After one of my talks with Nkrumah I sent a note to David Williams to fill him in on what I had learned, and added, 'I really have to go back to Nkrumah for more information. I'll phone him

and tell him that I am coming over to his office.' Presumably the
great man was readily available.

Looking back at the articles I wrote at the time, I am astonished
how knowledgeable, even authoritative they were. How did I learn
so fast about trends in the cocoa trade, about the timber trade, about
the prospects for the country's economy? Nkrumah certainly seemed
to be impressed. He kept in touch, and two years into his presidency
he proposed that I should set up a Ghana information service in
Paris. Flattered, I toyed with the idea of taking a sabbatical from
West Africa. Fortunately I came to my senses and realised that the
proposal made no sense for me.

Nkrumah was the most charismatic leader to emerge in British
West Africa. In 1999, BBC listeners in Africa voted him the 'Man
of the Millennium'. He made himself well known in Britain as a
freedom fighter several years before Ghana achieved independence.
Born in 1909, he studied sociology and economics in the US, first at
Lincoln University and later at Pennsylvania University. He earned
degrees in Philosophy and Theology and founded the African Studies Association. By the time he came to London in 1945, intending
to study law, Nkrumah's left-wing politics were firmly set. But that
was only part of the story. He had become a committed fighter for
African independence, and after he met George Padmore, the pan-
African activist, they jointly organised a pan-African Congress in
Manchester. Nkrumah established himself as a militant for African
independence – never losing sight of the ultimate goal of achieving
an African Union of Socialist States.

Nkrumah returned to Ghana in 1947 and became Secretary-
General of the United Gold Coast Convention, a fledgling party
campaigning to end British rule. Only a year later he was expelled
from the organisation for leading a campaign of civil disobedience.
His answer was to found his own party, the Convention People's
Party. It was the first mass party in black Africa. Seeking to stifle
the mounting pressure for independence, the British imprisoned
Nkrumah in 1950. They were forced to release him a year later
when his party won a landslide victory in local elections. By 1952

Ghana had secured limited autonomy and Nkrumah became Prime Minister.

Nkrumah reached the peak of his popularity on Independence Day. There followed a period of glory years when he worked to strengthen Ghana's economy while also pursuing his pan-African ambitions. This took him no further than a fragile, and as it turned out, brief Ghana–Guinea Union. In 1960, Nkrumah broke with the Crown and declared Ghana a republic. Never genuinely committed to democracy, Nkrumah became increasingly autocratic, and his government became tainted with corruption. He was preoccupied with the launch of the Non-Aligned Movement and neglected domestic needs. His popularity took a steep dive and in 1966, while he was on a visit to China, he was overthrown by a military coup. The Ghanaians who had danced with him for joy in 1957 now cheered at his downfall. Nkrumah lived in exile in Guinea for another six years and died in 1972.

Guinea was my first port of call in French West Africa. I arrived in the capital, Conakry, on a September day in 1956 and installed myself in the Hotel de France. At that period Sekou Toure was Mayor of Conakry. How best to contact him? I enquired of the affable concierge. 'No problem at all, *Madame*. His office is across the street. I will take your card to the house.' Simplicity itself, and it worked. Half an hour later Sekou Toure joined me at the bar. My friend Keita Fodeba came soon afterwards. The talk was about independence, about a clean break with France – and yes, about pan-Africanism. I had acquired a significant new friend – a charismatic figure who illuminated for me this twilight period of African colonies in search of their vocation. Slim, of average height, Sekou Toure's square-boned face could be forcefully forbidding, and yet when wreathed in smiles would be relaxed and welcoming. He was a man of humble African origin who had the courage to take on de Gaulle and refuse to be intimidated. On a one-to-one basis he was quiet and charming. As a public speaker he could be bombastic – his rhetoric could carry him for hours and keep his audience with him. After Guinea's abrupt independence, Sekou Toure became President, established a one-party system and gradually developed into an authoritarian and repressive figure. He died in 1988. My early admiration was long gone. Sekou Toure was a classic example of the corruptive force of power.

Unlike other key figures in French West Africa, such as Leopold Senghor or Felix Houphouet-Boigny, Sekou Toure never made himself an establishment figure in France. He missed out on a university education and worked as a postal clerk in Conakry before involving himself, aged 23, in trade unionism. From now on the trajectory was clear: socialism was his credo, and trade unionism was his launchpad to political activism. Pan-Africanism was the means to make the African voice relevant in world affairs. Initially Sekou Toure worked closely with Houphouet-Boigny in the 1946 launch of the RDA and saw the party as a vehicle for a united approach by French West African countries in negotiations for constitutional change. But General de Gaulle's animosity towards this left-wing trade unionist ran deep. Most of French Africa's black leaders had been regularly elected to the French Assemblée Nationale, including Sekou Toure. Some even served in the French government. But while the others took their seats, de Gaulle saw Sekou Toure as a radical socialist and blocked him from sitting in the parliament after he was elected first in 1951 and again in 1954. Only in 1956, after being elected as Mayor of Conakry, was he finally allowed to take his seat in the Assemblée Nationale.

After that first trip to Conakry, I kept up my contacts with Sekou Toure and my other new French African friends. Paris was often used as a venue by the RDA leaders to co-ordinate their negotiating position on constitutional transformation. A convenient place for me to pick their brains, and at the same time meet some of the officials on the French side of the negotiations. So, off I went to Paris on quite a few occasions. That was how I met a high-flying French diplomat named Paul-Marc Henri. Gregarious and attractive, he had a brilliant mind and a cosmopolitan approach to life. Paul-Marc and I took an instant liking to each other and our lives sporadically intertwined to the end of his life, in 1998. Not long after we first met he phoned to warn me that I had come to the attention of the French security authorities. My frequent meetings with French

African leaders had led them to suspect that I was involved in intelligence gathering for the British. I would be stopped at the border on my next trip to Paris. Me – a spy? I was incredulous. And also a little flattered! Of course, the French claim did not contain a single grain of truth. David Williams was seriously annoyed – not with me, but with the French, who were hampering my reporting. It took several energetic letters of protest before Paul-Marc could confidently advise that the coast was once again clear for me to come to France and resume my contacts with the African leaders.

In the year after my first meeting with Sekou Toure, I came across him again. It was in September 1957 in Bamako, the capital of Mali, where I was covering the third Congress of the RDA. The French West African countries already enjoyed a large degree of autonomy. Now they had to prepare for the decisive step, finalising negotiations to independence. Could the French African leadership achieve a common position? All of us journalists familiar with the various personalities felt much involved and were speculating wildly.

The Bamako meeting lasted the best part of a week. Houphouet-Boigny and Sekou Toure were the dominant politicians. But key figures such as Modibo Keita from Mali, Gabriel Lisette from Chad and Gabriel d'Arboussier representing Gabon also played important roles. All spoke immaculate French. But between them these men were a study in contrasts. Sekou Toure and Modibo Keita were fundamentalist in their interpretation of independence and had not allowed themselves to be absorbed into French culture. They were African nationalists, largely untouched by their connections with France. As they saw it, autonomy could only be a brief staging post to full independence and pan-Africanism. Most of their fellow politicians had led careers that zigzagged between France and Africa, and felt at home as much in France as in Africa. Houphouet-Boigny was even a member of the French cabinet and d'Arboussier ended up with the high rank of Ambassador of France.

Irrespective of their back story, at that RDA Congress in 1957 all of them were united in their determination to make their RDA grouping the dominant political force in French West Africa, and all of them declared their commitment to unity. There was much false optimism about the RDA cutting across tribal interests, and there were resolutions about economic development and integration across the region. After a debate on education it was decided that Arabic should be included in the school syllabus. Yet I cannot recall that there was any significant concern about the extensive Muslim populations in West Africa. With the wisdom of hindsight, I am amazed that so little attention was paid to Islam as an issue that has now become so profoundly divisive and murderous in large areas of the region.

Underlying all the debates were the tensions over future links with France. However much Houphouet-Boigny pressed, he could not secure the unanimous support of the RDA leadership for a French–African Confederal Community. Sessions were often delayed for hours while the top leadership argued amongst themselves. Party members tolerated these interruptions as much as the interminably long speeches. Many just slept in their seats. The journalists, unsurprisingly, were less generous. How much longer before we could write our stories? It was my first experience of a party congress in Africa, and I was trying to make the most of it.

So what did I do to occupy myself? I won myself my tiny place in West African history. How so? Nkrumah had come to the RDA Congress as an observer. I knew where he was staying. I had concluded that Sekou Toure and Nkrumah were soulmates and must get to know each other. The French authorities thought otherwise and wanted to prevent a meeting that might lead to collaboration between these two firebrands. So in the dead of night, I evaded their surveillance and surreptitiously took Sekou Toure to Nkrumah's lodgings. My instinct had been right. The two leaders had common ground. The meeting led to the formation of the Ghana–Guinea Union – a project launched with great fanfare in 1958, expanded in 1960 and disbanded as a failure in 1963.

Back at the final session of the RDA Congress, the fissures between the radicals and the conservatives had not been healed. Sekou Toure's closing remarks underlined his refusal to compromise. Independence meant divorce from France. Formal ties had to be severed. To resounding applause he concluded: 'A Franco–African

Community cannot stem from these territories.' Houphouet-Boigny had the last word and acknowledged that unity had not been achieved. Distancing himself from Sekou Toure, the Ivoirien leader again called for a confederal approach to relations with France and declared his commitment to a 'Franco–African Community based on complete liberty'.

A year later, Houphouet-Boigny was – almost – vindicated. France organised a referendum offering the countries of French West Africa a choice between a new federal community with France – the Communauté Francaise Africaine – or complete independence. With the referendum came de Gaulle's warning of economic rupture with any country that opted for independence. Sekou Toure was not deterred. He used every means at his disposal to secure support – even exhorting wives to withhold their sexual services if their husbands did not undertake to vote 'No'. He triumphed with a resounding majority of 'No's. He also received an even more resounding response from France. Overnight, French administrators were withdrawn, economic and financial aid was terminated. Guinea was left high and dry to fend for itself.

Guinea aside, all the other countries of French West Africa voted in favour of the 'Communauté Franco-Africaine' that General de Gaulle had sought. Under the federal constitution, the French African countries would be autonomous on all domestic matters. But France would remain responsible for foreign affairs, defence and economic policy. It may have been a worthy project. But it was destined to fail.

Less than two years later, in 1960 General de Gaulle had to recognise that such limited sovereignty was unworkable. The institutional links were jettisoned and each of the French West African states finally gained full independence. Guinea apart, warm relations and close economic ties, even security and military assistance, with France survived. While the institutional links now belonged to history, French Presidents have continued to nurture the concept of a Franco–African community. Comparisons can obviously be made between the French approach to relations with former colonies and Britain's solution: membership of the Commonwealth. Have either

of them made a significant contribution to economic progress and
political stability in West Africa?

My final visit to Guinea was in 1960, two years after independence. After France's vindictive departure the country remained
deeply impoverished. Sekou Toure's left-wing politics had done little
to attract new investment. Guinea's only major resource was bauxite.
I had flown in on an aircraft full of Slav faces. Evidence of Soviet
domination? They turned out to be a troupe of Russian dancers, part
of a cultural exchange programme. Later I was told that a Chinese
troupe had been far better. But at the airport, we had spotted that
the new national airline, Air Guinee, was flying Russian planes, and
it soon became apparent that there was a more significant Soviet
outreach in Guinea than the dancers.

In the Hotel de France – shabbier but name unchanged from
colonial days – the champagne and foie gras had gone, the wine
was Hungarian, and East European and Russian visitors were in
evidence. East European diplomats were also prominent. But the
hotel guests also included a scattering of Western business people
and American tourists. Sekou Toure was no longer ensconced across
the street but living and working much more grandly in the former
French Governor's residence, now designated as a 'Palace'. Life was
bustling. People were not as poorly dressed as reports had suggested,
and indeed a trade union dinner-dance revealed an astonishingly
up-to-the minute French fashion sense. I found that 15 countries,
most of them from the Warsaw Pact, but also including the UK, the
US and China, had established diplomatic missions. The Americans
had quickly secured one of the best villas with an ocean front. An
Algerian diplomat, a representative of the FLN (Algerian National
Liberation Front), lived in a small bungalow plastered with photos
of Algerian freedom fighters and used his modest establishment as
a meeting place for exiled nationalists from neighbouring countries.

Most of the economy, with the important exception of Guinea's
precious bauxite mines, had been nationalised. The larger part of
the country's ambitious development plan was to be financed with
loans and grants from the Soviet Union and China. Sekou Toure
insisted to me that 'No, I have not joined the Communist bloc. It

is simply a bread-and-butter matter.' These countries had been the first to offer help 'on conditions that were commensurate with our national dignity'.

In my notebook I wrote that Sekou Toure was still easily accessible. There were signs of Islamic influence, with the Presidential guards sporting beards, and there was 'little evidence of hard work'. After the departure of the French, the administration had been left in a shambles. It was a miracle that government offices had secured a modicum of able staff and that basic policies could be implemented.

Sekou Toure invited me to join a railway tour up country. The party included a sprinkling of potential investors. But it quickly became apparent that the main purpose of the whistle-stop trip was to resolve local problems and energise grass roots participation in the country's 'supreme organ', Sekou Toure's Parti Democratique de Guinee. Even as we left Conakry railway station the propaganda machine was at work, with loudspeakers blaring out a song extolling how happy Guinea was to be independent. Over the next three days I witnessed a series of enthusiastic public meetings – men and women, boys and girls always sitting separately. Speeches were usually followed by feasting, dancing and flag-waving. Sekou Toure's declarations, often delivered at great length, always carried the same message: an exhortation to unity and hard work. His party was 'the unique source of policy and was committed to social and political advance and determined to fight tribal and religious divisions'. He called on people to involve themselves at every level of society:

> Guinea's courage has won the admiration of the world. But independence without a goal – an educated Socialist society committed to African unity – is like a tractor that cannot be used because the seeds have not been sown. Democracy must not be confused with individualism. Democracy means that every citizen must be involved in a communal dedication to progress and within the confines of the unitary state and party.

Moscow would have applauded. But Sekou Toure was by no means alone in questioning whether the newly independent states of Africa were ripe for Western-style multi-party parliamentary democracy. In 1959, I was invited to a week-long symposium on 'Representative Government and National Progress' organised by the Congress for Cultural Freedom at Ibadan University in Western Nigeria. Central to the discussions was the feasibility of a multi-party system in newly independent states in Africa. Participants included a sprinkling of Western academics. But the majority were intellectuals, trade unionists and middle-ranking politicians from British and French West Africa and the Belgian Congo. The top leadership had stayed away.

In Ibadan the participants were probably unaware – as were most of the people involved in its widespread activities across Europe and many other parts of the free world – that the Congress for Cultural Freedom was a propaganda weapon in the Cold War. It was a CIA-sponsored organisation designed to counter Communist propaganda and promote liberal democracy and cultural freedom. Its main targets were intellectuals and other key opinion-makers. It launched highly respected journals including *Encounter* in the UK and *Preuves* in France. Participants at its seminars and contributors to its publications included a roll-call of the elite of Western intellectuals. Of course, I had my suspicions and so did many others. But the CIA's role was not fully exposed until 1966, some 16 years after the Congress for Cultural Freedom was formed as a counter to Soviet efforts to capture intellectual support in the West. I came to know it well, and indeed I owe my first experience of West Berlin to the Congress for Cultural Freedom symposia held in the divided city. I am the last person to defend CIA manipulation of public opinion. Yet here I am doing it in this instance. My experience convinced me that the Congress for Cultural Freedom not only promoted high-calibre writing but also encouraged far-reaching debate about the challenges to intellectual freedom and democracy likely to emerge in the post-war world.

Africa was within the sights of the Congress for Cultural Freedom as an out-of-Europe theatre of the Cold War. With the colonial empires close to extinction, the Soviet Union was in competition with the West to capture the hearts and minds of African states as they moved to independence. The Ibadan symposium was part of that battle. The discussions, often heated, demonstrated that the leaders of the new African states had little interest in the Western model of democracy. A multi-party system would be too divisive and would only serve as an obstacle to the consolidation of independence and national unity.

The colonial powers had done little to prepare Africa for representative government. Other ways had to be found to satisfy those who wanted to guarantee liberty and freedom of expression. Some participants toyed with a concept of 'guided' democracy under one-party rule. Others warned that the African elites simply wanted to replace white colonial dictatorship with black dictatorship. I wrote about the debates but set aside journalistic ethics and had no compunction about entering the debate. I was outspoken. One-party rule invariably leads to autocracy and corruption, and undermines freedom.

'There are so many urgent problems in newly independent countries,' countered a Ghanaian. 'A multitude of parties would only make for disunity. Only strong government can secure national cohesion.' Or again: 'Democracy is not an end in itself. We should not assume that Africa's institutions have to be a mirror-image of the West's . . . given the situation in which the new countries find themselves, democracy (in the Western sense) is not an immediate option. It may never be an option. But at the very least there must be a transitional period of unitary government.' Some argued that tribal chiefs had been used as puppets by the imperial powers. Others asserted that the tribal and religious chiefs connected Africans to their roots and deserved to have an influential role in government. Once again far too little attention was paid to the Islamic presence in West Africa. Nor did the concern over extremism make it onto the agenda.

Near the end of the Ibadan meeting, the discussions turned to pan-African issues and the prospects for a federation of West Africa. In the absence of Nkrumah or Sekou Toure, those fervent believers in African unity, serious doubts over pan-Africanism prevailed. A Nigerian participant spelled out the obstacles:

The African leadership is far too divided between Marxists and supporters of capitalism; there is no common language in the region. Economic co-operation would be hard to achieve. There are fundamental differences over the relationship with the former colonial powers.

Geography as a common denominator would never be sufficient to seal the bond.

By the time I went to the conference in Ibadan I had become a seasoned traveller over much of West Africa. I had been to Mali, all the way up to Timbuktu. I had been to tiny Togoland and to Nouakchott in Upper Volta (now known as Burkina Faso) and to Mauritania, once part of the Berber kingdom. I had made a brief stop in Gambia, but spent far more time in Sierra Leone, Ghana and, of course, Nigeria. I always tried to end my trips to Africa in Dakar, the capital of Senegal, then the most sophisticated city in the region and a tourist centre that attracted many French visitors.

Senegal is a barren country with scarce natural resources. Dakar's size and infrastructure is out of all proportion to its hinterland. It was built by the French Colonial Administration as its headquarters for AOF, the Association Occidentale Francaise, which included eight French West African countries. By the time I first visited Dakar in 1957, it had already lost much of its original purpose (AOF was finally dissolved in 1960) but had many of the characteristics of a prosperous city state and felt almost like an African extension of Paris. Racially it seemed a well-integrated city at the middle- and upper-class level. It was less integrated among the *petits blancs* and the grassroots (or rather desert-roots) Senegalese. Dakar had luxury, it had slums, it had commerce and it had culture. It also had Leopold Senghor to give it political and intellectual heft. The city centre housed banks and department stores, elegant boutiques and top-grade hotels. The Corniche had beachside clubs and nightspots. French women served at many counters, and in the hotels French waiters were ready to satisfy every whim. There was an efficient port and a medium-size industrial zone. There was a small theatre whose Director was in search of good African playwrights. There were modern blocks of flats with superb views to the sea and architect-designed villas for the well-to-do. But the larger part of the Senegalese population lived in the slums of the Medina.

Dakar's Woloff women were resplendent. Turbaned and dressed in colourful brocades, they carried themselves regally. I spent many happy moments just watching them parade down the city's busy streets. But my meetings with President Senghor were the most rewarding pleasure. Senghor's wife was French and they owned a home in Normandy where he lived in his retirement. As fluent in English as he was in French, our talks ranged way beyond African politics to the arts and especially to Senghor's love of poetry. Senghor told me how a young British diplomat looking after him on a visit to Sierra Leone had hesitantly asked him whether he needed help with English. Senghor shot back: 'Actually, yes. I am just translating one of Gerard Manley Hopkins' poems and there is one word that escapes me.' One of my treasured possessions is a limited edition of some of Senghor's own poems, with illustrations by his good friend Marc Chagall.

Even though Senghor had that big intellectual hinterland, he was an ambitious politician with a well-developed ego. In theory he accepted the logic of pan-Africanism. But only if he could be in charge – not the best formula for a confederal arrangement. This was exemplified by the short-lived nature of Senegal's union with its neighbour, French Soudan – better known as Mali.

I was in Dakar on the eve of the Mali Union's proclamation in April 1960, and was invited to a small informal gathering at the Prime Minister's house. Senghor, in shirt sleeves, was there with Collette, his wife – the only other woman present. The talk was all about the happy prospects for the Mali Union. After a while all was still for a musical interlude of traditional African songs played on a *cora*, a West African blend of harp and lute. The musician ended with a new composition – the Mali Union's newly composed national anthem. The formal Declaration of Union was made on the following day. President Senghor, speaking in the new Federal Assembly, announced that Senegal and Mali would merge their government machinery. A long-term economic development plan would be drawn up. France was expected to give more aid 'in return for our loyalty'. President Senghor drew himself up proudly: 'We are revolutionaries. The Mali Union is paving the way to African Union.'

It did no such thing. This was no revolution. It was a farce played out in a battle of egos that lasted two months. Senghor and Modibo Keita, Mali's leader, could not agree on which one of them was the titular head of the Union. The two countries came close to military confrontation. Senghor decided to cut his losses and put all the Mali officials in Dakar on a sealed train to Bamako. Modibo Keita was so angry that he afterwards destroyed stretches of the railtrack on his side of the border. It was the first of the pan-African dreams to shatter.

There were only very rare opportunities to interview the wives of the African leaders. Mariane, the wife of Modibo Keita, volunteered. Both Muslim, she had been in her mid-teens and had not met her husband before they married.

Mariane was the unchallenged Number 1 wife, but was reluctant to put up with his second wife: 'Polygamy has to end. Times are changing.' She told me only a small proportion of the 2 million women then living in Mali were literate. 'But all of them are militants, and working not just for their own emancipation, but for the progress of our country.' Few of Mali's women wore the veil in those days, and Mariane cheerfully said they were able to work alongside the men in schools and hospitals and even in road construction. Mali had not yet encountered Muslim extremism. That was to come later.

During my travels in West Africa, I had spent a fair amount of time with expatriates – civil servants or members of the business community. For many, their time in West Africa was ending. But for the most part, heads held high, they were determined to maintain their lifestyle right up to the end. During a trip to a forest concession deep in Western Nigeria's Benin Delta, I remember how I bumped around on rough tracks, watched huge trees being felled to the rhythmic chanting of fragile-looking Nigerian foresters, and then found myself at an etiquette-laden, formally served luncheon – not a mere *lunch* – with the British manager and his wife in their isolated company house. Downriver to the inland port of Sapele, I was soon sipping a gin and tonic with British hosts on the terrace of a luxuriously furnished house with perfect green lawns leading down to the Benin River. Almost but not quite a classic Thames river scene. From our comfortable perch we could see how the newly felled up-river trees had become sturdy logs floating down the river, soon to be hoisted into ships whose outlines were just visible against the darkening skies.

Nigeria's capital, Lagos, was a city teeming with life, with people of every race and nationality, overcrowded and with debilitating traffic problems. But the traces of colonial privilege remained. I wrote:

It has become a cosmopolitan city. The notion of Black Africa as the 'White Man's Grave' has become history. The symbols of those early days have become museum-pieces: the weighty toupees that men wore to protect themselves against the sun have become a curiosity occasionally seen on a few old 'coasters'. The heavy leather boots once worn to guard against mosquitoes have been replaced by the small bottles of anti-malaria pills on every white person's breakfast table. In the past only intrepid women like the missionary Mary Slessor or the explorer Mary Kingsley had dared to come out to the White Man's Grave. Today there are many British women working as teachers or nurses, as doctors and in business. And most expatriates bring their wives and during school holidays their children. The numerous bronzed children bursting with health are the best proof that life in West Africa has lost its hazards for expatriates. They live in good houses often provided free by their employers. There is an inexhaustible supply of servants. People have cooks and drivers, cleaners and gardeners, perhaps a 'wash boy' for laundry and a garden boy to spend his days watering plants and flowers. In the waning days of British colonialism expatriate life still has its compensations.

Nigeria holds a very special place in my life: it was where I had my first contact with the *Guardian*, in the shape of Geoffrey Taylor, the paper's Foreign Editor who was on secondment in Lagos to spend a year as Editor of the *Nigerian Daily Times*. He commissioned me to write occasional analysis pieces on African issues for the *Guardian*. It was thrilling – the first time I had been asked to contribute for a mainstream British paper. My intense learning curve at *West Africa* was beginning to pay off. Maybe? To be honest, I was so engrossed in the politics of Africa that it never occurred to me that the odd article for the *Guardian* could become a significant passport to the Editor's attention.

My main interest in Nigeria, as in the rest of West Africa, was in constitutional change and in the politicians who were driving it. Nigeria in many ways was unique, mainly because of its size, the multiplicity of its ethnic and religious groups, and because its regions were to a large extent ethnically divided between three key groups: Hausas in the North, Yorubas in the West and Ibos in the East. At the time of the independence negotiations, its population was around 53 million, far outstripping the other countries of West Africa. The country was also divided on religious lines, with the North overwhelmingly Muslim and the West divided between a smallish Muslim majority and Christians. The East was mainly Christian but divided between Roman Catholics and various Protestant denominations. An imbalance of size and economic resources added to the complexity. With roughly two thirds of Nigeria's population, the North is the largest region in territorial and population size. The much smaller Eastern region – well known for the Biafran War – has the advantage of extensive oil resources. The struggle for political control and access to economic resources became far more pronounced after independence but was already obvious during the six years before independence when Nigeria already had a large degree of autonomy. Under colonial rule, Nigeria had been administered on a quasi-federal basis, and it was self-evident that independent Nigeria would have to be governed as a federation. In 1958, a constitutional conference in London drew up a federal constitution that largely preserved the existing regions. Independence itself was set for October 1960.

I was able to follow closely the preparations for this complex country's independence. My Editor, David Williams, was an invaluable asset. David had the confidence both of the Nigerian politicians and of the British ministers and officials who were involved in the independence negotiations. During the 1958 constitutional conference I was often taken along to meet the participants. I already knew some from earlier visits to Nigeria. Lagos was used as the head office of the *Daily Mirror*'s group of West African newspapers. Percy Roberts, then the group's Managing Editor, encouraged me to travel and meet some of Nigeria's leaders on their home ground. As elsewhere in West Africa, I found open doors and a readiness to discuss the politics of independence.

I gained many friends among the diverse contacts I made during my travels in Nigeria. But my favourite was the modest, yet self-assured Alhaji Sir Abubakar Tafawa Balewa. Unlike other African leaders, he was never seen in Western suits and wore his white voluminous robes with great dignity. His wives did not appear in public. Given the northern region's dominant role, he was already serving as Nigeria's First Minister for a period before independence and became Prime Minister on Independence Day. His education, rare for a northerner, included a year at London University's Institute of Education. On his return he worked as an Inspector of Schools until opting for politics and forming the Northern People's Congress party. The party gained the largest number of seats in the new federal assembly and formed a coalition with East Nigeria's leader, Dr Azikiwe's NCNC party. He was knighted a few months before independence. As Prime Minister, Sir Abubakar was instrumental in forming the Organisation of African Unity. But at home he became embroiled in Nigeria's factionalism and though re-elected in 1964, he would be assassinated under mysterious circumstances in 1966.

I enjoyed many quiet talks with Sir Abubakar. On his visits to London, we had the occasional dinner, and I was taken aback when he turned up one day with a leopard skin from an animal he had personally shot. This was still a time when furs did not cause shock-horror, and I accepted the somewhat unusual present with pleasure. But when my mother saw it, she expressed shock – not because it was a leopard skin, but because of the donor. Why such a valuable present? What was my relationship with this Nigerian? The idea that it was simply a friendly gesture was incomprehensible to her. I kept the skin and had it made into a waistcoat. It was rarely worn. It no longer exists.

On an autumn day in 1959 I was at my desk in the Fetter Lane office of *West Africa* when Cecil King made a rare appearance. From on high I was informed that my services were no longer required. I was dismissed. David Williams was either unable or unwilling to intervene. No explanation was given, though I always wondered whether Cecil King suspected that I was toying with an offer from a competitor – untrue – and may have questioned my loyalty. Or he may have decided I was doing too much freelance work. But would he have behaved like this to a male journalist? Did he feel a woman was easy prey and could be dispensed with without fanfare or justification? At the time it was shattering. The National Union of Journalists intervened on my behalf. But got nowhere. My self-confidence suffered a big blow. Yet in retrospect, it was the best thing that could have happened to me. Suddenly unemployed after six years with *West Africa*, I discovered the erratic freelancers' world, where you live in uncertainty and are wise to accept every feasible commission that comes your way. Naturally I turned to the big beasts who had occasionally taken work from me: the BBC's World Service and the *Guardian* were my saviours.

I loved broadcasting and was doing frequent BBC commentaries, spouting forth in discussion programmes on West African affairs. But even better, I was able to go back to Africa to write some features for the *Guardian*. My assignment included coverage first of Nigeria's and then Sierra Leone's independence celebrations.

Nigeria's independence celebration in October 1960 will always stand out for me as a very special event. That is where I met the man who may have saved my life as a ten-year old girl in Austria. At one of the Independence Day parties I met Israel's envoy, Ehud Avriel – and made a surprise discovery. Without being overdramatic, I may owe it to him that I became a *Kindertransport* child and escaped from the Nazis and possible death. Austrian by birth, Ehud was 19 when Hitler marched into Austria. A Zionist, Ehud joined Aliya Bet, an underground immigration movement, and soon found himself working with the Vienna branch of the Jewish Agency for Palestine. One of his tasks was to deal with the Nazi authorities to secure the essential exit permits for *Kindertransport* children. Ehud did not remember my name. But I would certainly have been one of his 'charges'. He himself managed to escape from Vienna in 1940, and after Israel's independence in 1948 he became one of its most trusted diplomats. After our mutual discovery in Lagos, he also became one of my most trusted friends. At various times Ehud tried to convince me that I would be happier if I made my life in Israel. I could not be persuaded. But it's no wonder that I will always think of Lagos as a gold brick in the structure of my life.

In Lagos, just as it had been in Accra, the independence celebrations were exuberant expressions of great joy. But the ceremonies in Lagos were more formal, and the dignitaries more restrained. Nkrumah had been a militant fighter against colonialism, and he brought that spirit to the independence ceremony. By 1960 the political map of West Africa had been transformed. Nigeria's leaders had found a cooperative partner in Britain to negotiate their freedom. During the independence celebrations they were – almost, but not quite – content to lay aside their factional differences and celebrate their emergence as a major independent power in Africa with unanimous pride. The balance of power was wobbly. Nigeria's designated head of state was Dr Nnamdi Azikiwe from Eastern Nigeria. Sir Abubakar Tafawa Balewa, from Northern Nigeria, was Prime Minister – and as a quasi-consolation prize, Nigeria's Beauty Queen came from Western Nigeria! Princess Alexandra, who had represented the monarch in Accra, played the same role in Lagos. But on this occasion there was a great deal more ceremonial than in Accra and the proceedings extended over several days.

The Beauty Queen contest was held two days before Independence Day. The selection criteria were interesting: 50 per cent of the marks for beauty; 5 per cent for the contestant's dress; another 5 per cent for her personality; 5 per cent for excellence in the English language; 5 per cent for her sense of humour; and the remaining 20 per cent for her sense of diplomacy and her ability to act as a good ambassador for Nigeria. Miss Ibadan from Western Nigeria had the highest score. Thousands watched as the Beauty Queen was crowned at midnight by Nigeria's Finance Minister.

The gods cast a benevolent eye on the contest. The heavy rains that dampened other pre-Independence Day festivities held off for the crowning of the Beauty Queen. The genuine Royal, Princess Alexandra, fared less well and experienced her first soaking soon after arrival, during the open-car drive into Lagos. Worse was to come during a mammoth party on the lawns of Government House. Everyone of significance was there: politicians, senior officials, business leaders, foreign guests and African chiefs with one or more wives. The Nigerian guests were resplendent in their robes and headgear. Russians strode around as if the world belonged to them. The British were in their Royal Garden Party best. Suddenly the skies came down and there was an indecent scuffle for what little shelter could be found under mango trees. The wet mass that had earlier been my hat was abandoned to the rain-sodden lawns. In true British spirit, Princess Alexandra decided the show must go on. With the retiring Governor General holding a giant umbrella over the elegant Princess, she stood still while the Royal fanfare was drowned out under the heavy patter of rain, and then advanced slowly down the lawn. To the sounds of Scottish reels, a few stalwarts came forward volunteering for a regal handshake. The sun returned. The bedraggled guests emerged from the sheltering trees. The celebration was back on track.

The official transfer of power took place the following day. During the afternoon great crowds assembled at Lagos racecourse to welcome Princess Alexandra. She was treated to a cheerfully delivered hyper-energetic display of gymnastics and dancing. A few performers were so tired that they simply folded up on the ground but kept their broad smiles. Princess Alexandra had already left the scene when a group of horsemen from the north approached. Sporting white turbans and green tunics with red sashes, they gave a remarkable display of horsemanship. Then it was the turn of the outgoing Governor General to give a farewell message. He declared that it could well be argued that the process to independence had been too slow. Yet he added that it could also be argued that it had been too fast. However, what really mattered was that no blood had been shed and that negotiations had been cooperative; the break-up of Nigeria had been prevented and a united Nigeria had emerged. To great cheers, and visibly moved, Sir George Robertson proclaimed that 'Britain and Nigeria can now treat each other as equals'.

Then as midnight approached, Princess Alexandra returned, dressed in a formal white evening gown, with a richly sparkling tiara on her carefully coiffed head. Moving forward slowly, bearing the instruments of power, she handed them over to the Nigerian Prime Minister. The Union Jack was lowered, the white-and-green Nigerian flag raised. Nigeria's national anthem was given its debut, heard for the first time in public.

Now it was Sir Abubakar's turn. This was never going to be a 'Nkrumah-esque' freedom shout. Standing tall in his white robes and white turban, his 'golden' voice pitch-perfect, he declared:

This a wonderful day and it is all the more wonderful because we have awaited it with increasing impatience. We have been compelled to watch one country after another overtaking us on our road when we had so nearly reached our goal. But now that we have reached our rightful status, history will show that we have proceeded at the wisest pace and that our nation now stands on well-built firm foundations . . . Today's ceremony marks the culmination of a process that began 15 years ago and has now reached a happy and successful conclusion . . . Each step of our constitutional advance has been purposefully and peacefully planned in harmonious cooperation with the administering power which has today relinquished its authority . . .

In conclusion the Prime Minister declared with characteristic modesty: 'As I open a new chapter in our history, do not mistake our pride for arrogance.'

After all the ceremony, the evening was marked by a State Ball that was somewhat short of sweetness and light. The French African leaders discovered that no tables had been reserved for them and felt slighted. Hamani Diori, Prime Minister of Upper Volta, reacted violently. Nigeria's ethnic differences were highlighted by the pointed absence of Western Nigeria's Yoruba Chief Minister, Obafewi Awolowo. Princess Alexandra, careful to steer clear of ethnic rivalries, limited her dancing to a turn with Nigeria's Chief Justice. Sir Abubakar did not touch the dance floor.

On her final day, Princess Alexandra opened the first session of the new Federal Nigerian Parliament. Dr Azikiwe, as Nigeria's new head of state, formally invited her, as the Queen's representative, to read the speech from the throne and welcome Nigeria as a new member of the Commonwealth. Independent Nigeria was now in business. Chequered times, including civil war in Biafra, lay ahead. But the African giant has survived in one piece. So far at least, Abubakar Tafawa Balewa has been proved right – the country's foundations have resisted break-up.

There was one more independence celebration in store for me: Sierra Leone's, in April 1961. It happened to coincide with my 34th birthday. More significant for me, it brought virtual closure to the West African chapter of my life. I will probably need forgiveness if I suggest that Sierra Leone, at the moment of its independence, was still something of an oddity among its African neighbours. A mid-sized country, even at this juncture Sierra Leone still lived up to the colonial-style nostalgia so brilliantly caught by Graham Greene. The capital, Freetown, is named for the freed slaves who returned to the country in the 18th century. They had modelled themselves on their observations of British life, and this had been handed down through the generations. By way of example, it was striking, I told my readers,

that the generously proportioned ladies of Freetown scorned African dress and liked to show themselves in fashionable flower-patterned dresses and modelled hats. Church on Sundays brought out the sartorial in men when most appear in pinstripe trousers, waistcoat and black jacket complete with homburg; some even wear frock coats and stiff collars[!].

But search below the surface, and deep tensions were self-evident. Independence was simply an opening act for the upheavals and civil strife to come.

Freetown occupies a profoundly shameful place in Britain's colonial history. It was notorious as an important entrepôt for the slave trade. Not far from Government House where the Duke of Kent stayed during the independence festivities, there was an enduring reminder: a giant cotton tree where the slave auctions used to be held. Bizarrely, to mark independence, its protruding, spreading roots had been painted a vivid white. An old lady who made her home in the tree had been removed for the duration – together with all her pots and pans. They were surplus to the ceremonials – a long-drawn-out, very British affair lasting over a week. Noticeably, West Africa's leaders were beginning to tire of these independence celebrations – this, after all, was the fourth in British West Africa, and there was the rest of Africa to consider. Top-class VIPs were sparse. Sierra Leone had to welcome VIPs one or more notches down the scale. The Duke of Kent stayed the course, attending several church services, banquets and receptions. Naturally there had to be the staple of independence celebrations, a Beauty Contest. Unusually, there was an all-women jury, who stressed that they put intelligence above looks. The winning girl scored high points for declaring that she was opposed to polygamy because 'I am a jealous person.' End of argument.

When I returned from Sierra Leone, it was no longer to the dingy flat in Florence Road in Ealing. By 17 December 1960, I had saved enough to deposit £110 towards the lease of a bright two-bedroom flat on Ealing's Eaton Rise. The gods must have intended it for me. They just didn't know how to spell my name. The building was called Helena Court. My mother became adept at local auctions to buy furniture at bargain-basement prices – and we moved in. It was the first place where I could bring friends and which at last felt like a real home. Above all, it meant that wherever I might be, my mother now had the basics of her life secured.

Even if Africa remained my main focus during those freelance years, I managed to fit in my first trip to the United States. Once again I tried to find work away from Britain. I stayed with Grete

Marmorek, a distant cousin and close friend of my mother, who had settled with her husband in Boston. They did not encourage my restlessness. I also managed a short excursion to New York, where I finally had my epiphany after I saw that the city's Jews were amongst its most prominent citizens and formed a significant part of mainstream society. I felt liberated – at least to the extent that I no longer wanted to hide my Jewish identity. But I was still far from finding the confidence to talk about that identity. I was also far from finding a job in America, and had no inkling that I would soon be back in New York, and indeed back with a job – not with an American employer, but with an employer back in Britain: the *Guardian* newspaper. It took just over two years to escape the uncertain freelancer's lot. For better or worse, the *Guardian* took me into its fold. I had a new professional home.

CHAPTER 5

THE UN IS MY OYSTER

The scene: the UN delegates lounge in New York. It was November 1962 and UN diplomats were enjoying their pre-lunch drinks. As usual, journalists were in the lounge to prise out titbits of news from the diplomats. I was among them. Where was the British contingent? I couldn't see a single British face. The British had something to hide. They knew how persistent I could be and that I would try to charm them into giving away information. I was writing a story about the contentious British policy in Rhodesia and wanted British corroboration about some particular aspect I intended to emphasise. 'What's happened? Have the British suddenly become abstemious and are avoiding their pre-lunch tipple?' I asked a French diplomat. The answer came back: 'They are all in the men's cloakroom, hiding from *you*!' Should I brave it and walk in? That was one step too far. Moreover, even though those UN cloakrooms were luxurious, the British couldn't stay in there for ever. Correct. They eventually emerged – and I got my information and my article was duly dispatched.

At this point I had been the *Guardian*'s UN Correspondent for just over a year, had covered some of the momentous diplomatic manoeuvring at the UN end of the Cuban Missile Crisis, together with a rainbow variety of international issues, and could scarcely believe the great good luck that had brought me to this prominent posting. I had come to New York on a circuitous route via West Africa and Belgrade. I had seven years of media experience behind me – but most of it confined to covering West African affairs.

Preoccupation with the trajectory to independence in British and French West Africa had blurred my vision of broader international affairs. Though I had long harboured an ambition to work within the UN system, I had not imagined myself as an outsider writing from the vantage point of the United Nations about East–West relations, the Cold War, decolonisation, development issues and a myriad of other matters.

After losing my job with *West Africa*, I had had a busy time freelancing, still cashing in on my knowledge of African affairs. I had written for magazines, produced a report on the diamond mines in Sierra Leone, given talks, broadcast regularly on the BBC's World Service – and had my name under a number of features commissioned by the *Guardian*. My self-confidence as a journalist had strengthened. But I also learned that the uncertainty of a freelancer's life heightened my sense of insecurity. If I wanted the security of a salaried staff job, I had to broaden my range of subject matter. I recognised that I was not made to be a specialist on UK domestic affairs. My interest was in international affairs. I was also keen to write about some of the remarkable women I was encountering.

As I had done a fair amount of work for the *Guardian*, I tentatively enquired what future possibilities there might be on the newspaper. 'Sympathetic, but still no firm decision', came the answer filtered back from the Editor, Alastair Hetherington.

In the late summer of 1961, I saw an opportunity to prove my worth to the *Guardian*. Cold War tensions were extremely high. Berlin, under four-power occupation, was in relentless crisis. Nuclear testing was continuing. The world was in a dangerous place. For the past two years India, Indonesia and Yugoslavia had been searching for ways to stay clear of the East–West divide and find for themselves a constructive role in world politics. On 1 September 1961, the newly formed Non-Aligned Movement would have its formal launch at a summit hosted by President Tito in Belgrade. The aim was to establish a group of countries determined to remain outside the power blocs, while at the same time mobilising to reduce Cold War tensions and the nuclear threat.

Now the Non-Aligned Movement belongs to the dim recesses of

modern history. But in its time the Belgrade summit was seen as a major event on the geopolitical landscape. Its principal architects were Presidents Sukarno, Tito and Nasser, together with Prime Ministers Nehru and Nkrumah. Fidel Castro was also involved. For the leaders of the newly independent countries of West Africa, the summit would become their launch pad on the international scene. I had the advantage of knowing several of the Africans leaders. Access to them would give me unique insights of the summit deliberations.

So would the *Guardian* welcome help with coverage of the event? To my delight, there was a positive response. The paper's Diplomatic Correspondent, Richard Scott, would be in Belgrade. But given that it was such a multi-faceted occasion, I could be useful. So off I went to Belgrade, checked into my hotel, obtained my press passes and waited, curious to meet Richard. And I waited and waited until I finally heard from London that Richard had missed his plane and would be delayed by a day. Then the magic words: 'You will have to cover the opening day of the summit on your own.'

Quite a challenge: the eyes of the world, and especially the eyes of Western and Soviet leaders, were watching to assess the cohesion of this new Non-Aligned Movement and the impact it might be capable of making on the Cold War. The Soviet Union marked the day in aggressive mode: it launched a nuclear test in the atmosphere in Central Asia, throwing down a gauntlet not just to the West, but also to the Non-Aligned Movement and its declared aim of reducing nuclear tensions. My first challenge would be to secure the texts of the leaders' speeches. Key points would have to be summarised, and the day's events described with plenty of colour to keep the readers' interest. And all of this had to be transmitted (in Belgrade that meant dictating by phone) to meet an early evening deadline. I made it!

Next morning my name was under the *Guardian*'s 'splash': the leading story taking up much of the front page. 'RUSSIAN NUCLEAR EXPLOSION – Soviet decision condemned by neutral leaders', ran the headlines over two columns.

To pick up the *Guardian* in the conference centre (remember, this was still a prehistoric, pre-internet age) and see my name on the lead story – this was happiness; this was satisfaction. Childishly, I just read and re-read my splash. And here is where I must confess (and I think many other journalists share the feeling) that the pleasure of seeing one's work on the printed page never quite goes away. Online journalism is missing out on a very special aspect of a journalist's job satisfaction.

Of course, I quickly came back to earth when Richard Scott arrived in Belgrade and I duly took second place in reporting on the remaining two days of the summit. I 'worked' my African contacts and managed to make friends with a couple of Yugoslav generals who were to be helpful in later years when I was covering Yugoslav affairs. I met and was lucky to remain in touch with the legendary Fitzroy Maclean, the buccaneering British soldier and diplomat who, as Churchill's envoy, joined Tito and his partisans during the war. I had a reunion with many of my friends from West Africa. I felt that this summit was to some extent a continuation of their independence celebrations, but that it also marked the growing maturity of those new countries. I was not the only bystander who thought that we were witnessing the emergence of a significant new player on the international scene. Sadly, the Non-Aligned Movement never managed to realise its potential.

Together with Richard Scott, I went to the grand receptions, shook hands with Tito and joined media friends for gossipy meals. Low-key but charming and instantly likeable, Richard was a senior member of the Scott family, the *Guardian*'s founders. We established a quick rapport and over a relaxed open-air supper in a simple restaurant overlooking the Danube, Richard seems to have concluded that I was *Guardian* material. He had mentioned that he would soon be off to New York, a city he heartily disliked, to cover the autumn session of the UN General Assembly. But there was no hint of what he was plotting.

However, back in London, he consulted the *Guardian*'s Editor, Alastair Hetherington. Richard was in the middle of a difficult divorce. The prospect of a three-month absence while his personal life was in flux made the New York stint even less enticing. He suggested to send me to New York in his place. Alastair agreed. I was in seventh heaven.

A week later – still on a freelance basis, possibly on probation, but certainly without guarantee of a staff job on the *Guardian* – I was in New York, and at the United Nations. The Congo was in crisis. The UN was at the centre of efforts to calm the battling factions amid failing attempts to find a settlement. I found myself on a rapid learning process about the world of diplomacy within that curious UN bubble. Naturally, I also had to broaden my understanding of the Cold War divide and all the issues that were brought to the United Nations Security Council or to its General Assembly. And of course I had to make it my business to develop good contacts and sources among the movers and shakers, diplomats, and politicians at the UN.

I was instantly enthralled by the transformation in my life. Writing to my mother – I continued to act as a dutiful daughter, reporting on my day-to-day activities – I told her that I was 'installed like a Pasha. The hotel has given me a whole suite including a pink(!) bathroom for the price of a single room. Apparently that's what they do if you are the *Guardian* and are a long-stay guest. They are charging $14 a day. That's £5.' (Once upon the time the pound stood high!) I added that I had little time to enjoy all this luxury, as my days were spent inside the UN building, and that I was already being invited out every evening. Soon I was telling my mother about the VIPs I was meeting: 'I have at last had a long talk with Adlai Stevenson. On another evening I went out for dinner with Senegal's President Senghor and his wife.' I mentioned in another letter that Rudolf Bing, Director of the Metropolitan Opera, had been my neighbour at a dinner given by the Ghanaian Ambassador, and that I was promptly invited to the following day's performance of *Turandot*. Ralph Bunche was a fellow guest in Rudolf Bing's box. He became a valuable contact at the heart of UN affairs.

But the letters were not just about progress in New York. My mother had once again started to complain that I was working too hard and must be overtiring myself; that I should tell the *Guardian* to let me come back to London before the end of the General Assembly; that the paper was exploiting me and I should not try to get a permanent job there. I knew of course that much of this was a reflection of her sense of loneliness and inability to find contentment. I retorted:

You have sent me two letters in a row with nothing but complaints about what I am doing, and now suddenly you don't even want me to join the *Guardian*. You just don't know what you want except to complain. I have been happy here these past few weeks. I have made friends, and senior people here at the UN have come to accept me far more quickly than I gather is usual. And all you do is complain. Can't you ever begin to realise that not everybody thinks and feels like you?

After I spent a weekend in Boston with my mother's close friend, Grete Marmorek, she wrote to my mother and urged her to make more of a life for herself, instead of trying to live her life through me: 'These kids grow up as you and I did, and to them the mothers are just as far and as near as ours were to us.' My mother tried but never succeeded in taking such advice fully to heart.

Nowadays, no British newspaper would think of sending a correspondent to cover, full time, the long autumn weeks of the annual meeting of the UN General Assembly – let alone having a permanent correspondent at the UN. It was different in the early 60s, when the UN was a near-constant flashpoint for East–West confrontation and crisis. The Security Council was used as a Cold War battle arena. The General Assembly was the forum where members of the new Non-Aligned Movement were flexing their muscles to press for nuclear and general disarmament and an end to colonialism. Then as now, the Arab world used the UN to attack Israel and promote the Palestinian cause. I could soon sense the difference between the skilled Western diplomats at the UN and their Communist counterparts. The Soviet-bloc delegates were all party functionaries held to a strict discipline, with the Soviet Ambassador clearly in command. They worked as a group. Their speeches were always full of blatant propaganda and attacks directed at the West. Every Communist-bloc speech would include routine assertions that workers in the West were slaves, that unemployment was rife and that the West was preparing for war. It was all so predictable – and boring. But of course it also made everyone wonder how these *apparatchiks* could bring themselves to deliver such pronouncements while living in New York and experiencing the genuine face of capitalism. It probably worked because the top layer of the Communist-bloc diplomats were well-trusted party members, while the more susceptible junior diplomats were frequently rotated to deter any move towards defection.

To a newcomer the UN scene can be bewildering, and certainly when I first scoured the building with the benefit of my new UN press pass, I was indeed bewildered. The media had a reserved area with separate rooms for permanent correspondents. The Japanese media all liked to work in the same room. The British and Americans never wanted to share rooms with competitors. As I was only there on temporary assignment, I had no room choice anyhow and had to find myself a place in the open media space as best I could. There was a steady flow of diplomats – the UN-speak for them was 'delegates' – who would bring the texts of speeches, or offer little briefings and whispers in the ears of favoured journalists. Once a day the UN's head of press would brief. On special occasions there might be VIP press conferences. I also had to find my way into restricted high-level background briefings. I think I can allow myself to say I rapidly became quite adept at the art.

In those days, security had not yet become a major concern and journalists were allowed to roam the UN corridors fairly freely. When the Security Council was sitting, I discovered a good tactic was to befriend the BBC or the Reuter's wire-service correspondents, who had their own cubicles to observe and listen to the proceedings. It was a sure bet that sooner or later senior delegates would turn up to offer a little background briefing. I was soon doing regular broadcasts for the BBC's World Service, so I could count on a welcome in the BBC cubicle. Door-stopping outside the Security Council chamber could also be profitable by way of catching senior delegates as they came and went or huddled for consultations. But often the most profitable place for information-gathering was the big Delegates' Lounge. So of course I made myself a regular.

Yet my favourite memory of the Delegates' Lounge has nothing to do with those pre-lunch activities. It goes back to an early evening when I first set eyes on Alistair Cooke, the *Guardian*'s US Bureau chief. I had only just arrived in New York and he had suggested an early meeting. I had long been a devoted reader of his *Guardian* work and listener to his BBC *Letters from America*. I went to that first face-to-face encounter with a beating heart. He quickly put me at ease – indeed, very much at ease. He obviously knew the bartender well and provided me with a strong daiquiri – a cocktail that was new to me – soon to be followed by a second and third. I lost my somewhat unusual shyness, but seemingly not all my good sense. We bonded, developed an easy working relationship and gradually formed a friendship that lasted until a final conversation just a few days before he died. But Alistair became much more than a friend. He was my mentor. If my work, my knowledge of the US and my self-confidence improved, I owe much of it to him. He encouraged me to explore the nooks and crannies of the UN and its potential for newsworthy stories, and also to go outside the UN bubble for stories in the real America. As a journalist, Alistair had a unique gift of words that I would never have tried to ape. But he taught me so much about clarity in the use of words – be economic with the use of adjectives was one imperative. Another imperative was to get right the first paragraph of any article. 'If you don't capture the readers' attention in the opening sentences, you have lost them.' Sounds simplistic. But it is the best advice a journalist can take to heart.

Alistair had a deep understanding of America, and a little of it certainly rubbed off on me. When we had come to know each other well, I would go to see him on Wednesday evenings, sit in his study with its red-painted walls and loaded bookshelves overlooking Central Park, and listen while he tried out on me the draft of that week's *Letter from America*. He never took to computers and continued to use a well-worn typewriter. Typewriter ribbons were no longer being manufactured, and he scurried around neighbourhood shops buying up their remaining stock. Alistair was a household figure in America, not least because of his introductions to the *Masterpiece* TV versions of the British classics. Americans were securely hooked on those TV shows. I still remember going with him to the 1964 World Exhibition in New York. It was the nearest thing to a Royal tour, with people stopping Alistair to greet him every inch of the way. I took to dutifully walking behind him, ready to hold any flowers or presents that might be offered. My imagination had run too far. There were none!

But back to the UN and that first meeting with Alistair. Of course I was answerable to the Foreign Editor. But Alistair Cooke was now my immediate 'boss'. What did he expect of me? How demanding would he be? No need to worry. All he expected was a daily early morning phone call to tell him what I planned to write. Encouragement and ideas for articles would be given. Guidance would be available when wanted. I could not have imagined anything better. Of course, it did not always turn out to be so perfect. Later, when I had become more self-assured, especially when I was working out of Washington, there were the occasional turf-wars and appeals to the Foreign Editor to set out the rules. But this was so rare that it really did not affect our relationship.

The UN was without a Secretary-General when I arrived on the scene in September 1961. Dag Hammerskjoeld, a dynamic though controversial figure who had won the confidence of the Western powers, but not the Soviet Union, had just tragically died under suspicious circumstances in an air crash in Rhodesia. It took until November before the UN Security Council turned to South-East Asia and elected U Thant, Burma's Ambassador at the UN, to become the UN's third Secretary-General. Formal in manner and low-key, but familiar with the UN, U Thant had the temperament to cope with the endless pressures and crises that are the staple of the job. But he lacked the charisma and dynamism of his predecessor and never really succeeded in imposing himself on the UN body. I had already come to know him quite well. In a profile written the day after his appointment, I described 'the worldly Buddhist', U Thant, as a 'popular and much respected figure at the United Nations'. But I also asked whether he had the toughness and the patience to handle the huge UN machine and the pressing problems he inherited 'at a time when the purpose and usefulness of the UN is regarded with perhaps greater cynicism than ever before'. Sounds familiar? However, there was a difference between now and then. In the 1960s, member countries – great and small – brought their conflicts, demands and aspirations to the UN; high-level negotiations were conducted there; occasionally there was even good news to report. The UN was a place that really counted in the conduct of international affairs. Can that be said of the UN today?

Almost from the very first day, I was filing (normally dictating by phone) a constant flow of stories from the UN. Demands to halt nuclear tests and moves to resolve the crisis in the Congo that followed Katanga's secession were the two key issues to which I had to return over and over again. Chinese representation was another prominent issue in bitter contention between the US and the Soviet Union. The Republic of China (Taiwan) was a founder member of the UN and held one of the permanent seats in the Security Council. The Soviet Union insisted that the seat had to be passed over to the People's Republic of China. The US resisted, bringing in the heavy guns, with their Ambassador Adlai Stevenson forcefully denouncing Communist China. The General Assembly was divided. The Americans warned they might leave the UN, or at the very least withhold funding if Beijing was allowed to take a seat. I wrote 'that the very existence of the UN is at stake'.

Apartheid in South Africa was a constant in General Assembly debates, as were motions to end colonialism. Funding problems and Russian refusal to help pay for the peacemaking operation in the Congo also demanded frequent coverage. I was developing good antennae for news stories – and learning the trick of using even small events at the UN as useful pegs for writing bigger stories. Occasionally I would write profiles of prominent people. Unlike my time in West Africa, at the UN there was a good sprinkling of women among the press corps, and we learned to be helpful to each other.

The weeks went by quickly. Invitations to receptions, lunches, dinners, often opportunities to pry out information, became a constant – but of course had to be fitted into deadlines for writing and sending my stories. Remember, this was well before the 24-hour news cycle, the internet and the smart phone. The time difference between New York and the UK (London was five hours ahead) meant that my work was usually done by around 7 p.m. – though if there was a major story, the paper could be kept open longer. Among my new friends was the correspondent of Russia's Tass news agency. For some reason, he gave me a small stuffed elephant. I don't think I was important enough for the elephant to house a listening device. If it did, the Russians might still be listening now. The gift was taken back to London and just about survived a mauling by a friendly dog who naturally mistook it for a toy. I still have it. It was a gift that triggered a love, not of my Russian friend, but of elephants.

At the end of the autumn session of the General Assembly – and the end of my freelance assignment – I wrote a 'State of the Nation' verdict on the UN: 'With the UN Congo operation under heavy fire and the Security Council's failure to stop India's invasion of Goa, the effectiveness of the UN as a force for peace and international cooperation has been thrown seriously into doubt, and Mr Adlai Stevenson has pronounced words of woe resembling a funeral oration.'

In that pre-internet age, I did not always know how much of my work was actually being used in the paper – not for want of trying the patience of the Foreign Editor by constantly pressing to be routinely informed – and appreciated. It was my insecurity busily manifesting itself. Only when I was back in London did I fully learn how well the *Guardian* had done by me. There was cause for pride. Alastair Hetherington was well satisfied and warmly congratulated me. This persuaded me to risk an obvious follow-up: had I proved my worth? Could I now be taken on as a staff correspondent? Disappointment. Alastair said, 'If I offer you a staff job, I would be taking you on for a lifetime career, and I am not yet sure that I am prepared to do that.' Such an assumption may sound strange in today's world, where few journalists would expect to remain with a single news organisation for much of their working life. But back then, when I was making my case for a staff job with the *Guardian*, expectations were for a long-term stay. During my time on the *Guardian*, only a small number of my senior colleagues left to work for other media organisations.

Even if I had not yet fully landed on the *Guardian*, I was offered a foothold. Alastair proposed a short trip back to old pastures in Africa – first to the Congo and perhaps Lagos, where the Organisation of African Unity (OAU) was to consider, among much else, the secession of Katanga and the Congo crisis. I had already met the Congo's new Prime Minister, Cyrille Adoula, and knew many of the OAU leaders. This would give me an insight into the turmoil in the former Belgian Congo, which had become a situation of such pressing concern to the wider international community. I was told to keep expenses down, focus on features that could be written back in London and only send major news stories from Africa.

Within days of arriving in Leopoldville I was invited to dinner with Prime Minister Adoula. It was in his residence and I was busy quizzing him about the situation in secessionist Katanga. Suddenly our conversation was interrupted by an urgent telephone call. The US Military Attaché had been shot in his bed! An act of terrorism? A deliberate provocation? An incident with international implications? Would the UN Security Council want to go into action? Adoula was deeply alarmed.

I had a dilemma. Was this important enough to justify the expense of sending a short news story to the *Guardian*? I decided against it. My instinct was right. It was soon discovered that the shooting had been a matter of the heart: a jealous husband whose wife was having an affair with the Attaché. A good story for tabloids; less so for the cost-conscious *Guardian*.

A few days later, still in Leopoldville, a missive arrived from Alastair Hetherington: 'You could get both feet through the door as an unestablished, but semi-permanent member of the staff if you would be willing to start with leader-writing,' adding that I should fly back to London. It was such a happy surprise and I concluded (or maybe it was just wishful thinking) that the message meant, 'Come back, and welcome to a *Guardian* career.'

I had guessed correctly. By the autumn of 1962, not just my

size-eight feet were through the door, but also the rest of me. I was now the *Guardian*'s fully fledged UN Correspondent with a designated office space in the UN's media area, and instead of a plush hotel suite, I had a small apartment within easy walking distance of the UN. I had travelled to New York in style. Instead of flying, the *Guardian* had allowed me to sail to New York on the SS *France*. My travel companions were John Maddox, the paper's Science Correspondent, and Brenda, his journalist/writer wife, together with the buccaneering *Newsweek* correspondent, Arnaud de Borchgrave. We made a merry quartet. It is a mystery to me just how this trip was authorised. It certainly couldn't happen today!

I was happy to be back in the UN tower of Babel. This time I already knew many of the diplomats and journalists. It felt like a return to a private club. But I did not foresee that, by the end of the year I would also have established a temporary base in Washington and would be spending more time covering US politics than the United Nations. Nor, of course, did anyone predict that within weeks of the opening of the 1962 session of the UN General Assembly the world would be brought to the brink of nuclear war, and that the Security Council would be the scene of breath-taking drama, the forum where the US confronted the Soviet Union with irrefutable pictorial evidence of its missile mission in Cuba.

The US had been at loggerheads with Cuba since Fidel Castro had come to power. Since he was a Communist closely allied to the Soviet Union, the Americans considered Castro as a threat to their vital interests in the southern hemisphere. To sum up briefly, in April 1961 a group of Florida-based, CIA-financed and -trained Cuban exiles had landed in Cuba's Bay of Pigs in an attempt to 'liberate' the island. It was an utter failure, and President Kennedy was left looking weak and foolish. But there was no slackening of the US drive to isolate Cuba economically and politically, and to undermine the Castro regime. Another, better-organised invasion was on the drawing boards. For his part, Castro reacted to the Bay of Pigs operation by calling on the Soviet leader, Nikita Khrushchev, to reinforce Cuba's defence capacity. He met with a willing response. For a variety of reasons, some perhaps even relating to the East–West confrontation over Berlin, the Soviet leader took the dangerously provocative decision to construct a missile base in Cuba – a location from which nuclear missiles could target the US.

At the United Nations, it became a constant theme for the Non-Aligned members to attack America's anti-Castro drive. Only a few days before the news broke that Soviet missiles had been installed in Cuba, I wrote a lengthy analysis of the Cuba debates at the UN. The Non-Aligned countries had welcomed Cuba's President Dorticos after his verbose, excessively long and defensive address to the UN General Assembly. America's Ambassador, Adlai Stevenson, looked isolated when he denounced Cuba as 'the aggressor'. 'On balance,' I wrote, 'in the UN, the US comes out as a distinct loser in this struggle with Cuba – the Americans see Cuba as the USSR-on-the-doorstep of Florida.' I added:

> Many UN delegates deeply resent President Kennedy's strong-arm methods and threats over Cuba. This applies to Britain and France as well as smaller countries. America's Western Allies may agree that Cuba presents a strategic threat to the West. They do not necessarily agree that the best way of tackling this is to isolate Cuba; even more they resent the way in which the US is trying to force them into action against Cuba. The smaller countries, threatened by the US with a cut-off of aid if they help Cuba in any way, see this as a threat to their independence . . . President Kennedy's Cuba policy is wreaking long-term havoc with the American image abroad.

Reading these remarks in 2019, one only needs to replace the reference to Kennedy with Trump and conclude that nothing ever changes.

But of course the world did change in 1962. On 17 October 1962, US reconnaissance detected the first of three intermediate-range ballistic missile (IRBM) sites in Cuba. On the following day President Kennedy personally issued a strong warning to the Soviet Foreign Minister, Andrei Gromyko, that the US would not tolerate Soviet missiles in Cuba. Gromyko countered by denying the presence of the missiles. During the next two days, while President Kennedy and his military advisers considered their military options, more missiles were detected. The stakes were rising higher by the hour. Over ten days the world was on the brink of nuclear war. By 20 October, 42 nuclear missiles had been detected on Soviet ships approaching Cuba. The US responded by ordering a naval blockade and putting its forces on the highest state of nuclear alert.

Like the rest of the world, I was watching this progress towards Armageddon with a profound mixture of fear and yet disbelief. Could this really be happening? I joined a few friends to get away briefly from the febrile atmosphere at the UN and drove out to Jones Beach on Long Island. We sat there for a while and asked ourselves with dead seriousness whether we would still be alive the next day. Then we drove back to New York, and next morning we knew we had been safe for at least another day. But for how long? Would the US and the USSR be able to find a way of pulling back? On 25 October the Security Council held an emergency meeting. Once more the Soviet Ambassador, Zorin, denied that his country had stationed nuclear missiles in Cuba. He protested: 'Falsity is what the UN has in its hands, false evidence.' I was watching from the BBC's studio as Adlai Stevenson dispensed with niceties: 'I want to say to you, Mr Zorin, that I do not have your talent for obfuscation, for distortion, for confusing language and for double talk. I must confess to you that I am glad I do not.' Stevenson went on implacably: 'Let me ask you one question: Do you, Mr Zorin, deny that the USSR has placed and is placing medium-range and intermediate-range missiles on sites in Cuba? Yes or no? Don't wait for the translation – yes or no?' Zorin remained silent. Stevenson came back: 'You can answer yes or no . . . I am prepared to wait until hell freezes over. I am also prepared to present the evidence in this room.' Zorin still remained silent. Now was the moment of denouement. Stevenson's aides produced large-scale photographs of Soviet missiles in Cuba. With TV cameras in place, the whole world could see the evidence.

It was a crucial moment. But it was still far from the end of the crisis. Indeed, the impasse became even more acute until, finally, on 28 October, President Kennedy and Mr Khrushchev found a formula for compromise. The sense of relief at the UN was palpable, especially among the Non-Aligned countries, helpless bystanders to a US–Soviet confrontation that could have destroyed them all. Russia would remove its missiles from Cuba in return for a public US pledge not to invade Cuba. Even this would not have been enough to end the confrontation, had it not been for an undertaking, kept secret at the time, to remove US missiles from Turkey.

Both superpowers drew important lessons from the Cuban Missile Crisis: having come so close to a nuclear holocaust, it persuaded them to rein in the nuclear arms race. Next year a 'hotline' was established between Washington and Moscow as a high-level means of communication to enable the two countries' leaders to defuse tensions without again bringing the world to the brink of nuclear war. Fresh impetus was given to the conclusion of a test-ban treaty, and overall, the superpowers agreed to focus on negotiations towards balanced reductions in their nuclear arsenals. None of this meant that the Cold War was ending. It had only become a little less incendiary. In those dark October days, I little thought that in the years to come I would spend a great deal of time trying to master enough knowledge about nuclear and conventional arms to be able to report on the endless negotiations that were triggered in part by the Cuban Missile Crisis.

Inevitably, no other issue brought up during the 1962 UN General Assembly session could match the high drama of the missile crisis. But there was no shortage of UN involvement in other matters, and I was hard at work. Of course, Cold War issues were never absent. I have counted almost 100 articles and news reports – some short, some long – that I sent from the United Nations over those three and a half months. Efforts to oust the Taiwan government from China's Security Council seat and give it to the People's Republic of China again failed. Resolutions on banning nuclear testing were passed. When Monaco's relations with France were in trouble some delegates amused themselves by suggesting UN membership for Monaco, a transfer of UN headquarters to Monte Carlo and using the income from its casinos to strengthen the UN's finances. Might have solved a great many problems had the suggestion been taken seriously!

While getting to know many of the diplomats at the UN, I myself had had to become something of a diplomat – not so much in the UN arena as in the *Guardian* arena. Alistair Cooke was the Chief US Correspondent. But the paper also had a highly influential correspondent in Washington. Max Freedman was a personal friend of President Kennedy and was close to Vice-President Johnson and other senior members of the administration. He often took Jackie Kennedy out to theatres or dinners. He was superbly well informed.

For a long time Max and Alistair had been good friends and had few turf problems in working out how they would cover the US scene. But gradually that cooperation fell apart. It was made worse by the fact that Alastair Hetherington had the highest regard for Max's work and had rather less feeling for Alistair Cooke's colourful style. There was a further complexity. Hetherington and Cooke had little fellow understanding for each other. I was always trying to convince the Editor that Alistair's work was unique and deserved the highest respect. I never quite succeeded.

Relations between Freedman and Cooke came to a head after my return to the UN in September 1962. They would no longer talk to each other. So the two prima donnas used me as a go-between. I would have to phone Max to find out what he intended to cover that day. Then I would phone Alistair, pass on the information and find out what he was planning to write – and finally tell the Foreign Desk in Manchester. What a bizarre situation! Only the *Guardian* could tolerate such a state of affairs.

During the Cuban Missile Crisis, Max Freedman did an outstanding job reporting accurately on the inside track of the administration's efforts to avert nuclear war. Having won the Editor's highest plaudits, Max organised a high-level visit for him in Washington. Alastair Heatherington was invited to meet the Vice-President and even President Kennedy. Alistair Cooke, meanwhile, remained a bystander in New York. His only moment of real glory during the missile crisis had been to describe the confrontation between Stevenson and Zorin in the Security Council. Tough luck on me – this was one occasion where I was pushed aside.

With Max standing so high, it came as a complete surprise when he suddenly announced early in December that he was leaving the *Guardian* – with immediate effect. A rapid decision was taken that Richard Scott would take over as Washington Bureau Chief. But Richard was still settling his personal affairs and would not be free to take up the post for six months or so. What to do? Washington was far too important to be left empty. It could not possibly be covered by Alistair Cooke working out of New York. To my surprise, the lot fell on me. I would have to fill the gap.

I could hardly believe my luck. In less than two years I had made it from freelancer and occasional contributor to UN Correspondent. And now all of a sudden, for a time at least, I would be Washington Correspondent. Of course, it dawned on me that while I had followed US affairs quite closely from my UN perch, I would be coming to Washington as a novice with virtually no contacts or intimate knowledge inside the Beltway. That alone was a big challenge. Worse was to hit me when I set foot in the *Guardian*'s Washington office, a room on the editorial floor of the *Washington Post*. The room had a desk and a chair – and empty shelves and an empty filing cabinet. Though Max Freedman had apparently given his word that he would be helpful, in fact he had removed the entire contents – contact lists, reference books, correspondence files, cuttings. He had also redirected mail intended for the *Guardian* correspondent to be sent to his home.

I was at my wits' end. When I finally managed to track down Max, he made no excuses and said he had simply removed his own property. Pressure from the Editor made no difference. I turned for help to the *Washington Post*'s Editor, and of course also to Alistair Cooke. Both responded readily. At the *Post* I was given access to their reference library, and had the willing cooperation of its journalists. And Alistair Cooke zoomed in, happy to have a little revenge on Max, and organised a big 'welcome' party for me at the Mayflower Hotel. It was packed with key Washington figures. Among them was Pierre Salinger, President Kennedy's Press Secretary. He became a trusted friend who helped to open doors that I might not have managed on my own. My 'Mayflower Day' was my launch pad into informed coverage of US affairs. I relished it.

My long-term love affair with US politics had taken off. I quickly began to cover a daily menu of news stories. An early scoop about Polaris nuclear submarines raised hackles in Whitehall and won me warm congratulations from Alastair Hetherington. It was easy to make friends and develop helpful contacts. Washington is a company town. Professional and personal relationships are all part and parcel of an integrated way of life in the US capital. It helped that I was working for a newspaper known in the US for its integrity, but which was rarely read in Washington during the pre-internet era. As few of my contacts actually read my articles, I managed on the whole to escape the kind of strictures I would encounter later in the Communist bloc.

During my first few days in Washington, I stayed with Wilton and Virginia Dillon, friends I had met in Ghana. Wilton was a sociologist, working at the Smithsonian, and next to George Weidenfeld was the greatest networker I have ever encountered. I have ceased to count the interesting people I met thanks to Wilton, ranging from Margaret Mead to Gore Vidal. Wilton had a unique gift for friendship. Throughout the years I spent in the US, Wilton and his wife were my refuge – the home to which I could turn at my worst moments of crisis, and the place where I could go when I was simply tired and needed to relax. Both sadly have passed away. Their photo is on the shelf above the desk where I am writing this book.

Back in January 1963, I soon found myself a small flat in Georgetown, perhaps the most congenial part of Washington, where many of the great and the good – and the journalists – live. My social life took off happily. Among my earliest friends were Matthew and Judith Huxley – Matthew was Aldous's son. Their home, graced by Judith's fabulous cooking, was always a hub of social activity and political debate. Anybody who was anyone turned up at the Huxleys.

Another home where I was made welcome was Averell and Pamela Harriman's elegant Georgetown house. It was a singular privilege for me. Pamela's son, Winston Churchill – from her marriage to Randolph – often visited. We became friends. One Sunday afternoon he came to have tea with me. Before leaving he phoned the British Embassy to speak to the Ambassador. He was asked for his name. When he gave it, the security guard on Sunday duty at the switchboard laughed, obviously thought it was a hoax and put the receiver down. End of conversation.

On weekdays the British Embassy was more trusting and welcoming! Some of the diplomats I met then now number among my closest friends. I owe two couples among them – Richard and Gaby Fyjis-Walker, and Edward and Audrey Glover – my two god-children.

There was a dilemma when I was first invited to one of the Ambassadorial dinners. Apparently it was still the custom for the wives – the concept of a 'partner' was not in vogue – among the guests to 'retire' at the end of the meal, and leave the men to their port and cigars. But what to do with a professional woman like me, invited in her own right? It was a diplomatic dilemma of the highest order. For the time being I had to comply and troop off with the rest of the women to powder our noses and gossip until the men were ready to rejoin the ladies. Of course, I had nothing against spending time with the sisterhood. But it was the outdated idea that men could only talk high politics – or gossip – without the presence of the 'weak sex'. And this was still happening in the early 60s! How out of touch could the Foreign Office mandarins be? It was only when Shirley Williams made a Ministerial visit to Washington that the taboo was finally broken and an end was put to the notion that the male sex required private time for cigars, port and conversation, freed from those ignorant women.

All this helped to furnish, stimulate and inform a far busier working life than I had experienced at the UN. When I started in Washington, Alastair Hetherington told me to take it easy while I settled down to the new brief. 'We never expected you to go off to a scoop-like start. Indeed I would have been a bit suspicious if you had done.' But I was impatient to get to grips both with domestic and foreign-policy issues, and when I look at the plethora of subjects I covered during my first six months in Washington, I confess to being amazed at myself! It demonstrates once again how I tried to battle with my indelible sense of insecurity by using intensive work to prove myself and win approval. Though most of what I wrote was published and won me praise from inside and outside the *Guardian*, I continued to make a nuisance of myself with complaints to the sub-editors that some of my copy was cut!

Even in Washington, I never lost track of my African interests, and when African leaders visited the capital they earned full treatment from me. I was beginning to ask myself whether I had it in me to write a book about Africa. However, for now US affairs had priority. All aspects of US foreign policy interested me. Cold War tensions were self-evident. But the aspect that came up most frequently during that first half of 1962 concerned President Kennedy's efforts to strengthen the transatlantic alliance. On the domestic front, it was the civil rights movement that punctuated much of my writing. Pressures for desegregation and civil rights were mounting and I was witnessing the deep fissures in race relations that posed – and sadly, continue to pose ever more urgently and stridently – such a fundamental challenge to America's social fabric. For me, it was also a more personal matter: anti-Semitism is such a prominent expression of racial strife, and anti-Semitism is part of my experience.

In May 1963, I was at the Kennedy summer home in Hyannisport to cover a meeting between President Kennedy and Lester Pearson, Canada's recently elected Prime Minister. Pierre Salinger had included me in the press group invited to cover a US–Canada summit. It would give me an opportunity to meet the President. And indeed, I not only met him but fell straight into his arms. He was leaning against a bench. Pierre took me forward. I stumbled. I was briefly, very briefly, in the President's arms. He smiled, everyone else laughed and I was a little embarrassed, but certainly not displeased.

Just before my Hyannisport day, I had been in Birmingham, Alabama and had written a feature about this Southern city under intense pressure to desegregate. Peaceful demonstrations led mainly by students and even school children were intensifying. Business was suffering. The divisions ran deep, and seemed irreconcilable.

Martin Luther King had come to make the case for at least some mitigation of the harshest aspects of segregation. 'Negro' was the standard vocabulary to describe America's African-American population in those days. Even King continued to use the word as if he wanted it to be a constant reminder of the iniquities of slavery and race discrimination. Here is a taste of the atmosphere in Birmingham. I quoted some white denizens. Denouncing the civil rights demonstrations, they declared:

> This is part of the world-wide Negro movement to oust whites and take over world government . . . Martin Luther King is affiliated to every Communist organisation in the world . . .

I returned to Birmingham and also wrote about white citizens of the city who had progressive views and were battling to achieve change in their divided community. I also reported on the bitter civil rights demonstrations in Cambridge, Maryland that took their model from the young people's marches in Birmingham. A small town not far from Washington, a third of its population were black and forced to lead a totally segregated life, with 38 per cent of the men unemployed. For the 'Woman's Page' of the *Guardian* I wrote profiles of some of the women, white and black, who were fighting for civil rights, and from Washington I also described the Kennedy administration's tentative efforts towards desegregation on a nation-wide basis. Tentative was the key word – though the verdict would probably be different if Jack, and after him Robert, Kennedy had not been killed.

It was Kennedy's successor, President Lyndon Johnson, who finally overcame Congressional resistance and enacted the landmark 1964 Civil Rights Act that ended segregation in schools and employment and made racial discrimination illegal. But legislation alone could never resolve the underlying tensions. Racial discrimination may have been outlawed. But the law continues to be sidelined.

Inevitably my reports from the civil rights protest scene provoked a flurry of concern from my mother. I was allowing myself to be exploited by my editors; I was in imminent danger; I was forced to slum it in insect-infested hotels!; I should turn to other work. And yet again she stressed how proud she was to see my name in print. I had become used to her worrying about me, but I was upset to discover that she was increasingly phoning my editors in London to voice her concern. Even Alastair Hetherington was not spared – though he seemed to take it with good grace.

By mid 1963 Richard Scott was ready to take over in Washington. My six-months stint there sadly came to an end and I enjoyed a good summer break back in London and travelled to Europe. While my mother hoped that would be the end of my love-affair with America, I was greatly relieved to have it confirmed that I would go back to New York to continue as UN Correspondent.

One thing was clear: coverage of British domestic politics was not on the cards. The *Guardian* now regarded me as one of its foreign-affairs specialists. That was exactly how I wanted it to be. Cosmopolitan had become one of my key identities, and it was a boon that the *Guardian* allowed me to put that identity to good use.

CHAPTER 6

IN LOVE WITH NARENDRA

'Hella is such a good cook. My son is so lucky.'

We are in my New York apartment. The year is 1962. A small dinner party is coming to an end. The speaker is the Maharaja of Sarila, head of India's smallest princely state. He is visiting his eldest son, Narendra Singh, India's Deputy Head of Mission at the UN. The guests cheerfully endorse the compliment. But I recognise the subliminal message in his body language as well as in the words. The Maharaja indeed likes my cooking. He has nothing against me as Narendra's friend or lover. But I need to be put in my place. Marriage is out of bounds.

I have never forgotten this seemingly innocent occasion, even though it did not really tell me anything new. I probably sensed it from the moment I fell in love with Narendra. If I wanted marriage, or an enduring partnership and children, I was well aware that I had put myself on a roadway that could only lead to an immovable block. His family would never allow him to marry another European, let alone a Jewish girl. The Indian government was another impediment. It did not allow its senior diplomats to marry outside the subcontinent. In Narendra's case a rare exception had been made, when Jawaharlal Nehru had given Narendra a special dispensation to marry the daughter of a distinguished French diplomat, from whom he was now divorced. Narendra, a high-flying diplomat, was devoted to his career. He could not expect a similar dispensation again.

But there was more. On rare occasions when I allowed myself to be honest about my relationship with Narendra, I questioned whether he really shared the depth of my feelings. Yes, we had a deep-seated friendship. We enjoyed being together, travelled well together, shared a love of opera and classical music – Mozart's 'Haffner Serenade' became our signature tune – and we were deeply interested in politics and international affairs. We shared friends and were never short of conversation. And yes, we greatly enjoyed our sex life. But in his case, did this really add up to being in love with me? For a while I convinced myself that the answer was yes, and indeed there were periods when it could have been true. But it took a long time, far too long, before I allowed myself to accept that I was deceiving myself.

I met Narendra on one of my visits to Ghana. He was posted there as a junior Indian diplomat, living in Accra with his French wife Rita and their young daughter. It must have been in 1956 or 1957. It was a casual encounter at a party. He made no particular impression on me – or I on him. We would have forgotten each other had we not met again in 1961 soon after I arrived in New York as the *Guardian*'s UN Correspondent. Narendra had risen in the hierarchy and was a senior member of the Indian delegation to the UN. We were very quickly drawn to each other and soon became a pair.

He was single now. As a major gesture to Narendra's family, before the marriage Rita had converted to become Hindu. As he told me the story, after the birth of their daughter Rita warned her husband that if they had another child, she would revert to her Roman Catholic faith and have the child brought up as a Catholic. Narendra, who would succeed his father as Maharajah of Sarila, knew that it would be impossible to have a Catholic son as his successor in Sarila. Hence the divorce – even though it had been a happy marriage. This story alone should have convinced me that Narendra was not looking to me for an enduring relationship. He would want a Rajput wife to give him a Hindu son – as eventually happened.

But none of this was uppermost in our minds during the first years of our relationship. Our bond felt strong. We were the same age. Both of us had had a cosmopolitan upbringing. Yet our backgrounds could not have been more different. I was still gripped by the refugee syndrome, still exploring my identities, still wrestling with my Jewish identity, still in search of firm ground. Everything I possessed, I had worked for myself. Narendra had never had to face such challenges. He was a fierce Indian patriot, secure and certain of his Indian culture. He belonged to a generation that was born in British India and witnessed the fraught path to independence and partition. He also belonged to a highly privileged class. Sarila was the smallest, and possibly the least prosperous Princedom in India. But wealthy or merely affluent, the Princes and their families were a class apart. The Princedoms enjoyed an autonomous status in Colonial India, and the Maharajas were absolute rulers who only reluctantly acceded to India and accepted its democratic constitution after the country had secured its independence. Narendra was educated at Mayo College, India's Eton, at a time when admission was still limited to boys from princely families. Even before he came of age, he was appointed Chief Minister in the Princedom ruled by his brother, the Maharaja of Charkhari.

Early in 1948 Narendra was invited to become ADC to Lord Mountbatten, Britain's last Viceroy in India. From that position he had a close-up view of the final preparations for Britain's departure from India. He came to know Nehru and many of India's leading politicians and maintained links with the Mountbatten family for much of his life. In Government House, Narendra gained an intimate view of the Mountbattens' domestic life but kept it to himself until he revealed a few delicately written insights in a memoir, 'Once a Prince of Sarila – Of Palaces and Tiger Hunts of Nehru's and Mountbattens', published in 2008. I learned from the book that Lord Mountbatten is 'credited with inventing the zip to replace the fly button on men's trousers', as part of an explanation of how Mountbatten once only took three minutes to change from travel clothes to full dress uniform. Narendra also describes how he was obliged to dress up in that same uniform to spend many hours posing in Mountbatten's place for a portraitist.

When the staff referred to Lady Mountbatten, she was called 'Her Ex' (Excellency). One evening, bearing a message for 'Her Ex', Narendra came to her sitting room to find Prime Minister Nehru sitting 'on the Knole sofa facing Lady Mountbatten, their position revealing an extraordinary intimacy between them'. Quoting from his diary, Narendra also described one of the farewell receptions for the Mountbattens where 'Her Ex and the PM [Nehru] are getting infamous. They are all the time together. PM seems almost in love.'

The memoir includes vignettes of a princely childhood. 'An elephant was my pram' for early evening outings, 'where people bent low and swung their right arm forward until the palm came to rest on their brows in an obsequious salute to their future Raja'. Once asked as a child to give his name, he had no answer. He had never before heard the question. He had simply assumed that everybody knew who he was: the young Prince. As he grew up, once a year he had to perform a sacrificial rite, 'beheading a goat by a single stroke of the sword'. Yet at Mayo College, the fledgling Maharajas were taught to become English gentlemen, perfecting their English and 'reciting Shakespeare and Wordsworth and playing cricket and polo'.

But Narendra had no desire for life as a playboy. As an independent nation India was emerging as a major force in South-East Asia. He formed strong but controversial views on the role played by Britain in bringing about India's break-up and the establishment of Pakistan, and found it hard to come to terms with partition and the policies pursued by Pakistan's leadership. Divided Kashmir was a deep and painful thorn in the flesh. Late in 1948, after the departure of the Mountbattens, he joined India's new Diplomatic Service. It was the beginning of a highly successful career.

One of his tutors taught Narendra that 'without first inspiring a certain awe you cannot gain the friendship of another country – or the love of a woman'. He may have practised this in his diplomacy. I cannot say that awe had anything to do with my love for Narendra. Quite the opposite, perhaps. Early on in our relationship there was one of the recurrent crisis debates at the United Nations about the status of Kashmir. I wrote an article that Narendra interpreted as criticism of India's stance. He was deeply angered, accusing me of disloyalty. I was not awed by this and instead defended myself, arguing that private life and work had to be kept separate and that it was certainly not my task to underwrite, let alone defend, India's case. My arguments were not persuasive enough. Narendra decreed that our friendship was at an end. I was totally desolate and fled to Washington to be with Wilton and Virginia Dillon in search of consolation. They calmed me down. After a tearful weekend I returned to New York, and after a short pause Narendra and I made peace. The episode taught us a lesson. It was never repeated.

Narendra and I did not move in together. But I was able to rent an apartment in the same block where he lived and we commuted between the two. Several of his colleagues also became my friends, and thanks to Narendra I met many prominent members of the Indian community in New York, including the admired blind writer, Ved Metah, and another well-known Indian-born American author, Santha Rama Rau. The film-makers Ismail Merchant and James Ivory and their scriptwriter, Ruth Prawar Jhabvala, also became part of my circle of friends. At the time they were making *Shakespeare Wallah*, an acclaimed film about a troupe of Indian actors touring India with Shakespeare plays. Ismail was a good cook as well as a gifted film producer. There were memorable curry evenings in his apartment.

Happy weekends were spent in Westport, where my close friends, Jane and Fred Rosen, had a holiday home right on the beach. Highlights there were summer parties hosted by the two famous actors, Paul Newman and his wife Joanne Woodward. There were also occasional excursions to Montauk or the Hamptons.

In the summer of 1963, I overruled my mother and decided to spend the summer holiday in the US. The plan was to drive in Narendra's Mercedes across to the West Coast and back again. The car thought otherwise. When we reached Chicago, it broke down. A major component had to be replaced. It would take at least two weeks before the work could be done. So we continued our trip by plane and rental cars, with San Francisco a first stop. Primed by Alistair Cooke, the marvels of Zion National Park and Grand Teton were included on our itinerary. We revelled in all we saw of America's scenic beauty and of its people far removed from the metropolitan seats of power. But when we returned to Chicago to pick up the car, it was not ready. Narendra had to get back to New York. I would have to drive the car back. To justify the wait in Chicago, I wrote a couple of features about the city. A few days later the car and I safely returned to the owner.

I became used to long-distance driving after I began to spend more time in Washington. I had to give up my New York flat, but regularly drove to New York to spend the weekend with Narendra. Somehow I always managed to arrive like clockwork on the dot of my planned arrival.

Life, of course, was not just about holidays or leisurely weekends. Each of us was working hard, often seven-day weeks. But I must mention one more unforgettable leisure excursion. We flew to Puerto Rico. The short trip included a concert with Pablo Casals as soloist. He was around 90 and had to be helped to the podium. Then the great cellist played his 'signature' plea for peace, the Catalan 'Song of the Birds'. It has a haunting melody. The sight and sound of the great artist has remained sealed in my brain.

So far I have kept my mother out of this account of 'Narendra life'. But of course she was never absent. She berated me for 'wasting my life on a worthless man'. In another letter she told me that 'he is not worth a single tear. You are kidding yourself if you think he loves you . . . in his selfish way he only thinks what he can get from you.' Variations on this theme were frequent. They were particularly bitter when I opted to do the big summer trip across America instead of spending the time back with her in Europe. My mother's derisory comments distressed me to the core, even though I understood her viewpoint. She recognised that my commitment to Narendra closed my eyes to other men more likely to offer me the prospect of a stable family life. I also knew deep down that she was right to question the depth of Narendra's feelings for me. I was constantly asking myself the same question, and prodding him for confirmation of his love.

While we were together in New York, I can justify my blindness to other men. But at the time I failed to take on board what a foolish mistake it was to cling onto Narendra after he was posted to Burma (Myanmar) in 1965. We maintained a constant correspondence, interspersing discussion of our feelings for each other with comments on political affairs, especially on his nemesis, Pakistan. He tried hard to secure a visa for me to come on a visit. But

Burma was a closed dictatorship, and an intervention by U Thant, the UN Secretary-General, failed to overcome the Burmese government's refusal to allow a Western journalist even a brief glimpse of the country. I have no record of the letters I wrote to Narendra. But I have kept a pile of Narendra's letters from Burma and later ones written as he moved on to new postings. Re-reading them now, they confirm that I was totally unable to confront reality and understand the obvious: that once away from New York, Narendra's life had taken a different turn and that I could never again be more than a marginal figure in his world. For a longish while, he too was in denial. He was lonely, missed me, frequently asserted that I was and always would be part of his life. But I always wanted more and tried his patience and tested his feelings with demands for commitment, for faithfulness and a map for future togetherness.

While we were both still based in New York, but I was away on trip to London, he wrote a letter that gave me hope because its whole tone was to stress how much he cared for me and was missing me. He described how he had looked up to my flat or even fondled the *Guardian*; how he would have liked to receive a daily loving letter from me where I poured out my heart and told him of my joys and sorrows. He felt tied to me. But the letter ended oddly. He blamed himself for being grossly selfish, possibly even wicked, and asked whether he would have found me equally attractive if I had not also provoked some resentment.

Over to a psychiatrist: I should have seen the warning signs!

Depending on his mood, Narendra's letters addressed me sometimes as 'Darling'; sometimes with nicknames I had acquired back at school ('Hella Pick Plock' or 'Hellaphant'); sometimes as 'Helli' as my mother always called me; occasionally as 'Hell'; – and when in a bad mood, simply as 'Hella'. In a letter from Rangoon (Yangon) to 'Hella Darling' he questioned whether he had truly fallen in love with me, or whether he just saw me as a symbol of a life and culture in America from which he was now separated. He asked himself whether it was some kind of emotional transcendence which followed debauchery. Then the letter switched tone. Narendra repeated my name three times in a row to say how close he felt to me – closer than if I were physically present. Was it presumptious, he asked, for him to think that only he had reservations about our relationship and that I, for my part, had completely surrendered to him? He urged me to reflect and be honest with myself.

And yet a few days later Narendra's tone again changed radically. He wrote that he would be green with jealousy if I went out with others, got kissed and more. But as marriage with him was not on the cards, he urged me to marry someone else. He could not expect me to be satisfied with a relationship where we could meet only rarely; maybe only once a year. He could not ask me to live on such cheap rations. The letter rambled on. Because Narendra was lonely in Burma, love for me was uppermost in his mind. Yet he believed that if we were actually together he would find it easier to push me away. If I wanted to marry another man, he would feel happy for me and yet be very sad. But quite possibly neither of us would get married.

A later letter written in 1969 when Narendra was working in the Foreign Office in New Delhi, dealing with Pakistan affairs. Addressed to 'Darling Hella' he wrote that the past few years had only helped to convince him how fortunate he had been to have got to know me (he described me as fine and noble). His wife Rita had been his first love, and I was a very different person. But I too had given him a great deal. He went on to thank me for my companionship and stimulating his mind. Without me his mind was getting dull again. He admitted that he had had affairs, while I had always been faithful. Now that he was getting older, short-term relationships could no longer satisfy him. A many-sided relationship was essential. There was a hint that he believed we needed each other. In some ways the concept of the two of us together as a pair was a fixture in his mind. But regardless: he could not and would not marry me. Narendra was due for a diplomatic posting abroad. As a parting shot in that letter, Narendra asked himself whether he should go abroad again alone? And as he could not marry me, what was the alternative?

The alternative turned out to be Juni, a Rajput from a good family. They had known each other for some time. They married in the early seventies, when Narendra was India's Ambassador to Spain.

Juni was not yet on the horizon when Narendra invited me to India in 1966. As I spent the time mostly in the company of India's uppermost class, it was a lopsided initiation to India. We met in Calcutta (now Kolkata), where we stayed with one of Narendra's relatives who showered me with saris. I had the courage to wear one for a Rajput wedding of one of Narendra's relatives, and was paid the compliment of being told that I looked 'stately'! We went to Darjeeling and Sikkim and took photos of each other – this was the pre-selfie age – silhouetted against the icily white Himalayas. Then we flew to Delhi, and I was made genuinely welcome by his family. Next port of call was Jaipur and its Maharaja, and then Narendra took me to Ajmer to show me Mayo College, his *alma mater*, and on to nearby Kishangarh to see some of its famous paintings. The Maharaja of Udaipur, one of Narendra's close friends, had invited us to stay in his vast palace overlooking the lake where the now-famous hotel was just being completed. I had my first ride on an elephant, an outsize member of that wonderful species. As I was comfortably sitting on my well-cushioned lofty perch atop the elephant, escorted by his *mahout*, I understood how Narendra as a child must have felt that this stately animal was an ideal pram. For an adult, not in a hurry, this was a magic mode of conveyance.

My love affair with elephants was reinforced, and I have accumulated quite a collection of the inanimate variety. I also have a couple of paintings by a remarkable group of elephants, encamped on the outskirts of the Thai city of Chiang Mai, who are trained to paint trees and flowers. I have watched them exercise their painting skills and have heard them hoot with gratification when they are given sugar cane as a reward for their uncanny craftsmanship.

But back to my India trip. After Udaipur, Narendra finally took me to his home, Sarila, a pygmy compared to the seats of other Indian Princes. It was, however, far more user-friendly than the palaces I had

visited earlier. I could still get lost. But at least I could make myself
heard if I called for someone to extricate me. Narendra's sisters and
one of his brothers, the Maharaja of Charkhari, were in Sarila to
welcome me, and made me feel very much at home – though, of
course, just like Narendra's father, they had also drawn a line and
were quite clear that Narendra and I could never marry. I came back
to Sarila once more. But that was much later – about 12 years ago. I
came with a girlfriend as chaperone, and we were accommodated in
a separate wing of the house well away from Narendra's quarters. It
was a bitter-sweet visit.

Towards the end of my initial visit to India, Narendra organised
an overnight visit to Agra. We saw the Taj Mahal by daylight and
by moonlight. We sat together on that same bench where Princess
Diana would be photographed in all her loneliness. Outwardly
cheerful, I must have felt similar emotions. I knew that this was
some kind of conclusion to a relationship we had built since we first
met in New York. I would be on my own again. Or had I been on
my own all along?

Narendra and I never lost touch. The bond was never quite
broken. When I was posted by the *Guardian* to Geneva in 1967,
he was able to come for a short visit, and as he had a good eye for
interiors, I bought some *kilims* and a few pieces of furniture that
still live with me in London now. After his marriage he remained
true to his assertion that I would always be a part of him, and we
were able to maintain a long-distance friendship. When he first
married he also tried to persuade me to be friends with Juni. He
reminded me how happy we had been and asked if we could not
maintain good relations. He would like it if Juni could participate
in the friendship. That was one wish too far. I assumed, rightly,
that Juni would be in no mood for any kind of friendship with
me. For my part, I envied her for a marriage that had never been
open to me.

After Spain, Narendra served as Ambassador to Brazil, followed
by Libya, Switzerland and France. When he retired, he divided his
time between Lausanne, where he had bought a flat, and India,
where he had built a house in Delhi. He became chairman of the

Nestlé Company's subsidiary in India, and also took to journalism and authorship. With his experience as ADC to Lord Mountbatten, Narendra agreed to act as adviser to the makers of the film *The Viceroy's House*, which is about partition and purports to tell the inside story of the last days of the Viceroy in Government House. He did not live to see the film – which was probably just as well, since its storyline in several respects veered far from reality.

Narendra's first book, *The Shadow of the Great Game: The Untold Story of India's Partition*, became a considerable success not just in India but also in Britain and the US. It was controversial, a combination of Narendra's long-held views and deep research in British archives. He believed that blunders by India's leaders together with Britain's pursuit of ill-conceived strategic interests led to the partition of India and to Pakistan's determination to establish itself as a rival power on the subcontinent. A central theme of the book is to argue that Britain fostered partition as part of the longstanding 'Great Game' of keeping Russia out of the subcontinent and safeguarding British access to the oil fields of the Middle East.

While writing this book, Narendra sent me several chapters as he wrote them, and I became his unofficial first editor and critic. The same happened with *Once a Prince of Sarila*. He inscribed my copy of the book: 'To Hella – With love and without whose help I could never have written any book'.

Narendra died in 2011. I was able to speak with him briefly just once during his last illness. The friendship and bond were finally at an end. Of course I have asked myself innumerable times what it was in my character and background that led me to maintain such depth of feelings towards a man who could never have given me the familial and emotional security I so badly wanted. Perversely, I had pushed away in my early twenties two bright, attractive men in succession who had wanted to marry me. At the time I was still too engaged in establishing my professional independence and identity. I had had affairs before I met Narendra but had not tried to make them more significant than they were. And then Narendra came into my life and I did not want to let go. I was deceiving myself and knew it. Could it have been that my commitment to him not only blinded me to other relationships but also had the advantage of giving me full freedom to pursue my career? Or was it that I was so much in need of reassurance and proof of love that I battled on regardless of the boundaries that Narendra had set? I recognised that I wanted independence but also yearned for security, love and care from a partner I could respect. I had created for myself a make-believe world in which Narendra fulfilled that role. It took time to face up to reality – only to plunge into another ill-fated relationship several years later.

CHAPTER 7

SHUTTLING BETWEEN TWO 'U'S –
THE UN AND THE US

It was a grey and cold November day in 1963. I had just walked the few blocks from my flat to the UN building. There was none of the usual bustle. People were standing around in hushed sombre groups. President Kennedy was dead, assassinated. Friend or foe of the United States, the sense of shock among UN delegates was all-pervasive.

Just over two months later, another cold day, and I am on the tarmac at Idlewild – soon to be renamed John F. Kennedy – New York's international airport. I am in the company of 3,000 or so boys and girls. The mood is happy, excited, expectant. Wild cheering breaks out as their idols, the equally young Beatles, emerge from the plane on their first tour of the United States. The New York police stand there, bewildered – ambushed by the peaceful fervour of the crowd.

Move on again to October 1964 and I am in Quebec City shaking the gloved hands of the Queen, who has been receiving brickbats during a controversial visit to mark the centenary of the Canadian Federation. A month later I am sitting by a pool at the Camelback Inn in Phoenix, Arizona, writing an inquest on Senator Barry Goldwater's defeat in the Presidential election.

Roll on to March 1965 and I am in Selma, Alabama following Martin Luther King as he leads the epic civil rights march to Montgomery. And in between these landmark events, I am covering the diverse goings-on at the United Nations; occasionally I help out in the *Guardian*'s Washington Bureau; I write a frequent column on 'Women Talking' for the *Guardian*'s then Woman's Page; I plan books on Africa and the UN. At various points the Editor sounds me out, whether I would like to go Vietnam, or later whether I might be interested in becoming the paper's Moscow Correspondent, and at one point also suggesting an opening in a new post covering East and Central Africa. (No, thank you, to all three offers – they are never mentioned again!) With all that going on, I still manage to enjoy life with Narendra and a growing number of American friends. And I do not forget my mother and maintain my frequent letter-writing and make occasional trips to London to see her.

I have always admired America's art of patchwork quilting. And my life in those years was like the making of a patchwork quilt. I relished the opportunities to write about different events and situations, to travel in America, to meet new people, to expand the range of foreign policy issues I covered, to switch perspectives from UN affairs to US politics and policies. Somehow it all fitted together. The Kennedy assassination was the focal point of the quilt.

After the first half of 1963, when I was based in Washington, my friend Richard Scott was then installed there and I returned to New York to resume my job as UN Correspondent. Reflected in high-level speeches during the UN General Assembly debates, it was a pleasant surprise to discover a slight thaw in the atmospherics of East–West tensions. Soviet and Western ministers all at once seemed to agree, I wrote, 'that peaceful competition was a wholly acceptable way of pitting capitalism against communism. "Let the best side win" is the new slogan.'

Apartheid in South Africa came up again and again in UN debates during that autumn of 1963. Britain was in the dock over its resistance to the imposition of sanctions. Even the US distanced itself after the UK voted against a ban on arms sales to South Africa. The UK was also heavily criticised for the still unresolved crisis in Southern Rhodesia, and was also forced to defend itself against various territorial claims, including the Falklands, Gibraltar, and parts of British Guiana and British Honduras. Britain's Foreign

Secretary, Lord Home, could not refrain from a riposte. Those who tried to wave the big stick against 'neo-colonialist powers' should realise that this would discourage investment and hold back their development. The message may have touched a sore point but made no impact.

President Kennedy's mid-October appearance at the UN was one of the highlights of the UN General Assembly. It was the second time he had been to the UN. Listening to the youthful President, full of hope for a more peaceful future, nobody could have guessed that there would be no third visit to the United Nations. In a far-reaching speech, the President called for peaceful cooperation and sought to put the United States in the forefront to battle poverty, safeguard human rights, and, well ahead of his time, to protect and conserve the environment. He proposed that America and the Soviet Union should cooperate in the exploration of space and perhaps mount a joint expedition to the moon.

Mr Kennedy was still glowing from the successful conclusion, just over a month earlier, of the partial nuclear test-ban treaty, the first major disarmament treaty in 17 years of Cold War. The world no longer had to live in fear of fallout from nuclear weapons tests. But he went on to caution:

> We may have reached a pause in the Cold War. But that is not a lasting peace. The Treaty is a milestone – but it is not the millennium . . . If this pause in the Cold War merely leads to its renewal and not to its end, then the indictment of posterity will rightly point its fingers on us all.

That speech was made on 20 October 1963. Just over a month later, on 22 November, JFK was in Dallas and met his assassin. At the UN, the kaleidoscope of the world's nations stood, heads bowed, in grieving silence as US Ambassador Adlai Stevenson declared: 'the tragedy of this day is beyond instant comprehension. All of us who knew him will bear the grief of his death until ours. And all men everywhere who love peace and justice and freedom will bow their heads.'

I scoured around the UN building, asking diplomats for their reaction. Most felt they had lost a friend, a champion for peace who had recognised and respected the interests of smaller countries. What struck me most was the fervent concern of many delegates to be sure that the assassin was 'neither a Negro nor a Jew'! In the immediate aftermath, UN delegates were too shocked to give much thought to the new US President, Lyndon Johnson. Naturally they hoped he would rise to his new responsibilities, and that, like President Kennedy, he would put high value on the UN body, and support its work. But they also questioned whether LBJ had much understanding for the UN body or possessed the generosity of spirit they had seen in Mr Kennedy.

Three weeks later they had their answer – and LBJ passed with high grades. On a visit to the UN he proposed a Rooseveltian New Deal on a worldwide scale. He declared 'an unswerving commitment to the keeping and strengthening of peace'. He had a four-point plan: the US wanted to see an end to the Cold War 'once and for all'; the US would work to end the dissemination of nuclear weapons (the Nuclear Non-Dissemination Treaty was achieved in 1968); the US would work for nuclear arms control and reductions; and above all the US would seek 'sanity, security and peace for all'.

Alistair Cooke and Richard Scott wrote most of the immediate coverage of the assassination and its aftermath. I was given the task of writing about Jaqueline Kennedy. I described 'a luminous beauty' who won

the American nation's admiration for her steadfast bearing and dignity, her dazed calm and her dignified display of love and grief . . . No one will forget the sight of Jaqueline Kennedy in a simple stark black suit walking up the seemingly endless steps of the Capitol beside her husband's caisson, one child clinging to each hand. Her walk was upright, sometimes steadying her stumbling little son. Then standing stock still through the funeral oration; going forward again to the caisson with Caroline; kneeling and kissing it.

Come 1964, and I felt like an old hand at the UN, almost part of the furniture and a familiar face to senior members of the UN Secretariat and many of the diplomats. Throughout the year I reported the mini – and the maxi – problems and crisis situations preoccupying the Security Council and the General Assembly, ranging from the Congo to Cyprus, from peacekeeping to funding shortages, from Nelson Mandela's imprisonment to the need for UN observers in Yemen. I could go on and on. But in fact all this UN activity turned into something of a backdrop for writing about US politics and, in more general ways, about an American world outside the United Nations.

So it was that I found myself covering Beatlemania – and catching it myself – as the 'Fab Four' descended on the US for the first time. Physically the Beatle invasion was launched on 8 February 1964 when their plane touched down to pandemonium at Idlewild airport. Beatlemania had been around for some weeks and their arrival merely provided evidence of their existence in flesh as well as voice. Among the 3,000-strong army of teenagers, many in the reception party wept for joy. Bearing a Union Jack, the young Beatles descended from the plane as a look-alike quartet, smiling broadly, neatly dressed and coiffed with carefully rounded fringes. Everybody wanted to get close up, touch them, get a close sniff of the Beatle aura. But there was heavy police protection – the kind of protection normally afforded to Royalty and Presidents. Without the police barriers little would have been left of the Beatles. One policeman said the world had gone mad. Meanwhile, Beatle songs were being played on the airwaves virtually non-stop. 'Yeah, Yeah, Yeah' was on everybody's lips. In a supermarket, I spotted a transistor radio carefully poised on a pile of oranges, playing Beatle songs while the clerk was packing up purchases. Beatle wigs were in high demand and hairdressers were inundated with an unusual mass of new customers: young boys who demanded 'Beatle cuts'.

The Beatles' first live performance was, of all the unlikely places, at Carnegie Hall, the temple of classical music. Naturally tickets sold out immediately and the inevitable black-market price reached mighty peaks. Astute devotees thought they could beat the system. On the Beatles' day they went to an earlier concert at Carnegie Hall, suffered a dose of classical music and then hid themselves under the seats in the hope of ecstasy to come. Tough luck. They were spotted and inevitably turned out. Music critics attended in force. But they had taken care to consult their children before putting pen to paper. They made certain to avoid saying anything that could cause a subsequent domestic lynching. Actually it was hard to make a judgement about this Carnegie Hall debut. I was one of the lucky ones with a press ticket. The songs were drowned, overwhelmed by the constant shrieking of an over-excited audience. I emerged from Carnegie Hall slightly deaf – but went on to hear Ella Fitzgerald, the queen of jazz, still holding her own against all invaders – including the Beatles.

My companions that evening were Fred and Jane Rosen, friends I had met when Narendra had taken me to an India Tea Council reception. Fred was a big figure in the public relations world and his wife Jane was an experienced journalist. They seemed to know everybody who mattered on the New York political and cultural scene. Fred, who always called me 'Kid', cut a strikingly handsome figure with an outwardly extroverted but inwardly very private persona. Jane was highly intelligent, warm and a stickler for accuracy, which she had learned as a *New York Times* correspondent. They quickly entered my life, where they remained firmly implanted, until sadly, first Fred and more recently Jane died and left an unfillable hole in my existence. We spent many weekends in their second home in Westport. On the understanding that I never spoke or disturbed Fred while he was having his sacred breakfast read of the *New York Times*, the Rosens' homes became my homes on the frequent visits to America that continued after my base had shifted back to Europe.

I owe it to Fred and Jane that I met their close friends in the top echelons of the *New York Times* and was offered – though in the end it did not work out – the post of UN Bureau Chief. Naturally I often wonder how my life would have gone if I had joined the staff of the *NYT*. Would I have been happier and more settled? After all, until I found a home with the *Guardian*, an important ambition had been to settle and find durable work in the United States. What could have been better than to write for this prestigious American newspaper? But I suspect the answer would be a 'no'. I was used to the *Guardian*'s more relaxed, unbureaucratic ways of handling its staff and their work. The *NYT*'s culture was far more exacting and impersonal.

Admittedly, during this period in the 60s I was to some extent spoiled by Alastair Hetherington, who warmly supported my work. The same was true of the Foreign Editor, Geoffrey Taylor (who had commissioned my first freelance contributions to the *Guardian* way back in West Africa), and Mary Stott, who edited what was then still called the Woman's Page. They all felt it was important to have me, a woman, writing on political affairs for the main sections of the paper. At the same time they also encouraged me to write features from a woman's perspective for the 'Women Talking' column. I was free to choose any topic I liked – provided, as Mary reminded me, it steered clear of 'household and furnishing stuff and the like'. At the end of 1963, when Alistair outlined my working brief for the coming year, dividing time between the UN and US affairs, he stressed that my output should include 'some specifically female pieces. By this I mean the kind of strongly personal and human aspect you conveyed in the article about Mrs Kennedy after the funeral.' Mary Stott was more explicit about the special mix of writing that I brought to the *Guardian*. She told me that my occasional articles for the Woman's Page added 'lustre' to that section of the paper, precisely because 'you are best known as a foreign correspondent'. I loved writing those occasional 'Women Talking' columns. It allowed me to show a little of my own interests and personality and to communicate more directly with the readers.

My mother was of course my most loyal reader; also the most worried. She had taken to phoning the Editor to complain that I was being exploited, overworked and put in danger. It says a great deal for Alastair that he kept his cool and was kind to her. In one letter he described a long talk with her and said that he

must ring her more often. She says she is your fiercest critic and [you] have no right to be writing about American politics (as I told her you would be doing during the Presidential election) because you don't know enough about it. I told her she would be surprised how much you know, and that we were satisfied, even if she is not . . . I said you would be going to California this weekend and she asked how far that was. I said the full width of the continent, and she sighed. It was all fairly amicable. But I think your mother feels that everything is ultimately my fault. [!!]

There cannot be many editors, then or now, who would have such forbearance, such understanding for a refugee whose sole pole of love, affection and sense of security rested in her faraway daughter. Understanding this, and loving her, I made every effort at reassurance. But her worries were becoming an ever-growing burden.

They were not eased when she read my reports from Quebec, a city that had been put on high alert for a Royal visit. The British monarch stands above politics and is accustomed to deep respect. So it must have been a very novel experience to the Queen when she arrived in Quebec City in October 1964, only to be confronted by booing separatists screaming 'Elizabeth go home'. In the 1960s, French Canada's separatist movement posed a threatening challenge to Canada's unity. It associated the Queen with English-speaking Canada and refused to recognise her as their head of state. The Canadian authorities, fearful of another Dallas, put Quebec into a military straitjacket.

The *Guardian* does not normally pay a great deal of attention to the Queen's official travels. But on this occasion, where it was obvious that her presence in Quebec would be controversial, it was decided that a reporter had to be on hand. I was designated for the task. It was the first time I had covered a Royal visit and also the first time that I'd encountered a particular breed of journalists whose job it is to cover the Queen and senior members of the Royal family. To me, they felt part courtier and part media. I was treated as something of an intruder. On this occasion it was the women among the Royal correspondents who treated me with disdain when they discovered that I had neither hat nor gloves to wear for the

Queen's media reception on *Britannia*. The Queen herself seemed quite relaxed when she encountered my naked hand and even had a few words for me. A few years later, at a Commonwealth Heads of State meeting in the Bahamas, it was the self-appointed male cheerleader for the Royal correspondents who ousted me from a bus on its way to the Queen's reception, 'because you are not one of us'.

Untouched by the opprobrium of my 'courtier' colleagues, who described the separatists in lurid tones and sensationalised the alleged danger to which the Queen was exposed, I wrote about the politics of Quebec and tried to explain why the Queen had run into such public rejection of her position as Canada's, and by extension Quebec's, Head of State. This was about a divided Canadian Province where much of its majority French-speaking population was demanding greater autonomy, and where a small break-away movement had emerged demanding full independence. It was not until the 1980s, after constitutional concessions had been given to Quebec, that political calm was fully restored.

The Royal visit in 1964 had been set to mark Canada's centenary celebrations. The Queen was originally invited only to Prince Edward Island, where the separatists would have had little room for disturbance. The visit to Quebec City was thought to have been her own idea. Her advisers failed to discourage her, even though they anticipated trouble. The Canadian government may have felt that abrupt cancellation would make them look weak under pressure from extremists. So it was that, throughout her weekend visit, the Queen, riding in a bullet-proof Cadillac, was surrounded by a protective army of Mounties and by police armed with truncheons and authorised to use them freely – as indeed they did. She was booed, insulted or simply ignored. These were not the welcoming crowds to which she had been accustomed before – or since. The Queen's expression was inscrutable. The Duke of Edinburgh, however, was not amused and flailed out against Quebec's Premier, Jean Lesage. I reported that 'the vast majority seems to join in identifying the Crown with Britain, British culture and with English-speaking Canada. But there are also forceful strands of nationalism among French Canadians. And as a result this visit has come to be seen as divisive more than unifying.' Several times I was stopped in the street by young people who had spotted the press badge I was wearing. They explained: 'You see, she is not our Queen.'

The Queen herself, in the address she delivered at a state banquet in Quebec's Chateau Frontenac, made one of those mystic Royal pronouncements that touch on the far-out margins of sensitive political affairs. It conveyed the message that she understood Quebec's problems. Possibly acting on advice from Mr Lesage, she declared: 'A dynamic state should not fear to reassess its political philosophy. That an agreement worked out a hundred years ago does not meet all the needs of the present should not be surprising. Let the dialogue continue.'

On Presidential election day, 3 November 1964, I found myself in Phoenix, Arizona at the Camelback Inn – motto: 'Where time stands still'. Together with a large force of American and foreign correspondents, I was waiting for the election result of the Johnson–Goldwater campaign. Goldwater was a native of Phoenix. It was his territory. The Camelback's owner was his close friend. This was where, the next morning, Senator Barry Goldwater would come to make his concession speech while his aides were playing the familiar tune of blaming the 'Judas' media for their candidate's defeat. We had all predicted victory for Lyndon Johnson. It was only a question of how big. It turned out to be a landslide. It had been obvious from the outset of the campaign that Goldwater, a candidate from the conservative wing of the Republican Party and a favourite of the John Birch society, only had a below-zero outsider's chance of overcoming LBJ. Lyndon Johnson, a consummate political operator with a surprisingly liberal bent, had been Kennedy's Vice-President and had been catapulted into the Oval Office after the Kennedy assassination. He had already secured a major achievement – one that had defied President Kennedy's own efforts to secure an end to segregation. LBJ, as interim President, had managed to overcome Congressional opposition to his landmark 1964 Civil Rights Act, designed in part to end racial segregation in public places. Now, as the Democratic Party's Presidential candidate, LBJ was seeking legitimacy as President in his own right.

I had occasionally written about Goldwater, when he was still campaigning for the Republican nomination. So I was delighted when, in the final stages of the Presidential campaign, the *Guardian* decided its pockets were large enough to allow me to join the media group that travelled with the Goldwater campaign. It is a unique experience to be part of a Presidential campaign circus. We were criss-crossing the country, sometimes making five or six stops in a day. Given the constraints of time, campaign meetings would generally be held at the airport. It is hardly a way to get to know America, and after a while every airport looks the same. And every campaign speech sounds identical – most of the time they really were. The connoisseurs among the journalists, who had covered the Goldwater campaign from the beginning, could quickly spot whether it was the 'Chicago' speech or the 'New York' speech or could even be a newly concocted fighting speech. My personal battle all along the campaign trail was against time. At each stop, I would have to listen to the candidate, persuade a few members of vox pop to tell me their views of Goldwater, scribble fast and then capture a telephone to dictate my 'precious' words to the copytakers in Manchester. Be assured, you lucky journos who work with mobiles and laptops, those pre-internet battles just to get the stories back to the papers were no mean feat!

Occasionally plane travel was abandoned for campaign trains. That had its hazards. Travel was in slow motion with frequent stops. This was an opportunity for local politicians to come on board, meet the candidate and wander through the train until they got off at the next stop. Invariably, when they came to the media section of the train, they would pronounce on Barry Goldwater's eminence and deliver a diatribe against the media by denouncing their prejudicial reporting – 'fake news' had not yet entered into the popular vocabulary. The ensuing conversation did not necessarily stay polite. We all knew we were travelling with the losing side. Alistair Cooke, however, had warned me to be fair in writing about Goldwater and not be tempted to denigrate him for his rightist views.

While America was voting, there was time to reflect on the campaign. Lyndon Johnson had set out his vision for the 'Great

Society' and had fought on a civil rights platform with the commitment to complete his landmark legislation to secure full voting rights for all Americans. The Vietnam War glowered ominously as a near-dominant campaign issue. After Goldwater carelessly declared that nuclear weapons could be used tactically to end the war, Lyndon Johnson warned that a President Goldwater could plunge the United States into a nuclear conflagration. One of the Democratic campaign's most memorable advertisements had been 'Daisy', a little girl picking flowers that morphed into a mushroom cloud. LBJ won 44 states and 61 per cent of the vote.

Goldwater only won six states – except for his own state of Arizona, all were in the South. It was a significant political shift in a part of the country that had traditionally belonged to the Democrats. It reflected the Southern whites' resistance to desegregation. Barry Goldwater was their man. He had fought the campaign from a strident anti-civil rights platform, and had infused a great deal of rhetoric about black lawlessness and crime. He had a small constituency that loved what it heard.

Even before the election booths had closed, computer projections indicated a massive Johnson victory. It was obvious that Goldwater was the victim of an inexorable Johnson landslide. But Goldwater could not bring himself to concede. He sent word back to the Camelback Inn that he would wait until the actual figures were available. And he added a further delay because he also wanted to know how the vote had been distributed across the country. Wealthy Goldwater supporters, who had gathered at the luxurious hostelry to watch the election results, were devastated. With a super-heavy overdose of optimism, they had planned for a 'celebration' dinner to be climaxed with a victory ball and the crowning of a 'Cactus Queen'. But the computer projections only brought gloom. There was no celebration and the would-be Cactus Queens were sent home. The TV cameras were turned off. The guests ended their wake, sang no dirge and just collected their Cadillacs, driving away past the next-door house, whose owner had had the strange desire (or was it foresight?) to name his house 'Armageddon'!

Goldwater waited until the next morning before he finally brought himself to send a congratulatory message to President Johnson. The main thrust of that message was to stress the importance of law and order and a prosperous economy, and to declare that 'communism remained our number one obstacle to peace'. He made his actual concession speech in one of the Camelback's conference rooms. An inscription on one of the walls read: 'This is, my friends, the peace-time room with room for everyone but gloom . . . There is a happy peace, an end to strife.' Sure, there is always hope, and indeed Barry Goldwater was by no means at the end of his political career. He was re-elected to the Senate in 1967 and gradually turned himself into the Republican Party's influential elder statesman. He became a leading voice in persuading President Nixon to resign, and helped to pave the way for Ronald Reagan's election. In his final years he even became a small-scale libertarian. At the time of Goldwater's Presidential campaign, I certainly underrated his potential for political prowess.

Before leaving the glories of the Camelback Inn, most of us journalists wrote our own finales to the campaign. Being a sun-worshipper, I settled by the pool to write my conclusions. It was a warm day and I was in a summer dress. One of my abiding memories of that day was James Cameron, also in a deckchair by the pool, dressed in an unseasonable heavy tweed suit, a scotch by his side, scribbling away to produce a succinct and colourful account of a humourless politician in his hour of inevitable defeat. With James's unique gift for incisive, descriptive interpretation, he probably outwrote us all.

For my part, I looked back on the two defining issues of the campaign – civil rights and the Vietnam War – and speculated about LBJ's chances both of securing Congressional approval to sweeping civil rights legislation and also of finding a way out of the war. I was more optimistic on the politics of civil rights than on the peace prospects for Vietnam.

I had been writing, on and off, about civil rights issues since I had gone to Birmingham, Alabama in the spring of 1963 to cover the protest movement there. Nothing had prepared me for the Selma march in 1965. It was courageous, it was exhilarating, it was frightening, it was unifying and divisive. It was a successful attack on the old Southern order, and it gave President Johnson the muscle to secure his landmark Voting Rights Act that finally enabled all African Americans to have the vote. It will surely always be celebrated as the symbolic turning point in the battle for desegregation.

African-American disenfranchisement in the Southern states was the trigger for the Selma protest movement. It began in March 1965 when John Lewis and Martin Luther King joined local activists in a voting rights campaign in Selma, where only 2 per cent of African Americans had managed to get onto the electoral roll. Brutal responses from local sheriffs only served to reinforce the campaign. On 7 March a large group of activists, led by John Lewis, embarked on a protest march from Selma with the state capital, Montgomery, as their destination. As they crossed the Edmund Pettus bridge just beyond Selma, they were met by a solid blockade of state troopers, using tear gas and attacking the marchers with billy clubs. John Lewis was among the numerous wounded. Pictures of 'Bloody Sunday' produced national outrage, but only seemed to reinforce Alabama's determination to block an extension of voting rights. A second March on Montgomery, led by Martin Luther King, was attempted on 9 March, but it was halted in response to a federal injunction. However, a few days later, in a nationally televised broadcast, President Johnson identified himself with the protesters and followed up by submitting the Voting Rights legislation to Congress. This enabled the Selma activists to secure federal authorisation – and protection – for a new attempt to march to Montgomery. The aim, of course, was to reinforce pressure on the Southern states to end their resistance to desegregation and their refusal to extend voting rights to all African Americans.

On 21 March, 300 protesters set off on their five-day 54-mile-long march to Montgomery on what was to be designated the 'Selma–Montgomery Voting Rights Trail'. Protected by federalised Alabama National Guardsmen, the number of demonstrators swelled to around 30,000, including a fair proportion of white men and women on the last lap to the state capital. They had come in buses; they had flown in from all parts of the country. They had flocked in from the neighbouring countryside, and hundreds of Montgomery

black men and women were lining the streets to support Martin
Luther King and his civil rights companions as they enjoyed their
triumphal entry into Montgomery. The heroes of the March, who
had walked the entire route, were distinguished by wearing bright-
orange plastic jackets. The Governor had urged Montgomery's
white population to 'stand up for Alabama and stay away from
outside agitators'. But windows were open. Even the most diehard
segregationists were astonished to see and hear nationally famous
artists like Harry Belafonte among the demonstrators, leading them
by singing freedom songs. With Dr King and his wife and John
Lewis heading the March, it came to a standstill on the steps of the
Capitol. A solid line of green-helmeted police blocked any further
advance. The marchers wanted to hand over their petition for voting
rights:

> We present our bodies with this petition as a living testimony
> that we are deliberately denied the right to vote and are con-
> stantly abused by the so-called law officers in this state. We call
> on you [the Governor] . . . to assure the registration of every
> citizen of voting age . . . We call on you to put an end to police
> brutality . . . We call on you to end the climate of violence and
> hatred that persists in this state . . .

Governor Wallace, small of stature, unreconstructed and self-
righteously tough in his resistance to civil rights, must have been
watching. But he refused to appear. The petition was left in the
hands of the demonstrators. The hostile atmosphere did not deter
a series of defiant rallying cries. Martin Luther King, as always in
search of common understanding, used calmer words. At the end of
it all, he made one of his most memorable speeches, outlining his
goal of an America in which segregation has been completely eroded
and 'negroes' are free to use the ballot box to defend their rights. He
pleaded for non-violence:

> Our aim must never be to defeat or humiliate the white man,
> but to win his friendship and understanding. We must come to

see that the end we seek is a society at peace with itself, a society that can live with its conscience. That will be a day not of the white man; not of the black man. That will be a day of man as man.

Six months later, in August 1965, President Johnson succeeded in securing Congressional assent to his Voting Rights Act. The Selma marchers had overcome.

Together with a large bevy of journalists, I covered the Selma march through rain and sunshine from beginning to end, sometimes driving, sometimes walking, talking with the marchers and tempted to join in their singing with the constant refrain, 'We shall overcome.' The marchers were given overnight shelter by local supporters, while the journalists usually returned to their Selma hotel and its telephones. On the first day I gave a ride back to one of my American colleagues. He was an African-American and naturally sat next to me. I was blithely unaware that in the deep South such proximity could be a deadly offence. I was lucky. Nobody from the Ku Klux Klan spotted me. Five days later, Viola Luzzi, a 40-year-old white woman who had come from her home in Detroit to join the protest march, was ferrying home some of the black marchers. One was sitting next to her. Four Ku Klux members intercepted the car and shot Viola dead.

For me, the Selma march was one of those seminal experiences that reinforced my commitment to fight racial discrimination.

It was now my fifth year in America. I knew the *Guardian* wanted to free up New York for Clyde Sanger, the paper's correspondent in East Africa, who for family reasons was keen for a transfer close to his native Canada. The end of the year would be the end of my reign at the UN. I had to consider my future. I was fairly certain the *Guardian* did not want to lose me. But what would be on offer? Probably it would again be a foreign posting. Would I enjoy building up a new group of contacts and a new group of friends? Was I ready to leave America? Did I want a break from the daily grind of reporting and writing? There were so many other questions; not least, would I be anywhere within reach of Narendra, who was now in Burma? I did not forget to take my mother into consideration: what would free her from worry about me?

One morning the phone rings. Alastair Hetherington is on the line. Out of the blue, he asks if I would like to become the *Guardian*'s Correspondent in Vietnam? Instant explosion on my part: 'How could you inflict this on me? I am a coward. I could never be a war correspondent. Besides, my mother would have heart failure.' The proposal was dropped. Both my reasons were sound. I have the greatest admiration for the many women who have, in recent years, readily become, even enjoyed, their roles as war correspondents. But I know that I could never have been one of them. I am certainly not an armchair journalist. But to be embedded in a war is not for me. In that sense I really am cowardly – and not even ashamed to say so.

I had long toyed with the idea of writing a book about Africa, or about the UN, and had discussed this with George Weidenfeld as early as 1963. After a meeting in New York he wrote that 'I am determined that I should persuade you to write a book for us on one of the various subjects we have discussed . . .' Nothing came of this, as I felt unable to tackle a big subject while at the same time focusing on my *Guardian* work. But now, with the prospect of losing my UN perch at the end of 1965, I contacted Tony Goodwin at Penguin, who suggested a book on 'the Castration of the UN'. But then I talked again with George Weidenfeld. He wrote that if two publishers to whom he had sent my proposal were prepared to accept his terms, he would be able to offer me an advance of $3,000.

So I asked Alastair whether I could have some time off early in 1966 to write a book. This was agreed. I could have the first four months of the year. However, early in January, the Editor asked, somewhat gingerly, how the book was going. 'If by any chance it's going badly – but only in that event – read on . . . We are thinking of putting someone experimentally in Moscow to cover the Soviet Party Congress in March. If it were to prove worthwhile then we might perhaps send someone in permanently.' Was I interested? I had realised by then that the book project was indeed falling into the category of 'going badly'. But all the same, I was genuinely doubtful whether I was the right person for Moscow. All else apart, I didn't speak Russian, and to be dependent on interpreters is unsatisfactory. Moreover I had already planned my trip to meet Narendra in India.

With my future undecided, I was working hell-bent throughout 1965, sending my last piece from the UN on 28 December. I regularly wrote my 'Women Talking' columns, roaming far and wide from the Vietnam War protest movement to the 'Name Droppers', rich American women who insisted on pure gold needles for embroidering and using Limoges china for dogfood . . . I had fun in New Orleans, wore a Mardi Gras costume and described the scenes. Way before anyone had thought of Donald Trump as President, and when hardly anyone had even heard of him, I went to Palm Springs and wrote about this enclave of what would now be billionaires, but in those days were mere millionaires. It being the 1960s, I wrote, 'Negroes come here only as servants. Jews only come here by mistaken identity and never settle.'

In New York I sometimes wrote about its politics, sometimes about more trivial matters such as the dismissal of the French White House chef who refused to cook Texas recipes for LBJ and his friends. I was doing a fair amount of broadcasting as well as writing. When the UN General Assembly opened in September, my mind had to run once again helter skelter from UN funding problems to the Rhodesia problem; from the still abortive efforts to seat Communist China to tensions with the Soviet Union over arms control issues; from the crisis in Cyprus to the never-ending Kashmir crisis. There were interviews with U Thant and other senior figures. The Pope came on an official visit, pleading for peace, and annoying non-Catholic delegates by inserting into his message an indictment of birth control. Then there was the sad day when Ambassador Stevenson died. It was unexpected, and there was almost the same kind of stunned disbelief as there had been when news of President Kennedy's assassination spread through the building – perhaps all the more so, as Adlai Stevenson had been a familiar figure at the UN.

It was also during this session that I first met Kurt Waldheim.

He was there in his incarnation as Austria's Ambassador to the UN. The *New Yorker* magazine famously wrote of him: 'If he stood on the other side of the bar in the UN Delegates lounge, everybody would say he is a terrific waiter.' Waldheim was courteous, bland, unremarkable – and behind the mask, hugely ambitious. Later he was to have two terms as UN Secretary-General. It was only when he made his second, this time successful, bid for the Austrian Presidency that the storm burst over his alleged criminal wartime record; a storm that finally persuaded Austrians to confront their complicity with the Hitler regime. I maintained my contact with Waldheim for the rest of his career. Always keen to be in the spotlight, he allowed me to interview him even though my articles became consistently more critical.

On and on went the UN carousel. How much would I miss the UN? I had probably come to know it too well, and for now at least I'd had enough of it. How innocent I had been all those years ago when I had pined for employment in the UN system!

How much would I miss writing about American affairs? A great deal. I would strive to return – and the striving brought results a few years later when I came back as Washington Correspondent.

These first years of my *Guardian* existence had been heady times, and when I look back on all this activity now, I am a little breathless. I had matured as a journalist. I had an audience on the BBC's World Service. I was establishing a name and a sound reputation. I should have been happy with the plaudits I was receiving, not just from my Editor and Alistair Cooke, but also from respected outsiders. Surely I should have understood that my professional identity was now firmly in place. But I was still not persuaded.

CHAPTER 8

GENEVA – GATEWAY TO EUROPE

In my home I have a few treasured posters carefully framed for preservation. One proclaims: '*Halte au Chomage*' (A Halt to Unemployment); a second has a tight fist pointing fiercely at General de Gaulle, declaring '*Point de Non Retour*' (Point of No Return); and another demands a '*Presse Libre*' (Free Press). These were among the flood of campaign posters made in May 1968 by striking students at the Ecole des Beaux Arts in Paris. It had been a wet day in Paris on 29 May. It was the last day of the general strike that had paralysed France for more than two weeks. Students were marching through the Left Bank streets. Nobody took much notice of me and an American friend, Dick Dudman of the *Christian Science Monitor*, as we carefully stripped a few damp posters off the walls they had adorned.

Earlier during the strikes, we had gone to the Beaux Arts and asked the students if we could buy any of their posters. It was a fierce '*Non*.' Those placards were not for profit. They were for a cause. So we had to bide our time. My revolutionary haul is far more than a souvenir. It is a reminder of a magic few days that inspired social change and liberation. Wordsworth's 'Bliss it was to be alive' expressed my feelings.

I had come to Paris early in May for the opening of peace negotiations between the US and North Vietnam. It was an achievement of no mean proportion that the two warring sides were at last prepared to sit at the same table. Everybody knew the risk of breakdown and everybody knew that if the two sides continued talking, it would be a long, drawn-out process. In fact, there were more than 50 meetings in Paris strung out over nearly five years before a peace treaty could finally be signed and a ceasefire could come into force. It had never been the intention that I should stay in Paris for more than a few days to write about the opening moves of the talks. But I was caught out by the French Revolution. All transport was at a standstill. There were no trains, no planes and petrol pumps were dry. We were caged in France. Most certainly not the worst fate that could happen to anyone. For the duration of the strikes, I had two jobs. The Vietnam talks required almost daily news reports. Coverage of the French crisis was naturally led by the *Guardian*'s correspondents in Paris, Nesta Roberts and Margot Mayne. But thanks to my usual determination, I was allowed to pitch in and encouraged to write a number of features.

The student revolt had its origins in 1967 on the bleak, unfinished campus in Nanterre outside Paris. Their leader was Daniel Cohn-Bendit – nick-named 'Dany le Rouge' (Dany the Red) both for the colour of his hair and for his politics. He became the face of the spreading student revolt. After the dean of Nanterre shut down the university early in May 1968, the students took their protest to Paris and called for solidarity from the Sorbonne's student community. On 3 May the rector of the Sorbonne asked French riot police to clear the courtyard where around 300 students had assembled. Mass arrests prompted violent protests from bystanders. Cobblestones were torn out of pavements and hurled at the police, who responded with tear gas. Next day the Sorbonne was closed down. It was a dress rehearsal for far worse street battles on the night of 10/11 May. The student protestors had grown in number to at least 40,000. The plan had been to march to ORTF, the French broadcasting corporation. But they were met by riot police using truncheons to beat students and bystanders. Cobblestones were again torn up, barricades were erected and 500 students were arrested. Many were wounded. The battle continued almost until dawn. Next morning the Latin Quarter lay in semi-ruin. Two days later, the students were joined by the trade union movement, and France lay paralysed.

Told in short-hand this prelude to the General Strike hardly sounds like the promise of Wordsworth's 'Bliss' to come. I was installed in the small Left Bank Hotel Solferino, which had become my quarters years earlier during my 'Africa period'. The weekend before the revolution went live, I had been invited for lunch by Richard and Margot Mayne. Richard at that time was Paris Correspondent of *Encounter* magazine and a close collaborator of Jean Monnet, the 'father' of the European Union. The Maynes lived in a cottage outside Paris. Dick Dudman joined me, and we decided to hire the cheapest car available to get us there. It was a little blue Fiat. After churning over the political unrest with our friends, Dick and I decided to fill up the tank and hold on to the car. It might be useful if – and it was still a big if – the strikes spread to the public transport system. It proved to be a wise decision. On the night of 11 May, the car was kept well away on the Right Bank where Dick was staying in the five-star Hotel Bristol. That night of bloody riots I was out and about, a witness to the street battles. I was simultaneously enthused by the students' actions, horrified by the aggressiveness of the riot police and all the time deeply fearful of getting into harm's way – remember my coward's reaction to the proposal to post me to Vietnam.

When the General Strike began, the Fiat came into its own – almost literally. As petrol ran out, the number of cars on the streets diminished dramatically. Bar the Left Bank, where student unrest and police menace ruled, Paris became a city of pedestrians and cyclists. Only the police cars created big noise. Paris became a silent metropolis offering its layout and architecture to unencumbered admiration. I stood at the Place de la Concorde, and could embrace the long vista of the Champs-Elysées without the interruption and hullaballoo of cars and buses. But I also had the advantage of the Fiat. I could if necessary drive up and down the avenue, or indeed anywhere else in Paris. Dick and I used it to interview strikers in outlying factories, or to get a measure of the political mood in the suburbs. I had friends working at the Organisation for Economic Co-operation and Development, where they had a petrol pump with plenty of reserves. We were allowed to refill our little tank and were able to stay on the road for the duration of the strike. How lucky we were to be able to get around. Naturally, it was not just gallivanting – though it sometimes felt like it. There was hard work, interviewing, observing, listening and of course writing to be done.

It was stirring to go to the great courtyard in the Sorbonne, where students were huddled in groups debating, or spend time in its grandiose amphitheatre listening to the students' rolling-ball discussions about their aspirations, their goals, their tactics and strategy. With growing support from the wider public, the students were demanding radical reform: an opening up of France's encrusted privileged-based society; democratisation of key institutions, including, of course, education and the media; an end to Gaullism; and an end to the Cold War. Their dream was of a radicalised new world. They were euphoric. In the committee rooms where the students' leaders were plotting their actions, and in the corridors, the walls were plastered with slogans, manifestoes and instructions for dealing with tear gas or concussion. One of their innumerable slogans read: *'La Revolution est incroyable parce que vrai'* (The Revolution is incredible because it is true). The student groups included Marxists, Maoists, anarchists and Trotskyites, with a fair number of moderates aiming to sustain a unified front against the establishment. Not easy in such an overheated atmosphere. But somehow it held together. They called themselves *'Force d'occupation'* (Occupation Force), and even set up nurseries where children could play and sleep overnight. Students at the Beaux Arts made the posters and other colleges had their own debates. Outside in the streets, older adults took their cue from the students and discussed the need for social change. The Latin Quarter was transformed into a giant debating forum. Each evening there was a public meeting in the amphitheatre with around 7,000 people allowed in to join the students and take an active part in the debates.

I was there on one of the evenings when Daniel Cohn-Bendit addressed the assembly. Already under attack from the authorities for being a firebrand, there had been attempts to discredit him as a Jew. The students countered with a slogan: *'Nous sommes tous les Juives Allemands'* (We are all German Jews). On that evening there were

no interjections, no proposals or new manifes
Still and attentive, they listened and interrup
Cohn-Bendit declared the struggle had to cont
ist system could be shaken up and, with the s
destroyed; that this movement in France was r
the world. They were the agents of fundamen...

change. So much of the rhetoric chimed with the prevailing change of mood of the 1960s. Conservative views on authority, ethics and morality were under challenge from a younger generation infused with radical views on lifestyle, sexuality, human rights and freedom of speech. The student revolt in France was so inspirational because their slogan, 'Point of No Return', was transported to societal change.

On some evenings I visited a friend made through my earlier contacts with the Congress for Cultural Freedom. He was Francois Bondy, Editor of *Preuves*, the French equivalent of *Encounter* – both magazines sponsored by the CIA and channelled through the Congress for Cultural Freedom. Francois lived high up in an apartment building straddling the Left and Right Banks, close to the Ile St Louis. From his terrace we had a panorama of demonstrations on one side and a still cityscape on the other. It provided just the right setting for the small group of notable intellectuals conducting their own searching debates about social transformation. I had the courage to join in.

In the factories strikes were solid. But the talk among the workers was about their pay, their rights, material conditions, worker–management relations. The debate about ideas and a reordering of society was left to the students. Dick and I spent a day with striking workers at a Citroën factory on the outskirts of Paris. They were unequivocal in their determination to use the present febrile situation to extract better working conditions. But was there more at stake? 'De Gaulle has become an antique. He must go.' What about the students? 'Well, up to a point we have things in common. But each of us has their own interests that we must defend.'

Almost everywhere I went in Paris, I could spot posters of a man with a microfilm in his hand and a gag on his mouth. Written across

e was the slogan *'Information Libre'*. Journalists working
state-owned French Radio and Television (ORTF) were
anding an end to government controls over their output. But in
act they were already well on their way to making themselves heard.
The ORTF journalists had succeeded in occupying their building
and facilities, and were achieving the impossible to broadcast a
truthful account of the revolution. They told me of inconclusive
debates about a future ORTF modelled on the BBC charter. They
feared for freedom of speech in France and were convinced that independent broadcasting in France demanded even tighter safeguards
than the BBC enjoyed.

Reporting on the French Revolution was becoming emotionally
and physically draining. Dick and I decided to take a day off. We
headed for Chartres. The roads were empty; the countryside was
blooming in warm May sunshine; the air around us was scented.
After all the tumult in Paris, this world, just 50 miles distant from
the metropolis, felt strange, almost unreal. Then Chartres Cathedral
zoomed into view. This majestic edifice dating its Romanesque origins
back to the 12th century was virtually empty. We had it almost to
ourselves. As I sat there looking around at the famed sculptures and
mighty stained-glass windows, I suddenly felt at peace in a way I had
rarely known before. I was still, silent, just allowing myself to feel. I
had no words to describe it. I still have no words. All I know is that
it was not a religious experience, not some recognition that God was
speaking to me or that I was connecting to some element or being in
outer space. Those moments in Chartres Cathedral did not make me
a more aware and conscious Jew or tempt me to Christianity. Time
simply stood still. Was the spiritual peace I sensed at Chartres some
kind of message that I am capable of surmounting my restlessness
and insecurities? I kept it to myself and did not talk about it with
Dick. We paid our farewells to Chartres and drove back to the
mayhem of Paris. I have never forgotten how I felt that day. But did
I learn the lesson? Only off and on, is the honest answer.

With France still paralysed and the students getting more and
more vociferous, General de Gaulle was embattled but remained
defiant. On 28 May he disappeared, secretly flew to Germany to

meet with General Jacques Massu to assure himself that French forces would remain loyal if troops were needed to put down what he considered to be a popular insurrection. Then he returned to Paris. On 30 May General de Gaulle, armed with his familiar all-knowing forcefulness, addressed the nation. I had joined friends who were staying at the Hotel de Crillon. On a balcony overlooking the Place de la Concorde, loudspeakers boomed out the General's words. The message was unambiguous. He would not be hunted out of power. He would remain. His Prime Minister would remain. The National Assembly was forthwith dissolved and new elections would be held in June. Workers must return to work and students must return to study. The insurrection had been illegal, all part of a dark plot. While we listened, demonstrators came down the Champs-Elysées. But this was a different species. No longer the strikers. These demonstrators were bearing banners supporting the General. The Gaullists were back in force. And next day the traffic was back. The Fiat had done its duty and was given up. Just for a moment, on that balcony at the Crillon, I fervently wished for cement to be poured over the streets of Paris and for the buildings to be allowed to speak for themselves, and for the romance of a beautiful city. It was not to be!

For two months, France had been gripped in civic upheaval, economic paralysis and public debate. Now the workers drifted back to work, and the students ended the occupation of the universities. The Gaullists won the election, but General de Gaulle failed to regain his old authority. Ten months later, after a failed referendum, General de Gaulle finally accepted that his only choice was resignation. There was no way back to the *status quo ante*. The events of May 1968 triggered profound social change in France and inspired young generations around the free world.

Throughout the strikes, I had not been allowed to forget the main purpose of my stay in Paris: the Vietnam peace negotiations. This was the first glimmer of hope that this bloody war – for America, an unwinnable war – might be drawn down and negotiated to a halt. The sorry history of US involvement in Vietnam went back to General Eisenhower's Presidency and the first Indo-China War. But it really only began to escalate during the Kennedy administration when around 20,000 US Special Forces and advisers were sent to stabilise the South Vietnam regime in the mounting battle with North Vietnam's Viet Cong. Put at its simplest – even though there was never anything simple in the Vietnam War – the US supported the regime in South Vietnam. Communist Hanoi, under Ho Chi Minh's rule, was fighting for the unification of the country. Under President Johnson the US involvement grew exponentially and in 1968 it had grown to almost half a million US military fighting a bloody war that had already cost 30,000 American lives. In parallel with the administration's stubborn commitment to the Saigon regime, Americans at home became embattled in bitter, ever more vociferous opposition to the war. President Johnson was in a trap that had closed in on him after losing the New Hampshire Primary in the spring of 1968. Caught in the eye of the storm, LBJ decided to abandon the quest for a second term. But the war continued, even intensified. So did the anti-war demonstrations at home.

The willingness of the Viet Cong to come to the negotiating table in Paris offered a flickering prospect of a way out. Ambassador Averell Harriman, one of America's most experienced diplomats, was in charge of the US delegation. It helped that we had already met socially, and I was probably one of the rare non-American journalists to have access to him now. An off-the-record briefing with Mr Harriman a couple of days before the talks began gave me a fair idea of America's aims for the initial phase of the negotiations. It was obvious that the Vietnamese would call for a halt to US bombing. The Americans appeared to calculate that rapid progress on this demand could serve as a trigger towards engaging the Viet Cong in substantial negotiations. But Harriman was a realist and allowed himself no optimism. I gathered that the American delegation had been given little flexibility to their negotiating positions, and indeed that the US team in Paris included hawks, deeply opposed to any concessions to the North Vietnamese. The administration's hard red lines were self-evident. President Johnson was in attack mode and still sending reinforcements to Vietnam. While I was with Mr

Harriman in his office, a couple of men in working clothes appeared and said they had to make some adjustments to the heating system. They were obviously not what they purported to be. They were rapidly shown the door. When I think back on this little incident, it is yet again a reminder that once upon a time, not that long ago, security measures had a different dimension to the ones we have come to live with today.

The American delegation was installed in the Hotel de Crillon, not far from the US Embassy. The hotel bar became a familiar place for informal conversation with American diplomats and chatter among the journalists. It was a peaceful haven away from the uprising on the Left Bank. The Viet Cong delegation was accommodated more frugally, the lower orders apparently two to a room, in the Hotel Lutetia, a slightly louche Left Bank hotel beloved by émigrés and French intellectuals. The negotiations themselves were in the Hotel Majestic, back on the Right Bank. As the opening of the Vietnam talks coincided with the acceleration of the student protest, the French government was forced to take extraordinary measures to safeguard the business of diplomacy at the Majestic. Emergency power supplies were installed; telephone lines to the outside world were secured; plentiful food and non-alcoholic drink supplies were stored on the gloomy premises of the 'International Conference Centre'. Provision was made that the well-protected motorcades to ferry the delegates would not be troubled by the scarcity of petrol.

The assembled press corps was probably larger than the delegations and their aides. Unsurprisingly, American journalists made up the largest contingent. But Europe and Asia were not far behind. Most of us had had no previous contact with the North Vietnamese. It was a welcome discovery that some members of their delegation had obviously been authorised to brief Western journalists. Our new Viet Cong friends made little secret of their determination to use all possible means, militarily and now supported by diplomacy, to destroy the Saigon regime. They even speculated that Washington would welcome this strategy as a way of getting rid of what Hanoi described as the 'Quislings' in Saigon. But their key message was to assure all and sundry that the Viet Cong had come to Paris in good faith. Ho Chi Minh, their supreme leader, was ready for negotiations. They calculated, very hesitantly, that LBJ was of the same mind.

The kind of last-minute hitches that often occur before a difficult negotiation is underway were quickly resolved – thanks to American good will. The Vietnamese wanted an oblong table for the conference room instead of a hollow square table, and that was agreed. They wanted their side to make the opening statement and the Americans deferred. They wanted communiqués to refer to the 'Democratic Republic of Vietnam', and the Americans agreed, even though this was tantamount to tacit recognition of the Hanoi regime.

The formal opening of negotiations was indeed very formal, very polite, with the heads of the two delegations shaking hands – a significant mutual concession – and setting out their wish lists for the first stage of the talks. For this unique occasion, animosity was put under cover, but there was no way of hiding the mutual distrust. For starters, Hanoi called for an unconditional halt to US bombing. The Americans were unequivocal: no halt to the bombing without corresponding concessions from Hanoi. Both sides knew well enough that they were far distant from translating wish into deed. Progress, if at all, would be at a snail's pace, and it was unlikely that anything would be achieved during the remaining months of the Johnson Presidency. It would take another five years, until 1973, before Henry Kissinger, during the last stages of the Nixon Presidency, succeeded in making a deal with the Viet Cong 'on ending the war and restoring peace in Vietnam'. Even then it took two more years before the South Vietnam regime collapsed, the last American forces made their ignominious departure from Vietnam and the country's unification was finally achieved.

During the first two weeks of the marathon negotiations, the Paris meetings consisted of set-piece speeches, each side faulting the other for aggression and searching through the fine print for subtle messages about taking the talks forward into secret meetings. At this stage the Vietnamese had virtually no informal contact with the US delegation. They used the American journalists with close contact to the administration as a channel.

I was writing almost daily pieces about the Vietnam talks, using briefings by both sides to speculate about possible concessions and about obstacles, and describing as best I could the personalities and motivations of these little-known North Vietnamese, most of whom were in the West for the first time. But for me, all this came to a halt at the end of the month after General de Gaulle's defiant proclamation, reasserting his power and declaring an end to the May uprising. Time to leave Paris and go back to the grindstone as Europe Correspondent.

Where was 'back'? It was Geneva. That was where the *Guardian* posted me, nominally as European Economic Correspondent, in 1966. After my long stint in America, the leap from New York to small, slow-paced Geneva was not that easy. For the next four years, it was to be my home and also my jumping-off point to other European countries – and, as it turned out, even for short stints in the US. From the outset I knew that I would have to beef up my understanding of arms control issues, as Geneva had established itself as a suitable location for these complex treaty negotiations. My experience of the United Nations in New York gave me a head start at Geneva's European UN headquarters. Geneva also hosted several other international organisations, including the WHO, the ILO, the UNHCR, the World Council of Churches, the EFTA and other, less well-known international agencies. Between them these bodies would always keep me busy with newsworthy stories – when I was not deployed elsewhere.

Geneva is part international city, part patriotic Genevois city. It is a small place with a disproportionately high international community. The Genevois do not readily mix with the foreigners in their midst, and I had no particular ambition to break those barriers. The international community in Geneva leads a separate life, and social integration between the two groups is rare. That certainly became my experience. I was destined for the international sector and the priority was to settle into this new environment. Luck was on my side. I managed to find a small furnished flat in a big apartment complex called Parc de Budé that lived up to its name and was indeed situated within a beautifully kept park. It was just a few minutes' walk from the United Nations. My guess was that Parc de Budé's population was nearly 100 per cent foreign. The closest friends I made in Geneva lived in the complex.

I was quickly made welcome by Macha Levinson, an American friend and a former US diplomat, whose husband, an international trade union leader, was based in Geneva. Macha, whose family was of distinguished Russian origin, is an arms control and Russia expert. She gave me insights into these two worlds that were of enormous help. Her husband, Chip Levinson, was head of the International Trade Union Federation and ahead of his time in arguing that the trade union movement could only remain effective if it built a multinational framework to match the power of multinational companies. He was an early prophet of globalisation. There was no shortage of stimulating conversation in the company of the Levinsons and their friends.

Narendra also knew Macha from New York, and there was a convivial reunion when Narendra came briefly to inspect my new existence. For a few days it was like old times.

My old friend, Ehud Avriel – the Israeli diplomat who had helped to engineer the *Kindertransport* out of Austria – introduced me to two of his friends in Geneva, Norman and Alena Lourie. Norman was an Israeli of Lithuanian origin who had lived the early part of his life in South Africa before opting for Israel as his home. Alena was Czech and a survivor of Theresienstadt and Auschwitz. Alena's identical twin sister Irena, marked by the same terrible experience, was also living in Geneva when I first met her. During those early years of our friendship, neither of the twins was able to talk about their survival of the Holocaust. That came only much later when I wrote a family memoir of Alena's life. Irina eventually married Lane Kirkland, the head of America's AFL/CIO trade union organisation. In their hospitable Washington home I learned to enjoy Thanksgiving, and just as in the home of my friends, the Huxleys, I met many of the movers and shakers of the Washington scene.

Alena Lourie became a close friend and confidante. Her succession of dachshunds bellowed with pleasure when I turned up. We helped each other in good times and in bad, we quarrelled and we made up, we travelled together and we shopped together – and we were fierce competitors in Scrabble. Norman Lourie was an idealist and a gentleman in the true meaning of the word. He loved Israel, believed in the goodness of mankind and thought that a peace settlement was possible. In Geneva he was one of the founders of the Liberal Synagogue. He was a good Jew. I had a huge respect for Norman. But even his commitment to the synagogue and the progressive Rabbi he had helped to appoint, only rarely drew me to services there. The struggle over my Jewish identity was still very private and unresolved.

The Levinsons and the Lourie family were the nucleus of my social existence in Geneva. But they became much more and remained tightly intertwined with my life.

Barbara Mossu was the daughter of one of my milliner mother's clients. She was married to a French journalist in Geneva and we formed a firm friendship. Prince Sadruddin Aga Khan, uncle to the Aga Khan, became another Geneva friend of mine. When I first met him he was High Commissioner for Refugees. An interview led to an invitation for lunch in his lakeside home and a meeting with his wife. They were committed vegetarians and refused to wear leather. Guests were served non-vegetarian food, while they had their own separate menu.

Now that I was back in Europe and within easy reach of London, my mother could at last relax – to a degree. I was able to make excursions to London, and of course my mother could visit me in Geneva. The plaintive letters were suspended. It was a relief for me, and for her. It drew us closer – especially as she realised that Narendra was no longer a 'threat' to the life she wanted me to have. As ever, she pressed me to find a husband.

The atmospherics of the UN in Geneva were very different to New York's. Geneva was less febrile. Politics were less bombastic. Diplomats at the Geneva UN were often chosen for their expertise in arms control, international trade or human rights. Ministerial meetings produced few dramatics on the New York scale. And there was no replica of the convivial Delegates Lounge. The press corps at the Geneva UN was small, and I had almost no women colleagues.

Few major news organisations thought it worthwhile to have full-time correspondents in Geneva. Thanks to its scarce financial resources, the *Guardian* was almost unique in using a Geneva-based correspondent both for UN coverage and as a jump-off point for covering events across Western Europe.

In August 1968, I was looking forward to my first sight of Prague, the city where my grandmother had spent her last days of freedom before being forcibly transported to Theresienstadt. Alexander Dubcek, installed as Czechoslovakia's leader since January, was tampering with Communist orthodoxy. The aim was to create a 'Communism with a human face' with a programme of economic reform and a loosening of political control. By March, Dubcek felt ready to abolish censorship, a move that was guaranteed to be seen in Moscow as a challenge to its authority. Overnight the Czech media changed from automatic support for the regime to open discussion, analysis and criticism. Writers felt liberated. The excitement generated by the student uprising in France caught on among Prague's intelligentsia. Dubcek's 'Prague Spring' turned into a phenomenon carefully watched by the outside world, warmly welcomed in the West and deeply suspect in Moscow. Czechoslovakia's Party loyalists were aghast. But for a while President Brezhnev and the hard-core Communists in Prague were biding their time.

Prague was full of Western media, talking with the writers and the politicians, gauging public opinion and speculating whether this liberal version of Communism had a future. The *Guardian*'s Bill Webb had written some great pieces about the outpouring of new writing. Just after mid-August the paper asked me to go to Prague for a brief foray. I never got there. Late in the evening my phone rang in the Geneva flat. It was one of my British colleagues. 'Warsaw Pact tanks are pouring into Prague. It's an invasion.' He had seen the news on one of the wire services. Immediately I called the *Guardian*. 'Get to Prague on the first flight in the morning.' I didn't have much cash at home and there would be no time to go to the bank. I woke up the Louries and rushed to their flat to borrow money. Come the morning, I discovered the inevitable. All flights to Prague were cancelled. Instead I took off for Vienna, hoping that I could get into Czechoslovakia by road. The borders were sealed for incomers. The guards were less strict with the flood of refugees trying to get out. Not that Austria was keen to have them. Kurt Waldheim was now Austria's Foreign Minister. He sent instructions to the Austrian Ambassador in Prague, Dr Rudolf Kirchschläger, to turn down all visa applications. Dr Kirchschläger honourably ignored his Minister's order and the refugees came tumbling into Austria after all. I talked to some and wrote about their plight. Little did any of us think how many more refugee stories would have to be written in the years to come!

The Soviet Union together with components from Hungary, Poland, the German Democratic Republic and Bulgaria, had sent over 600,000 well-equipped troops into Prague. Only Romanian troops were missing from the Soviet-ordered Warsaw Pact intervention. The Soviet leader was applying his newly formulated 'Brezhnev Doctrine' under which the Soviet Union secured itself the right to intervene in any country where Communism was threatened. Russia's satellites had to play by Soviet rules. Free speech was anathema to Moscow. Dubcek's Communism with a human face could tempt others to follow suit. Dubcek was brought to Moscow and made to sign a humiliating declaration that obliged him to rein in his reforms. In April 1969, he was forced to step down, and his reforms were reversed. Czechoslovakia was back in the Communist orthodox fold. Dissidents were not to be tolerated.

After I failed to get into Czechoslovakia in the immediate aftermath of the Warsaw Pact intervention, it was pointless to stay in Vienna. Like many other journalists, I moved on to Belgrade. There was much speculation that Yugoslavia could be Brezhnev's next target. Tito, after all, had long ago detached himself from the Soviet empire and had developed his own model of 'self-managed' Communism. Personally I did not believe that Brezhnev would try to challenge Yugoslavia militarily. Tito was no Dubcek. Tito had a loyal, well-trained army at his command and would offer powerful resistance to invasion. He was no walk-over. Then there was the question of America's reaction. Washington had of course protested against the Soviet intervention in Czechoslovakia but had not retaliated. With respect to Yugoslavia, the response might be different. I interviewed senior officials and met with the Yugoslav generals I had come to know from earlier visits. I told readers that 'Yugoslavia is leaving no doubt in anyone's mind that it means to fight back an aggressor, and that the resistance would be long and tough. The country's unity has undoubtedly been reinforced under the present strain.' But not reinforced enough to prevent the country's bloody break-up after Tito's death in 1980.

During those August days back in 1968, speculation about Yugoslavia's fate quickly switched to speculation about Romania. Would Moscow move to put an end to President Ceausescu's attempts to woo the West with his stabs at an independent foreign policy? Had his outspoken condemnation of the intervention in Czechoslovakia – 'a grave error and serious danger to peace in Europe' – gone beyond the limits of Soviet patience? The media pack decided to move on from Belgrade to Bucharest so as to be in place when the Soviet tanks rolled into the city. Most of us had missed the show in Prague. The second round, in Romania, must not be missed. Our news organisations wanted us to have premier seats for the forthcoming display of Soviet strength.

One problem: the Romanians refused to issue visas to the media. The solution: we were simple tourists looking forward to the pleasures of Romania's thriving Communist capital, Bucharest. We just happened to be travelling with typewriters and heavy camera equipment. Officials turned a blind eye. Our presence was seen as a welcome insurance against Soviet intervention. Without us even asking for them, extra telephones were installed in the hotel, the Lido, where several of us stayed. Pretend tour guides turned up offering to show us Bucharest's landmarks and its happy people. This was my first lesson in Romania's devotion to the art of make-believe. On later visits, I realised that they had few equals in that art. Romanians could make black look white, could make food shortages be interpreted as mountains of plenty, could explain lack of heating by claiming the freezing country was suffering from heatwaves.

Censorship was tight and Romanians were told very little about the rumours of Soviet intervention or the diplomatic manoeuvres to deter Moscow from such action. 'The Romanian capital is relaxed and calm. There are no signs of concern; no general mobilisation, and the only invasion here is of the world's media holding what amounts almost to a wake,' I wrote. But below the surface, there were plenty of signs that Ceausescu was under heavy pressure from Moscow to conform. He toned down his loud criticism of the Soviet intervention in Czechoslovakia and used several speeches to affirm his loyalty to Moscow and the Warsaw Pact. He promised to accelerate the renewal of the USSR–Romania Friendship Pact. All this was just about enough material to keep me writing while the wake continued. It was hardly dramatic stuff.

In the evening, many of us would congregate at the Lido's bar. We would discuss conflicting rumours from East and West. Would the US intervene if Moscow moved against Romania? Would Britain? Marooned in Bucharest, we could do no more than make intelligent guesses – until one of the senior American correspondents, Arnaud de Borchgrave of *Newsweek* magazine, came rushing in. Important news! He had just been with the Romanian Foreign Minister: 'He has told me that everything is going to be all right.' From the back of the room a young reporter from the rival *Time* magazine hesitantly interjected: 'You know, this is rather curious, because the Romanian Foreign Minister isn't in Bucharest. He is in New York at the United Nations.' So the uncertainty and the waiting game continued. But not for long. Two days later President Johnson announced that he had received firm assurances from Mr Brezhnev that Romania was safe and would not have to suffer Warsaw Pact forces arriving uninvited on its soil. Anticlimax was present and correct. We received our marching orders. The media invasion was over and we beat a hasty retreat. Bucharest lost most of its international 'tourists'. I was back on my way to Geneva.

A footnote: in 2000, when British archives relating to 1968 were opened, it turned out that throughout that autumn of 1968, British intelligence was convinced that the Soviet Union was planning military intervention both in Romania and in Yugoslavia. Even a date, 22 November, was put on the anticipated action against Yugoslavia. Britain weighed up giving military help to Yugoslav partisans.

I knew none of that and simply returned to my wide-ranging coverage of UN matters in Geneva. September is always high season for meetings of major and minor United Nations agencies and other international bodies. The sprawling UN buildings in Geneva become a vast talking shop and cocktail party campus. Endless resolutions are proposed, haggled over, voted on, put into the record books – and mostly ignored and forgotten. When I asked delegates for a succinct explanation of what was going on at any specific meeting, and what results were being sought, mostly they would shrug their shoulders, say it was pleasant to be in Geneva at this time of the year, and that it was always helpful to have contact with colleagues from other countries.

In October, I found myself once again in America. In a new twist to a busy year, it had been decided to send me back to New York for a brief survey of the UN General Assembly, and even better, to let me share in the coverage of the Nixon–Humphrey Presidential election battle. I knew how lucky I was. I knew I had become hooked on American politics. I was high over the moon.

Naturally, I was happy to renew old friendships at the UN and in New York, and, dare I say it, people were quite happy to see me again. My first welcome-back lunch in New York was with my good friend Curtis Roosevelt, the President's grandson. We already knew each other well. It was always a thrill when he reminisced about life with his grandparents. Back in the UN building, I rediscovered the old routine: listening to the set-piece speeches by Presidents, Prime Ministers, Foreign Ministers and U Thant; chatting with diplomats; searching for newsworthy stories. But in truth, this side of the UN, the one that operates as a showcase political talking shop, had come to feel musty, repetitive – and powerless. I was growing cynical. I was also impatient to get back to Washington and onto my major assignment for the late autumn of 1968: the Presidential election.

I spent much of the time with the Nixon campaign, but ended up on election night in the losing camp with LBJ's Vice-President, Hubert Humphrey, in Minneapolis. I surveyed San Antonio, where LBJ would have his base after he left office. I went to Little Rock to get a sense of whether Senator Fulbright, the Senate's liberal foreign-policy guru, would be re-elected. I hopped from one campaign stop to the next: to Albuquerque to Pittsburgh to New York to Los Angeles and many more cities. The bitterly controversial Vietnam War coupled to the moribund Paris peace talks constantly vied with domestic issues in shaping the campaign and the candidates' stump speeches. Nixon addressed himself to what he coined 'the silent majority' and fought on a law-and-order platform and the promise of new initiatives to end the war. Humphrey stood to defend LBJ's 'Great Society', to fight 'a war on poverty' and to strengthen civil rights. Controversially, he called for a halt of the bombing in Vietnam.

Nixon at close-up was no more attractive than from far-away. It was hard to find anyone on the press plane who liked him or felt that he inspired trust. But most of us also recognised Richard Nixon's sharp intelligence and his clear focus on the campaign issues. This was not a first-edition Trump.

In a letter to my mother – who was as usual worrying about my work overload – I gave her the bare bones of my reaction to Nixon. Writing from New York's Madison Park Gardens, I told my mother that this was

> where Nixon is having yet another rally – the hall can hold 30,000 supporters and the place is full. I hate Nixon by now with a deep abiding hate. Watching him these past few days has been awful. He is so much worse, so sly, so insidious and dangerous. I feel sorry for us all that he will almost certainly be President . . . It is good to be with the Nixon campaign only because I have some good friends in the media group. We all band together in self-defence against the awful man. Last night on the plane from Cleveland we had a great party celebrating that Nixon had had an empty hall at a campaign rally there.

In that letter I added that before going to Madison Park Gardens, I had spent a happy afternoon with Alistair Cooke and that he had read me a preview of his next *Letter from America*. Alistair was a good antidote to Nixon.

Travelling with the Hubert Humphrey camp was a far more good-natured experience. The Vice-President was a real human being, not a machine, like his opponent. He was conciliatory in speech and manner; he listened to the voice of growing radicalism. Towards the end of the campaign massive crowds rallied to Humphrey and the polls showed a sudden upsurge. For a few days there was a fleeting thought that Humphrey might, against all the odds, make it after all. In Los Angeles on the final evening the travelling press corps was invited to join the Humphrey campaign at a star-studded Hollywood party. We danced deep into the night, and took off at 3 a.m. in the last of the four campaign planes to the Humphrey headquarters in Minneapolis, landing bleary-eyed on election day. I remained bleary-eyed for a further 24 hours, after which the candidate appeared at 9.45 in the morning to concede. Nixon had just won the Illinois vote, which brought him over the top to give him the required 270 Electoral College votes. There had been a seismic shock in the South, where Republicans had captured a whole bunch of traditionally Democrat states. The fun was over. Humphrey had lost. The Nixon era, Part I, would soon be upon us.

I thought back on that day to four years earlier at Camelback Inn in Scottsdale, Arizona, where Barry Goldwater had also appeared after a sleepless night and acknowledged defeat. In his case there had never been the slightest doubt that he would lose. He must have known that, and fighting the election campaign, he had become a champion in self-defeat. I disagreed with his politics, but came to feel quite sorry for him. I need not have worried. He made a strong political comeback in the Senate. With Humphrey it had been different. I agreed with his political message, liked his character and thought he would make a good President. There was good reason to feel sorry. Not just for Humphrey's personal loss. It felt like a loss for all of us.

I had a few more days of grace in Washington, and watched with bemusement when Richard and Pat Nixon arrived at the White House to look over the building that would soon become their home and office. A week earlier it had still been uncertain whether they would win a lease to that handsome property at 1600 Pennsylvania

Avenue. But now they had it and knew they could move into the White House at the end of January. They had come to view it under the guidance of the present tenants, and to make sure there were no ill feelings between them. They wanted to have a smooth change of occupancy and warn outsiders, especially warring factions in Vietnam, against harbouring any illusions that there were divisions to be exploited during the interim before the Presidency changed hands in January. How civilised and unlike the Obama-Trump transfer of power. For the Nixons, it had been a long road from Whittier in California and taken a hard fight to win a lease to their new home. To the extent that Nixon was capable of showing any feeling, he stood there, next to President Johnson on the doorstep of the White House, looking quietly triumphant.

At the end of November 1968 I was once again in Geneva, but I was able to spend the Christmas and New Year period in London making up for lost time with my mother and catching up with friends. It had been an extraordinary year in modern history, and I had had the great good luck of a front-row seat for its game-changing events. The coming year would probably be an anticlimax, though perhaps I would have a little more time to reflect on my life. Once again looking at the balance sheet, had growing experience and success at last made me feel reasonably secure? Not really. I was still battling over my identities. And my mother's disappointment and frustration over my failure to bring home a suitable husband remained a constant reproach.

I tried with little success to convince her that the *Guardian* wanted me to continue in Switzerland for the time being. She asserted that Switzerland was a dead end where my future was concerned. To be honest, I myself would have preferred to come back to London. But I suspected that if I fought against remaining in Geneva, the Editor would have insisted on sending me to Brussels. I had no desire to head there. I harboured an inexplicable dislike of Brussels.

If 1968 had been a busy year, 1969 was certainly no slouch. When I look back on the events and subjects I tackled, the number of trips I made, I am once again bemused. Versatility was my mentor.

Coverage included a girl on trial as a 'Devil's disciple'; the Pope demanding justice for the poor; President de Gaulle lording it over President Nixon during a state visit to Paris; central bankers in conclave in Basle hiding from financial journalists and me; Britain tabling a draft treaty on Germ Warfare; the US and Russia planning Strategic Arms Limitation negotiations in Geneva; a review of aircraft security after a tourist on his way to a big-game hunt in Africa carried a hand-gun on board, undetected; President Tito presiding over his Party Congress in Belgrade; Red Cross help for Biafra; the High Commission for Refugees pleading for adequate funding; frustration over the lack of progress in the Vietnam peace negotiations; Hella Pick turning into fashion correspondent at a St Laurent fashion show in Paris. That is just a small selection from my 1969 reporter's kaleidoscope, which also includes another October trip to the UN in New York and on to Nixon's Washington.

Inevitably, some of the reporting was tedious. Most of it was challenging, interesting, often even amusing – and almost always hard work. Some of it was collegiate. Some of it was solo work. No matter what, I was always single-minded and competitive but managed to make a few new friends among fellow journalists. At the UN in New York, and even more in Washington, the number of women journalists was growing. Yet I still found myself in a largely male, white media world. Journalists of colour were a rarity. Keeping up with a diversity of issues and contacts was a constant process of learning. But I was getting to know many of the movers and shakers of big and small events, and I was, as so often before, pushing out of sight and mind my personal struggle with identity. Work had established itself as my best form of escapism.

There was one story that demanded attention again and again – not just in 1969 but right back to the moment I'd arrived in Geneva, and which remained in my baggage until after I finally moved to London in the spring of 1970. Guess what? It was the United Kingdom's efforts to become a club member of the European Economic Community, as it was called before it became the European Union. Harold Macmillan was an early convert to the European project. Harold Wilson, initially an opponent who believed a revitalised

Commonwealth would better satisfy British interests, became a convert in the late 60s – when I began to cover European affairs – and fought hard to overcome tough opposition within the Labour Party. Edward Heath firmly believed that British standing and interests in the world would be strengthened by EEC membership. The first hurdle – a very high one – was to overcome General de Gaulle's veto to British membership and to secure the support of the other founder members just to open the gate to EEC membership negotiations.

When I started to report on European issues in the late 60s, Britain was still merely at the stage of periodically knocking at the Brussels doors which had been firmly sealed by de Gaulle's veto. Depending on who was in power, British Ministers, of Labour and of Conservative persuasion, were pushing hard, their knuckles raw. Do any of the Brexiteers remember, let alone understand, the mindset of their forerunners? In that former age, over an extended period, the political and economic benefits of joining up with the European project were largely undisputed – though to be fair, political minds were focused more on economic benefits than on prospects for political integration. Brexiteers take note!

Looking back on what I was writing during my Geneva years from mid 1966 to mid 1970, I have found over 300 pieces that refer one way or another to British efforts to apply for membership. Coverage of EEC and EFTA affairs took me to Paris, Brussels, Strasbourg, Rome, Lisbon, and sometimes even kept me in Geneva. Much of it was about bread-and-butter issues: the financial cost of joining the EEC; the Common Agricultural Policy; Commonwealth trade policy; the UK's economic fitness for membership. But it was also about the relationship between Britain as a founder member of EFTA (the European Free Trade Association) and the EEC; about the feasibility of a European currency; and yes, also about the advantages of closer political integration. It required much patience and a degree of ingenuity to keep the reader onside in describing and analysing the tortuous diplomacy that slowly carried the UK to the negotiating table. I did my best to make even the dull sound quietly stimulating to the reader.

There were many opportunities to meet the British Ministers leading the diplomatic effort to join the EEC. I silently applauded when I heard the down-to-earth George Brown, Foreign Secretary in 1967, declare in ringing tones that

> by joining the EEC we would be strengthening Europe and Europe's position in the world. We can bring to the Community a large industry and an outstanding agriculture, great scientific knowledge. Above all we should bring our world standing as a country, rich in endeavour and achievement over the centuries.

Unlike a later generation of politicians, Mr Brown never suffered from the delusion that a 'global' Britain, standing solo on its island, was a more attractive proposition.

Around 1968, when the government's efforts to overcome de Gaulle's veto on membership negotiations were stepped up, I interviewed Labour's Anthony Crosland, who was then President of the Board of Trade. He understood how 'intolerable' it would be to reduce the European Community to a mere trading arrangement. 'The Community has attained a genuine reality . . . We must build on this and not throw it away. It means that the Community must be much more than merely the machinery for free trade.' Time and again, in the drive to secure membership negotiations, Britain's leaders on both sides of the divide asserted that Europe's common interests, its security and its prosperity, demanded union – a union that included Britain inside the club. Membership negotiations finally began in 1970, and it was a Conservative Prime Minister, Edward Heath, guided by the same powerful convictions, who, two years later, secured victory

Memories can be so short. Who still remembers those urgent pleas for membership? Even I, who covered them, had forgotten just how eager Britain's politicians were to belong to the club, and how determined they were to lead a successful diplomatic offensive for acceptance at home and abroad. Yes, I know that the six-member EEC was a long way removed from the 28-member EU and its complex web of institutions. But as I see it, what has not changed is the underlying concept of a European Union with common interests, a shared cultural identity and an influential place in the global community.

I had been a convert to the cause even before I began to write about British efforts to join the EEC. Following the story only re-inforced my conviction that I am European by instinct, as well as in heart and mind. This was the world I recognised, which spoke to me and set a framework to my uprooted life. I feel myself out of place in a Brexit Britain.

CHAPTER 9

A LONDON BASE

FOR THE WANDERING JEW

It was 5 May 1971. The *Guardian* was celebrating its 150th anniversary. Germany was still a divided country. German Chancellor Willy Brandt was the guest of honour and keynote speaker at a mega *Guardian* birthday dinner at London's Dorchester Hotel that brought together Britain's political, business and media elites. Brandt delivered a rallying call for European unity and declared that 'Europe needs Great Britain'.

I was seated close to the top table. No reflection of a sudden boost to my rank. It was simply designed to have me within easy reach to buttonhole the German Chancellor after the dinner. Europe and America were locked into a serious dispute over trade and exchange-rate issues. The *Guardian* wanted to seize the opportunity to secure a comment from Brandt about the mounting crisis in transatlantic relations. The tactic worked. I managed to get close before the post-dinner throng surrounded Brandt. Could I have a few words before he left the Dorchester? 'Here there are too many interruptions. It's better if you come back to my hotel,' or words to that effect.

Yes, I was aware that Willy Brandt had a certain reputation. Shock horror – and with apologies to #MeToo – I readily went off to the Hyde Park Hotel, determined that I would not allow myself to be diverted from my agenda: a short interview followed by a trip to the hotel lobby's telephone to dictate Brandt's words of wisdom to the *Guardian* and then off home. But of course it didn't work out like that. I never did get around to the interview I had come to do. Nor, for that matter, did the alternative turn out to be a groping or Brandt's bed. The reality was both more banal and far more profound. We sat on a window seat in his sitting room and talked into the early hours of the morning – not about the political situation and transatlantic problems, but about Hitler, the Holocaust, German history, anti-Semitism, guilt, conscience, morality, reconciliation; also about my past as a *Kindertransport* child and about Brandt's political activism before and during the war. This was not Willy Brandt the German Chancellor. This was Willy Brandt the charismatic human being, a German with a powerful sense of right and wrong, and a strong belief in the power of reconciliation.

That nocturnal talk was, for me, cathartic. Willy Brandt had worked his magic on me. For the first time, I understood that I could come to terms with Germans and the German nation; that I could stop thinking 'Nazism'? and Germany were synonymous and could open up to Germany as a solid post-war democracy. It may sound illogical – and indeed it was illogical – that it took until 1971 for me to be able to think of Germany as a 'normal' country where I could spend time happily without any qualms, feel at home, not ask myself whether any German I encountered had been a Nazi. I was ready for friendship with Germans as with other nationalities. Of course the Nazis hadn't all evaporated. But after that Brandt conversation, they no longer dictated my view of Germans as a whole or made me see Germany as an outcast nation. How to square the belated reconciliation with Germany with the fact that I had started visiting Austria soon after the war's end and had felt comfortable about being there – even though I was of course fully aware that Austrians were far more reluctant to confront their Nazi past than the Germans? How contrary that it was Germany rather than Austria that troubled me and was my hang-up – until that seminal encounter with Willy Brandt. The best explanation I can offer myself is that Austria was in my blood, while Germany was a 'foreign' country with deeper barriers to overcome.

Happily, my first encounter with Willy Brandt led to many more meetings. It became a friendship. One of my great regrets is that I have no record of Brandt's great store of anecdotes. I particularly remember a couple of dinners with him and his good friend, Francois Bondy. During long evenings the two men complemented each other non-stop with jokes and stories, and the laughter never stopped. I can recall the laughs but not the stories. Shame on my poor memory . . . my loss!

When the *Guardian* celebrated its anniversary, I was no longer working out of Geneva. I had been living in London since the beginning of the year and now had my own desk and ample filing cabinets in the London office, then in Grays' Inn Road. To my very agreeable surprise, my mother had at long last recognised that I needed my independence and had understood that we could both live in London without sharing a home. She had gone out of her way to help me find a flat. One of her customers was Bridget d'Oyly Carte. Her company had a property in Knightsbridge. I was able to move into a small flat with my favourite number – '3' – at 33 Knightsbridge. It was hard to shut off the noise from the heavy traffic below me. But I loved it and continued with my habit of having fairly frequent Saturday or Sunday evening dinners where I cooked favourite Austrian dishes and our little polyglot group dissected the world and life itself late into the night.

Over the next two years, my work was much as it had been in Geneva. I was still the European Economic Correspondent. During the months leading up to the UK's accession to the European Economic Community, my main focus was on the negotiations in Brussels. Transatlantic strains over economic policy also featured large in my coverage. I was still covering arms control negotiations in Geneva and keeping an eye on the Vietnam peace negotiations. Both in 1971 and in 1972 I was again let briefly off the European hook to fly to New York to cover the opening high-level weeks of the UN General Assembly, with a brief look-in on the Washington scene included. In short, I remained a part-time travelling nomad. The wandering Jew continued to wander; only the base had changed from Geneva to London.

But for the first time I also had the chance to plant my feet firmly in the ground of the London editorial office. And before long I also had one of my memorable experiences of irrational sex discrimination – not at the *Guardian* but in the Foreign Office: to be more precise, from a small elite group of British Diplomatic Correspondents. Drawn from the leading British newspapers – no foreigners, please – and the BBC, around a dozen journalists were given a daily background briefing on the foreign policy issues of the day. The practice mimicked the parliamentary lobby. The *Guardian*'s Diplomatic Correspondent, Patrick Keatley, was a member of the group. The Editor decided I should act as substitute. 'Over our dead bodies!' cried the BBC's member of the group. 'Women have no place here' was the obvious message. This was a men's club. A woman clearly would not be capable of understanding the finer points of British foreign policy, nor presumably would she respect the confidential nature of the briefings. I did not take this lightly. But I was powerless. Fortunately, Alastair Hetherington decided he would not let this pass. Both the BBC and the Foreign Office experienced some interesting lashings from a Scots tongue. End result? Hella was deemed fit to join the background briefings – and to be fair, once the insiders had lost their battle, they acted fairly with their new female member. Before long there were more women in the group – and in due course, the whole idea of selective daily background briefings was abandoned. The insider group was no more.

I had never been in any doubt that the *Guardian* would stand up against any attempt at sex discrimination. Yes, in those days it could be badly faulted for failing to recruit enough women. But once on the staff, my experience suggests that equal opportunity reigned. As for equal pay, the management had little choice. The powerful National Union of Journalists set equal minimum levels of pay and equal annual increases in pay. The Editor had a small degree of freedom to top up salaries. At one point, when I made one of my frequent pleas for more money, he claimed I was the highest-paid correspondent on the paper. It still left me well below Fleet Street levels. But if true, then, selfishly, I am all for salary discrimination in favour of women.

I had fought hard to be allowed to return to London. The paper wanted me to move to Brussels on the perfectly correct assumption that coverage of the UK–EEC negotiations would be a near full-time occupatión. I countered that I had worked for the *Guardian* from abroad for a full decade, and surely it was important for me to have first-hand experience of the London office and get to know many of the colleagues whose by-lines I was reading but whom, often, I had not even met. I 'generously' offered to go to Brussels as often as necessary. And I found an ambitious and crafty young journalist, Richard Norton-Taylor, who was willing to act as a *Guardian* stringer and become my eyes and ears for searching out the subterranean workings of the entry negotiations. Once again, Alastair Hetherington humoured me and accepted 'the deal'. I was allowed to live in London. Richard was taken on for a miserly fee. The two of us made a good team and were helped by the *Guardian*'s part-time correspondent in Belgium, a journalist with the apt name of Henry Scoup. I became a frequent flyer to Brussels and Luxembourg – Eurostar was barely a dream – and Richard made himself indispensable enough to become a staff member and eventually the paper's distinguished Defence and Intelligence Correspondent. I think I can safely say that our little team never missed an important development in the dramatics of the UK–EEC negotiations, and occasionally we even managed a little scoop.

There was one immovable, ever-darkening shadow overhanging my life. Early in 1971, my mother was diagnosed with acute cervical cancer. She was operated on immediately. The doctors held out little hope of remission. They prescribed radiation, though they doubted it would do much to prolong her life. Yet she came out of hospital and seemed well enough, and for a few weeks was able to maintain a cheerful front. I think I pretended to myself that all would be well for a while to come.

And then there was 31 March, one of the deep-black days in my adult life. I was in Brussels. My phone rang. It was Eric Silver, a close *Guardian* friend. My mother had collapsed in the street at a bus stop in Ealing. She had been on her way to the hospital for her radiation treatment. When the ambulance arrived she was already dead. Eric met me on my return and the next few days are a blur. There had to be a post mortem because she had died in a public place. Then we – a small group of cousins and close friends – were able to have her cremated in the Mortlake Mortuary, not far from her favourite walks in Kew Gardens and the river path to Richmond.

To my lasting regret, my mother and I never acknowledged to each other that her end was near or that this was the time for deep heart-to-heart talk. We left so much, so very much, unsaid. I should have asked questions about her marriage and my father and her sub-sequent private life that I had never brought myself to ask. I will never know whether she had an abortion around the time she arrived in London. I should have insisted that any resentment I felt over her protectiveness was insignificant. I should have told her how much I loved her, how much I had always depended on her love and her faith in me. I should have thanked her for the sacrifices she made for me. I should have . . . oh, so many 'should have's. The list is long; the conscience is bad. The regrets have not withered.

I never called her 'Mummy' or 'Mother'. For some obscure reason, she was my 'Trummy'. I have probably been overly harsh in portraying the relationship between my mother and my adult self. I may have overstressed the tensions that developed when I failed to become the happily married wife and mother she had longed for me to be. But of course this was just one layer of a complex relationship burnished by all the experiences of mother and daughter, from a carefree early childhood to emigration, followed by the tough war years, and her struggle to give me a sound education. She sacrificed so much for me. Yes, she saw me as a child long after I had moved to adulthood. I should not have allowed this to upset me so much. After all, my love for her was always profound and has remained profound. Without her, my life lost its key firmament and the direct link to my family past.

With my mother gone, decisions had to be taken about the Ealing flat. I had few friends in the area, and I had no wish to live there. I decided to sell the lease. But I also realised I could not long remain in the rented Knightsbridge flat. The owners wanted it back. Where to go? A good friend who lived in Hampstead informed me that I was a natural for the area. He took me to look at various properties that might be within my limited range of affordability. We hit on a treasure trove: a two-bedroom flat with an unusually large living room, a balcony and, below ground, a lockable garage. It was not quite in Hampstead, not quite on Primrose Hill. Belsize Park is my nearest reference point. Insurance companies rate it as Hampstead and adjust their premiums accordingly – upwards. I raised £3,500 from the Ealing flat, secured a £7,000 mortgage, sold my modest holdings of stocks and shares and, in March 1972, acquired a new home for the princely sum of £22,000.

The Ealing flat had to be emptied. My mother's work room – one of the flat's two designated bedrooms – was a jumble of worktop and ironing board, an ancient sewing machine, a couple of wooden heads used to model hats. A bed stood crowded against one of the walls because my mother insisted on sleeping there when I was in the flat and occupying the other bedroom – considered to be 'my' room. There was also a small chest of drawers filled with letters and documents. She appeared to have kept every letter I ever sent her, together with any missives from my grandmother Olga after she had fled to Prague in 1938. I realised that I had inherited from my mother the habit of keeping letters from people close to me. However, during those days in 1971, when I was clearing out the Ealing flat, I was overcome by some kind of perverted rage over my mother's death: I tore up and threw away far more papers, documents and letters than I kept. I will never know what I lost. I will never quite forgive myself for destroying some part of my already scarce family history.

But at least I had the good sense to keep much of the furniture my mother had bought at those Ealing auctions years ago. Some of those pieces live with me still in my home. I also kept a typical Austrian *dirndl* that my mother wore in the mountains and an elegant black lace dress, both of which had survived emigration. My mother had good taste. I have them still. I have never worn them.

My mother had died in the spring of 1971. In the late autumn of that year, I suffered another blow. This time no other human was involved, only me and my anatomy. I had to have a hysterectomy. It was probably already too late to have a child. But this was the definitive end. I had always wanted a child – but I had not wanted it enough to face up to being a single mother. I could not see how to combine motherhood and my career. I had no independent means. But to be honest, I could not contemplate motherhood without the father's partnership. After the hysterectomy all this became academic. The line would end with me. 1939 had been the first big rupture in my life. And 1971, with my mother's death, was another crucial rupture. And now the hysterectomy. I had many friends. And yet I was very much alone. How to cope as a solo act?

Grieving over the loss of my mother had to be reserved for sleepless nights. Condolence letters were warm, well meaning, stressing how lucky 'Hanna' – her English name – had been to pass away suddenly, painlessly. But that was only marginal consolation. Brooding, however, was self-forbidden. As always, work was the obvious escape, and I flung myself into it. Until agreement on EEC membership was reached in January 1972, the Brussels commute had high priority. In London I was able to contribute to the coverage of domestic politicking over Britain's place in Europe.

During the early part of 1971, France was still resisting British efforts to join the EEC and was using issues surrounding the future role of sterling to block progress. Much of that changed in May. Christopher Soames, Britain's Ambassador in Paris, had been in secret talks with President Pompidou to arrange a summit meeting with Prime Minister Heath. It was set for 20 May. On arrival at the airport, Edward Heath immediately set about creating the right mood music and bravely uttered a few words in laboured French, saying that decisions taken at the EEC enlargement negotiations would be decisive for the 'political future of Europe'. The summit turned into a success. The Pompidou bar to British entry was lifted. Now Brussels could focus on the tough bread-and-butter issues.

The happy outcome of the Franco–British summit could probably not have been achieved without the diplomatic skills of Christopher Soames. Married to Mary Churchill, Winston's daughter, he had carefully prepared the ground to convince President Pompidou of Heath's commitment to the construction of closer European integration. In Paris, diplomacy can always be well oiled with hospitality in a grand setting. The British Ambassador's Residence is housed in the 18th-century Hotel de Charost built by Napoleon's sister, Pauline

Borghese. She sold it to the Duke of Wellington in 1814, leaving behind its valuable furnishings, including her ornate bed.

The Residence provided Christopher and Mary Soames with a perfect setting for cultivating their diplomatic contacts. Mary had a singularly warm personality and an instinct for making people welcome. Soon after we met, I was invited to lunch with just her and Christopher. It was my first time in the Embassy and Mary took me on a small sight-seeing tour that included one of the bedrooms. It housed Pauline's famous bed. Previous Ambassadors had slept in it. Christopher Soames was a large man. The bed was too short for him. Eventually it was moved downstairs to be exhibited as one of the Haus treasures. A small footnote to my links with Mary: in later years we happened to have the same hairdresser and often ran into each other there. The connection that started in Paris continued during the rest of her life.

In the autumn of 1971, with France on board, Britain's Common Market negotiations had finally reached their end spur. They became more intensive, more detailed, more technical – more taxing for the lay observer. In parallel, the EEC was also negotiating Irish, Danish and Norwegian membership. Geoffrey Rippon was the Minister in charge of the negotiations with Brussels. Jovial, rotund, pipe-smoking, media-friendly, he was a true believer in the European project, but was naturally also a fierce defender of British interests. At the negotiating table he earned a mixed reception – he was not always as sharp as his continental colleagues.

Largely for the benefit of France and the other EEC members, the Prime Minister was still emphasising the political importance of European cooperation. But at the negotiating table British officials were sticking to the straight and narrow and were warding off any European initiatives on political integration – that would have been too controversial in the UK. Economic issues were on the table, and politics only came in at the margins. This was most obvious in relation to Commonwealth affairs. The UK was intent on preserving Commonwealth interests and was so concerned that New Zealand's agricultural exports would be allowed to preserve a privileged place in Britain that they even toyed with the absurd idea of proposing

New Zealand's membership of the European Community. Fishery rights caused even more problems and bedevilled the negotiations right down to the wire – and beyond. British and continental fishing rights and access to British waters have become a dispute that defies solutions. An insignificant factor in the economies of both Britain and France, fisheries nevertheless became defining issues both in the UK's entry negotiations and four decades later, again in the exit negotiations, and yet again in the post-Brexit trade negotiations. In 1972, the *Guardian* used the headline 'Stinking Fish' over an article where I described why the negotiations over fishery rights were giving Europe a bad taste:

Why should Foreign Ministers of major European countries be knowledgeable about crabs and oysters, sole and herring – fishing mind you; not even eating them? Until recently the British government had thought that the Fisheries issue with the EEC was a comedy of errors that would resolve itself with a good laugh and a meal all round . . . Mr Rippon is puzzled why the Community cannot be persuaded that the need to preserve the interests of British fishermen is genuine and must be taken seriously.

It was not the first time that I had faced the challenge of sustaining the readers' attention on dry and complex issues. Arms control negotiations had already taxed my ingenuity. Now I was writing about technical, often obscure matters that nevertheless touched on the everyday lives of British farmers and fishermen, and on housewives' purses as well as on the heartstrings of a country that was emotionally linked to the Commonwealth connection. My passion for the European project had strengthened. Pleading my case for adequate space in the *Guardian* when more colourful news stories were competing for coverage, I surely caused plenty of irritation among the paper's editorial staff.

Champagne flowed in Brussels on 18 January 1972. The last hurdles over Commonwealth food imports and over fish had been papered over. Even more champagne flowed three days later when the Prime Minister, Edward Heath, came to Brussels to sign the

Treaty of Accession. I was not there to share it. I was for once out of action, recovering from my hysterectomy operation and convalescing with Embassy friends in Dakar. It was luxury in the sun. Even so, it was obviously frustrating to miss out on the climax of the EEC saga after following the process through all those long months of negotiations. They had lasted 19 months, involved summit meetings and 13 ministerial sessions, and had required the full-time work of countless senior civil servants. But even if I missed out on the celebrations, it was still some time before I 'retired' from writing about the European Economic Community.

The domestic politics around the Europe issue were bubbling away. I had a small share in covering the festering debate about European integration. Even while he signed the Accession Treaty in Brussels, Mr Heath was still seeking parliamentary support and trying to bring on board that first generation of Conservative MPs who were adamantly opposed to British membership of the EEC. Mr Heath only secured a majority of 21 when the House of Commons voted for the Treaty. The Labour Party voted against it, and Conservative Party opponents manifested themselves in no mean way: 17 among them ostentatiously abstained and four Conservative MPs, led by Enoch Powell, voted against the Treaty.

I had interviewed Enoch Powell earlier, in May 1971. As I see him, he was a precursor of the ERG ultra-Brexiteers. He pioneered the sentiments and arguments that successive Tory hardliners have developed all the way to Brexit. Britain would lose its identity; Parliament would lose its sovereignty; contributions to the Community's budget would cripple the Exchequer; there were no economic advantages to be gained from membership. He told me that 'the British people are preponderantly averse to Common Market membership'. He would keep up his crusade by visiting the six existing members of the EEC to persuade them that it was not worth negotiating with the UK because the British people would reject membership. Mr Powell stressed his 'devotion to European culture'. Yet he believed he was speaking for the majority of the British people in declaring his opposition to joining Britain's fortunes to those of the EEC. He was confident that the British 'instinct' was leading the British people to 'an intense negative' against Common Market entry.

Powell, delivering a speech in Frankfurt a few months after the UK's Accession Treaty was concluded, also produced a self-serving argument specifically designed for German consumption: the six existing EEC members would oppose German reunification because they would not want a giant in their midst. Britain outside the EEC might be useful, possibly 'indispensable', in framing a new balance of power in divided Europe that would allow reunification to take place 'without catastrophe'. Surely a rather exotic concoction of strategic thinking.

Enoch Powell and his fellow Tory rebels were not alone in taking their message abroad. With rare exceptions, such as Shirley Williams or Roy Jenkins, much of the Labour Party, including their leader Harold Wilson, was just as fiercely opposed to EEC membership. Shortly before Enoch Powell spoke in Frankfurt, influential German politicians were treated to a massive dose of anti-EEC sentiments by leading Labour Party politicians. Spearheaded by Richard Crossman and Barbara Castle, a group of Labour's participants at the annual Anglo–German Koenigswinter conference argued powerfully against British EEC membership. They too asserted that British public opinion was firmly opposed to entry into the EEC. The nearest any of them came to compromise was to suggest a formal test of public opinion – a referendum. It took until 1975 for a referendum to be held, for Harold Wilson to change his mind and support membership, and for British public opinion to endorse membership with a hefty 64 per cent vote. But that is not how it looked at Koenigswinter in 1973.

Koenigswinter is a small village on the shore of the Rhine more or less opposite Bonn. Beginning in 1950, it played an outsize role in forging Anglo–German friendship and collaboration, long into the post-war era. Dreamed up by a small group of far-sighted German and British individuals who formed the private Anglo–German Society, the Koenigswinter conference started as an informal initiative to bring about Anglo–German reconciliation and understanding. Its success went far beyond expectations by creating a network of close contacts across the two countries. Koenigswinter has annually brought together politicians, diplomats, business people, trade unionists, media and academics. They meet in alternate years in Germany and the UK. The UK conferences are most often held in Cambridge. Even though they no longer attract top-level power players, the annual two-day meetings continue even now. The discussions focus on topical issues in world affairs and their impact in Europe, and can range from European integration to defence policy, from the welfare state to globalism. Koenigwinter's greatest asset has always been its ability to build trust between opposites. Many friendships have been formed at these conferences. In the early days accommodation at Koenigswinter was spartan. Early mornings found participants in their dressing gowns, towel in hand, waiting for a bathroom. A unique camaraderie developed. It was a novel way of getting to know people. That was how I first bonded with several prominent Labour Party politicians.

I was lucky enough to be invited to join the Koenigswinter conference for the first time in 1970, and to remain an annual participant until well into the 80s. It opened many doors for me (even bathroom doors!) and gained me new friends both in Britain and, significantly, also in Germany. The Koenigswinter conferences enriched my education in German affairs. They reinforced my interest in and admiration for the country.

1972 was Presidential election year in the US. Richard Nixon was campaigning for his second term. He stood high in the ratings. The Democrats lacked an outstanding candidate. The outcome was predictable. Having come to New York to write a profile of Kurt Waldheim, I was also given the opportunity to join the *Guardian*'s Presidential election coverage. In October I was back in Washington. The Watergate scandal had already broken but had not yet come close enough to President Nixon to dent the near-waterproof prospect of his re-election. Paradoxically, he was being carried to a massive victory not by popularity, but mainly by indifference and by a poorly performing opponent, George McGovern. Reflecting the wave of cynicism that gave Nixon his second term, the *Guardian* headlined my report: 'Yes, it's Nixon with a Yawn.'

Barely back from the US, in November 1972 I found myself sitting in a sauna in Helsinki. The sauna was in the British Press Attaché's house. I was a house guest. But this was not a holiday. I was there for the first tentative moves towards the staging of a Conference on Security and Cooperation in Europe – CSCE, as it became known. On and off, when European and American leaders had met in recent months, the subject of such a conference had come up. It was a long-standing Soviet proposal that NATO had pushed aside, interpreting it as a device to tighten the Iron Curtain and secure formal recognition of the division of Europe and the borders of Moscow's satellites in Eastern Europe. The Western allies, especially the Americans, were dubious and suspicious. Only France was keen to go ahead, calculating that such a conference had the potential to open Pandora's box to improved East–West relations.

In the end, the Western allies agreed to test whether such a conference could also serve their interests. Helsinki offered itself as a neutral venue for preparatory talks involving every European country, bar Albania, together with the transatlantic allies, the US and Canada.

I had been following the debate around CSCE for some time and managed to persuade the paper to let me go to Helsinki for the opening of the talks. It helped that I could produce willing hosts – as I could also do in New York and Washington – and would not cause the *Guardian* a financial crisis over hotel expenses in costly Finland. So it was that I found myself in Dipoli, a stark ultra-modern conference centre some distance out of Helsinki at the beginning of a risky diplomatic exercise with no clearly defined goal. It was a cold and dark November day. Few that day would have guessed that the negotiations would last almost three and a half years, and even fewer would have guessed that it was the beginning of a process instrumental to the break-up of the Soviet empire and ending the division of Europe.

The opening was low-key. The setting was inauspicious. I described it in a piece called 'No sex please. We are Finnish'. The building offered neither the dignity nor the creature comforts of the surroundings in which international conferences are normally held. One Ambassador said the principal conference room reminded him of a circus tent . . . There are no dark hidden recesses for the traditional corridor bargaining that is such an essential element of international negotiation.

Worse, the Finnish hosts had decreed closure of the 'Sexy Bar', which had plenty of dark corners 'where young good-looking waitresses in sexy clothes serve and dance with their guests'.

It took just over six months, until early June 1973, to reach agreement on a detailed agenda and a timetable for a full-blown Conference on Security and Cooperation in Europe that was set to open in July. The West was now fully committed. The CSCE negotiations had the potential to achieve a free flow of information and lower tensions between East and West. It could even become a tool in defence of human rights. The Russians for their part had become more confident that the CSCE process would allow them to cement the division of Europe and confirm their hold over the Warsaw Pact countries.

I was back in Helsinki in July 1973 when the Foreign Ministers of the participating countries came to launch the CSCE Conference negotiation. It was a brilliant summer day with sun shining well into the evening hours. The Finnish government hosted a festive garden party. The journalists were scouring the crowd to tackle senior politicians. I was part of a trio that found Eduard Shevardnadze, who would become Gorbachev's choice for Soviet Foreign Minister. I introduced myself. He smiled. 'My wife is also a journalist,' the Minister told me. A banal exchange. But it was evidently enough for Shevardnadze to remember me. In later years, he was always accessible – hardly ever the case with Soviet leaders. My contacts with him convinced me that he was a realist and had understood earlier than President Gorbachev that the division of Europe could not be sustained indefinitely.

After the great and the good had left Helsinki, the diplomats of all the participating countries settled down to detailed work. It took two years to agree on an ambitious road map for détente. That map would become known as the Helsinki Declaration.

And as I left that garden party in July 1973, I had not the remotest inkling that the Helsinki Declaration would propel me to become the *Guardian*'s East European Correspondent and allow me to witness at close quarters the closing years of the Cold War.

CHAPTER 10

A TALE OF LOVE

It is a September day in 1973. I am at my desk in the *Guardian* office in Grays' Inn Road. I receive a phone call from Professor Ralph Dahrendorf's office in Brussels. He is one of Germany's commissioners in the EEC, and is currently responsible for education and science policy. I barely know him. So it is a surprise to learn that I have an invitation to meet the Professor for tea at London's Lancaster Gate Hotel in a couple of days' time. No explanation of the purpose for this meeting. But of course curiosity is aroused and I duly accept the invitation.

A medium-sized bespectacled man with a neat moustache is waiting in the hotel lobby. But it is only when we have settled down for a sedate afternoon tea that Professor Dahrendorf explains why he is in London – though not why he has invited me to be the first to hear his news: the Governors of the London School of Economics met earlier in the day to approve his appointment as the school's next Director.

He would take up the post in mid 1974. I was surprised: this was the first time that LSE had picked a foreign head. And though the 44-year-old Dahrendorf already possessed a highly distinguished academic pedigree in sociology, he also counted himself as an active politician and a leading member of Germany's Liberals, the FDP (Free Democratic Party). He was known as a passionate European and had been a Commissioner in Brussels since 1970, initially responsible for international trade. He had proved himself to be a controversial, often critical activist in the EEC's governing body.

From the way he talked, I gathered that Dahrendorf had been looking for a new outlet for his very special mix of academia, administrative skill and political work. The LSE appointment amply satisfied his ambitions. I suggested that he might not find it easy to deal with LSE's turbulent student body, much of which was then virulently anti-Common Market, describing it as 'a club for monopolists'. Dahrendorf, a European by deep conviction, quietly said he had concerns but would be able to cope. All along, he was speaking in perfect English without a trace of an accent. Maybe, he said, 'I could gain added distinction, and win over my new flock, if I take a leaf out of Henry Kissinger's habit of sticking to a strong teutonic accent.'

Satisfied that I had a little scoop ahead of the public announcement of Professor Dahrendorf's prestigious appointment, I thanked him and went back to the office to write up the story. On the following day, when the LSE decision had become common knowledge, I wrote another short piece about Dahrendorf after he used press conferences in London and later Brussels to stress his intention to remain a fully engaged – and controversial – member of the European Commission during the period before taking up his LSE appointment. The decision to leave the EEC Commission had nothing to do with 'disappointment and frustration' with the European institutions. It was all to do with the LSE offer, which was 'so unique that I could not refuse'.

That news story out of the way, I never for a second thought that my brief encounter with Ralf Dahrendorf was anything but a rather quirky way of disclosing his LSE appointment. I was flattered that he had singled me out. But I didn't waste time trying to find out why. I had no inkling of a personal attraction. Once out of sight, he did not remain on my mind. And for quite a while that held true. But the day came when, much to my surprise, contact resumed – and this time it had nothing to do with news gathering. It was about mutual attraction, about our feelings for each other, and ultimately about a relationship that brought me close to suicide.

I felt well settled in London that autumn in 1973 when I had my anodyne tea-party meeting with Dahrendorf. I had overcome some of the grief over my mother's death. Britain had joined the EEC and I could forget about New Zealand's butter exports or Grimsby fishermen's woes. I was covering a broad canvas of foreign affairs and building trust among a growing number of contacts. Professional satisfaction was on the rise. Social life was stimulating, and I strengthened my friendship with Evi Wohlgemuth, like me of Austrian origin, who had first come to Britain, then settled with her parents in Chicago, but returned to marry a fellow student, a refugee from Germany. She became my soulmate and confidante in good times and in bad times.

Back in late 1971, Alastair Hetherington had offered me the opportunity of succeeding Richard Scott as the *Guardian*'s US Correspondent. Instead of the temporary assignments in Washington, which I had always relished, this was a chance to settle there for at least three years or so. I was strongly tempted, but to my own great surprise, I turned the offer down. I was afraid of becoming the classic wandering Jew, unable to set down roots anywhere. Simon Winchester was appointed Washington Correspondent. So here was my opportunity to give a good try to my root-planting in Britain. But come autumn 1973, there was another chance to move to Washington. President Nixon and the Watergate scandal were dominating the news. High oil prices and other economic issues were putting a great strain on transatlantic relations. There was a worldwide audience for the unfolding drama in the United States. The *Guardian* decided to expand its US coverage by having two permanent correspondents in Washington. I could not let such an opportunity go by again. I successfully applied for the new post and by the beginning of 1974 I was happily back in America.

The return to Washington was a return to familiar, well-loved territory. I managed to rent a spacious ground-floor garden flat in the heart of Georgetown. With Simon Winchester already in place, we had to share the work between us. Not easy. Both of us were fiercely competitive. The paper treated us as equals. There was a rough division of labour. My main job was to cover stories that had a bearing on America's foreign relations and its standing in the world.

I have conveniently brushed out of my memory any friction with Simon. I have never been given a full account of the frustrations we must have caused at the foreign desk in London. But on the whole we managed to avoid any embarrassing overlap in our reporting. The end product, the *Guardian*'s coverage of the Watergate epic and its aftermath, passed muster with colours flying.

When I had last seen him at the end of his 1971 Presidential campaign, Richard Nixon was as triumphal as his dour face could allow him to show. He had won his election with a landslide. There was nothing triumphal when I saw him again in early 1974. By now he was so deeply implicated in the Watergate burglary of the Democratic National Party headquarters that he was already fatally discredited in the court of public opinion. The discovery that the President had consistently taped conversations with senior aides made his situation still more precarious. Nixon's unusual strategy – to put it mildly – to secure a second term had been an act of self-destruction. Impeachment seemed inevitable. Only the deluded could imagine that Richard Nixon would serve a full second term.

Was Nixon among the deluded, or was he just acting out of desperation? Did he really think he could save his Presidency, or at least his good standing in the world, by negotiating arms control agreements with the Soviet Union, strengthening the transatlantic Alliance and generally acting on the international stage as if he had few domestic worries? Those were questions that I, like many others, inevitably asked myself that spring and early summer while writing about Henry Kissinger's efforts simultaneously to set up a Nixon–Brezhnev summit in Moscow; massaging and reassuring the European allies; and pursuing Middle East and Vietnam peace efforts. Foreign policy had always been Nixon's strongest card. Nixon and Kissinger worked as a team, with Kissinger widely seen as the brains behind the duo's diplomacy. The opening to Communist China, culminating with Nixon's visit to Beijing in February 1972, was a brave but controversial decision seemingly taken as part of a strategy to strengthen the administration's hand in negotiations with Moscow – typical Kissinger logic that Nixon had supported.

Kissinger had also succeeded in bringing about the 1973 Vietnam ceasefire accord that brought home the US troops and prisoners of war – but failed to stop the fighting – and earned him the Nobel Peace Prize.

Now, in March 1974, as Kissinger set off on his 'save the Nixon Presidency' mission to Moscow, his first task was to try and repair Nixon's tarnished image. In a curtain-raiser, I described that his tactic was to focus on arms control negotiations as the most fertile issue for a Nixon–Brezhnev summit. At their first summit in 1972 they had concluded the first Strategic Arms Limitation Treaty (SALT I), but talks towards a vital follow-up treaty (SALT II) on further cuts to US and Soviet long-range nuclear arsenals were stalled. Kissinger would try to convince the Russians that a Moscow summit with SALT II heading the agenda could be fruitful. Kissinger also wanted to urge the Russians to stop meddling in Middle East affairs, claiming that the Russians were undermining US peace efforts by encouraging and strengthening Syrian resistance to US proposals. Still sound familiar today? I concluded that the Moscow trip

> may turn out to be one of his most difficult encounters yet with the Russian leaders. After this visit he may want to eat the words he used the other day when he suggested it was easier negotiating with America's enemies than securing the cooperation of its friends.

Kissinger made little headway in Moscow. The Russians were not averse to a June summit. But there was no prospect of giving Nixon a tangible success story to take back to Washington as evidence of his indispensability. Nixon wanted the summit to be seen as another milestone in his pursuit of détente and wished to leave his mark on history as the President who converted confrontation with the Soviet Union into constructive negotiations. But the Russians rightly judged that the Moscow trip was far less about promoting détente than about Nixon's survival in the White House. Moscow was not ready for genuine progress on the SALT II negotiations and had put forward new hardline proposals which America would find impossible to accept. Kissinger conceded that the Moscow talks may have been affected by Nixon's weakened position over Watergate. But he rejected claims that the trip had been a failure. He made it clear to friendly journalists – I was among them – that he was very unhappy about the negative interpretation that was being put about. He completely rejected the view that 'Watergate has dragged American foreign policy into the gutter'.

Many years later I came to know Kissinger better. But back in 1974 he could recognise me just about enough to know that I was the *Guardian*'s correspondent. I doubt that he had bothered to look at me long enough to notice that there was a hint of a resemblance to his wife Nancy. Their recent marriage had been prominent in the news. I only knew her from photographs, and it certainly had not occurred to me that we looked alike. Others, however, did see a likeness. I first discovered it when a couple of taxi drivers addressed me as Mrs Kissinger. Then there was the local supermarket. I came to the checkout ready with cash to pay for my purchases. 'But Mrs Kissinger, you have an account here,' the saleswoman reminded me. I was honest, murmured, 'Mistaken identity,' and used my cash. There was further surprise for me at a reception where Kissinger was spotted and soon surrounded by a bevy of guests, eager to hear the great man's views on the latest state of relations with the Soviet Union. Someone pointed a finger at me, and shouted: 'Does your wife agree with you?' Kissinger replied: 'She is not my wife. My wife doesn't criticise my work.' I was thrilled. Kissinger must have read something I had written.

Maybe he had seen a tongue-in-cheek piece about his wedding. 'Henry Kissinger's marriage has put an end to one of the few light-hearted and more amusing asides of this unsophisticated scandal-ridden administration,' I wrote. 'His social life has been the subject of unfaltering attention, and he has cultivated his reputation as a swinger with wit and considerable relish. Chancellor Brandt likes to call him "Henry the Kiss" and even President Sadat and Mr Brezhnev have been encouraged to crack jokes about his extra-curricular activities.' In real life Kissinger and Nancy had been close for several years. Just fitting the marriage into his crowded diary may have delayed the marriage ceremony.

On 9 May 1974 the Judiciary Committee of the House of Representatives initiated impeachment proceedings against President Nixon. With senior Republicans, including Senator Barry Goldwater, warning that the President risked downfall if he did not yield up all his tapes, it already looked inevitable that a majority would form in the Judiciary Committee to vote for impeachment.

In early June the Washington commentariat began to throw doubts on Dr Kissinger's integrity. Old rumours that the Secretary of State had ordered wiretaps on close associates and on leading journalists were revived and again strongly denied. Congressional critics questioned whether Kissinger had lent his authority to support President Nixon's efforts to use foreign policy achievements as a strategy to stave off impeachment. There were rumours that Kissinger made secret concessions to the North Vietnamese to obtain his Vietnam ceasefire agreement. There were also rumours of secret commitments in the Middle East that led to the Syria–Israel disengagement agreement early in 1974. Now Kissinger's critics feared that dangerous concessions would be made in the arms control negotiations with the Soviet Union to secure agreements that would boost the President's stature.

Kissinger was plainly angry that his integrity or his motives were being questioned. But the preparations for the Moscow summit went ahead, and on 25 June the Nixon caravan took off for Moscow, via NATO headquarters in Brussels. I was part of the expeditionary force that Nixon took with him on the campaign to save his Presidency. *Air Force One* carried the President and a series of VIP supporters, together with Kissinger and their senior aides. Two other planes were filled with journalists. The White House had encouraged as many media outlets as possible to cover the Presidential foray. They hoped for positive news stories to come out of the Moscow summit that would bolster Nixon's survival ratings. From the outset, I doubted that many of us would be seduced. We had already been warned against expecting any spectacular agreements to come out of the Nixon–Brezhnev meetings. We also anticipated that the NATO allies would give Nixon a polite but strictly guarded reception. The transatlantic relationship was in one of its wobbly phases, and the European Allies were in no mood to boost a lame-duck President.

It would be fair to say that the majority of the 300 journalists who came along on this trip viewed it as an exercise in *schadenfreude*, an opportunity to watch the wounded President in a vain search for a healer. During a few moments of naked fear, some of us had cause to wonder whether we would live to tell the tale of Nixon's agony. We were on a Russian Ilushin plane transporting us from Yalta to Minsk. The sky was a crystal-clear blue. There was no evidence of heavy winds. Suddenly the plane dropped deeply down a vertical line. My heart stood still. Was this the end? Moments later, just as suddenly the plane corrected itself and resumed a steady flight. The Secret Service officer accompanying us was just as white as the rest of us, and whispered: 'We just lost an engine.' Luckily, the injured plane managed to fly without the missing component. There were no further engine drop-offs, and we safely landed in Minsk. The *Guardian*, in one of its famous misprints, printed that my news story from Minsk was written by 'Hella Pinsk'. Obviously somebody on the *Guardian* desk was in a poetic frame of mind.

The Moscow summit was drawn out, lasting from 27 June to 3 August. After their first meeting in Moscow, Leonid Brezhnev and Richard Nixon met again at the Soviet leader's property at Oreanda, close to Yalta. Following the stop-over in Minsk, it was back to Moscow, and amid suitable fanfares the joint Soviet–American communiqué was festively signed. Small steps forward on strategic weapons limitations had been made (though the SALT II Treaty was still nowhere in sight) and further limits on powerful underground nuclear tests were agreed, but not before 1976, when both superpowers would have completed their current series of tests. After it was all over, Dr Kissinger summoned the travelling media to an 8 a.m. briefing in the Intourist Hotel's nightclub. The 'hostesses' who had offered their services in night-time phone calls to individual journalists were kept at bay. But the dark-red plush surroundings, the dim lighting and a spotlight on Dr Kissinger's head were enough to provide an aura of surrealism to the occasion. The Secretary of State's assertions that the summit had fulfilled expectations and would lead to a distinct improvement in US–Soviet relations fell on mostly deaf ears.

The President himself had made a broadcast to the Soviet people. But he had not been tempted into meetings with the press. In fact, very few of us even had a close-up view of Mr Nixon. The opportunity to fire questions at him was non-existent. He would never have come close to winning a prize as a communicator.

Back in Washington, Nixon had to accept that the Moscow trip had only been a brief distraction from the domestic drive to impeach him. He adopted a twin-headed defence: to portray himself as the victim of a political vendetta and a martyr; and to warn Republican candidates who did not stand by him that he would not support them in the mid-term Congressional election. Neither tactic succeeded. Throughout July the calls for Nixon's resignation intensified. The Judiciary Committee steadily worked on building evidence against the President for his involvement in the Watergate cover-up and preparing for an early vote. Much of the outside world was following the high drama in Washington almost as keenly as the American nation. Simon Winchester and I were never at a loss to find stories to regale our paper's readers.

'Buried under the avalanche of calls for the President's resignation, the Administration is now under a virtual standstill.' I wrote this on 6 August as an opener to an article which asserted that America's foreign policy and its standing in the world had become victim to the Watergate crisis. My argument was that, having consistently tried to use foreign policy as a defence against impeachment, Nixon's judgement had become clouded. Unlike his sound, well-targeted foreign policy performance during earlier years, now, in the last period of his second term, Nixon's dealings with the outside world were largely reduced to cosmetics and showmanship. It was a sorry performance. America had failed to assert itself to break the crippling oil crisis caused by a deliberate shortfall of output by the Middle East members of the Organization of the Petroleum Exporting Countries (OPEC). The Soviet Union had held back on arms control negotiations. The opening to China was at a standstill. The European allies had been neglected and needlessly criticised. British efforts to strengthen the Special Relationship had been rebuffed.

The article turned out to be my obituary for Nixon's foreign policy. But with adrenalin at fever pitch I wrote a second piece headlined 'Nixon is dead – but he won't lie ⟨⟩ ⟨⟩ my obituary for Nixon's record on the domestic scene, ⟨⟩ ⟨⟩rance relation- ship with him since his first P⟨⟩ ⟨⟩ how Nixon was still resisting the ⟨⟩ from the Republican leadership th⟨⟩ ⟨⟩itably lead to a guilty verdict at th⟨⟩

Next day, 7 August, Ni⟨⟩ ⟨⟩ to hand over the tapes that incrim⟨⟩ ⟨⟩r-up. But he also reiterated at a c⟨⟩ ⟨⟩ to defend himself against impeac⟨⟩ ⟨⟩oon. I had broken away from a g⟨⟩ ⟨⟩, one of my good friends at the F⟨⟩ ⟨⟩ in his small Georgetown garden ⟨⟩ much longer Nixon could hold t⟨⟩ ⟨⟩ instinct made me break up the lu⟨⟩ ⟨⟩House to see if there were any new developmi⟨⟩ ⟨⟩a virtually empty press room, an announcement was in p⟨⟩ ⟨⟩sident Nixon had finally recognised that he was no longer a bona fide presence in the White House. Resignation was less ignominious than impeachment. He would address the nation the next day. Within seconds I was through to the *Guardian*. They heard it first from me, seconds before all the wire services were reeling out the glad tidings. A stupid sense of achievement?

Sitting in the Oval Office for the last time, Richard Nixon addressed Americans and the entire world by announcing that 'I have never been a quitter. To leave office before my term is completed is abhorrent to every bone in my body. But as President I must put the interest of America first. America needs a full-time President and a full-time Congress to face the problems the country faces at home and abroad,' and without the distraction of a President trying to vindicate himself. Hours later, ex-President Nixon was on his way home to San Clementi in California, and ex-Vice-President Gerald Ford had been sworn in as the 38th US President.

There was a new buzz in Washington. Ford was a more relaxed character. But he was far less experienced than Nixon. He would have to rely on Henry Kissinger and some of Nixon's other key aides. And of course there was much speculation over his choice of Vice-President. The odds were on Nelson Rockefeller. The diplomats and the journalists had new ground to explore and new gossip to enjoy.

I was in distinguished company among the British press corps, and was fortunate to be made welcome by the likes of Henry Brandon, Andrew Knight, Stephen Barber and Charles Wheeler. I was now well settled with a steady set of friends, with plenty of invitations to interesting tables and good access to the Administration and well-informed diplomats. I always had a great time at the parties hosted by the Embassy's Press Attaché, Dick Fyjis-Walker and his wife Gaby. Our friendship cemented, and when their son Matthew was born, I was invited to be his godmother. The Huxley house I had first come to know more than a decade earlier remained a home from home. As before, it was the place where power brokers and informality twinned – and where one could always share one of Judy's convivial meals. The other important social attraction in my life was Irina and Lane Kirkland's home. I was a frequent guest and was often likely to meet a wide panorama of decision-makers from home and abroad, from trade union leaders to leading bankers, with politicians and influential commentators thrown into the mix. I was enjoying myself in Washington, and I also knew that I was doing good work.

And dimly I perceived there was also a novel factor in my life. It was called Ralf Dahrendorf. As had happened in London, now in Washington, I received a totally unexpected message proposing a meeting with Professor Dahrendorf during his forthcoming visit to the city. Only this time it came not from his PA but from Ralf directly. It was spring 1974. Washington was resplendent in blossom and fresh greenery. Dahrendorf, still EEC Commissioner, was attending a conference and wanted to spend his spare time with me. I learned that he had a difficult and mostly unhappy marriage and three young children. Very dimly I recognised that Ralf was a complex character. But, far more brightly, I found that the spark that eluded me at the London meeting readily emerged on this occasion. Ralf's own spark needed no reminder. It was the beginning of what I took to be a casual affair. His Washington visit was brief, and he had no idea when he would next be in the US. During the rest of 1974, Ralf turned up a couple more times and we exchanged the occasional letter. We were probing each other. But it still felt very low key and undemanding. My focus in social life was on my friends in Washington. And as always I was deeply absorbed in my work.

President Ford was a familiar face in Washington. He had been a member of the House of Representatives for many years and was its minority leader for almost a decade until 1973, when Nixon made him Vice-President to replace the disgraced Spiro Agnew. Nixon and Ford could not have been more different. Unlike the tortured, introverted Nixon, Ford was uncomplicated, outgoing, relaxed and had no pretension to brilliance. Even some of his best friends sometimes admitted that he had a tendency to dumbness. All of this came as a relief. Nixon in his last days had looked close to mental breakdown. With Ford, 'nobody has the slightest fear that he will ever have a moment of insanity', I wrote. 'He is "Mr Normal" incarnate and doesn't look like changing just because he is President. He's gregarious, doesn't seem to like paperwork, and prefers to take his decisions by talking matters out with as many people as possible – even the press.'

Even if Gerry was no genius, the relief to have a new incumbent in the Oval Office was so great that a generous honeymoon was on firm offer. With Nixon the White House had become a forbidding place. Ford was determined to restore it as a frank, open and friendly Presidency. He also brought in brainpower and the glamour of money by appointing Nelson Rockefeller as Vice-President.

Ford's initial ratings put him on a high pedestal. It did not take him long to squander them. Exactly a month after Nixon's resignation,

President Ford gave his disgraced predecessor a Presidential pardon. It meant that Nixon, unlike the other Watergate conspirators, would not have to face a criminal trial and was free to enjoy (that is, if he was capable of enjoyment) his retirement and establish himself as a foreign policy pundit.

For the most part, Americans were outraged at President Ford's decision, and some were convinced that Nixon and Ford had made a devil's bargain: in exchange for being made Vice-President, Ford had promised Nixon a pardon if he was driven out of the White House. Whatever the reason, it was a fatal political blunder. Ford never recovered from it. His popularity plummeted. He was charged with poor judgement, poor leadership, poor decision-making. Ford almost certainly destroyed his hopes for the 1976 Presidential election, which he lost to the Democrats' Jimmy Carter. In one of my reports, I concluded that Ford had certainly restored integrity to the White House, but 'the Presidency has yet to demonstrate that it has brainpower and decisiveness'.

Shortly before the mid-term elections I went back to Montgomery, Alabama to meet Governor George Wallace. Nine years earlier I had been there with the Selma marchers, and had witnessed Martin Luther King at the head of some 30,000 supporters marching to the tune of their freedom songs and demanding their voting rights. A solid block of National Guardsmen had stopped them outside the Capitol. Governor Wallace had remained inside, unwilling to take up the challenge. Now, in 1974, he was again inside – but this time open to be interviewed by the *Guardian*. To a casual visitor, Montgomery looked prosperous and no longer quite so segregated. The Alabama State University now had hundreds of black students. The Alabama Democratic Party had a sizeable number of members of colour. A new civic centre apparently served all races without discrimination. 'Wallace is a realist,' I was told. No longer clinging to segregation, he was positioning himself as the incarnation of America's ignored middle classes – a pre-Trump populist who castigated big government and needless government give-aways. Though paralysed after a shooting two years earlier, and increasingly hard of hearing, he was still toying with the thought of running for the Presidency and certainly expected to be re-elected to the Governorship. Wallace claimed that Alabama had always been in the mainstream of American thinking. Just hyperbole? Or was there a grain of truth in that?

With the solid Democratic majority established in Congress after the mid-term elections President Ford found himself under heavy scrutiny and often at odds with the lawmakers. He was steadily criticised for his failure. The problems did not just stem from the Democrats but also from the growing strength of the conservative wing of the Republicans, whose elder statesman was Senator Barry Goldwater and whose hero was Ronald Regan. The conservatives accused the Vice-President of ushering in socialism and sharply criticised Ford for selecting a liberal bastion of capitalism – Nelson Rockefeller – as his Vice-President.

Prime Minister Wilson came on an official visit to Washington in January 1975. He had not yet decided whether to support British membership of the EEC in the referendum he planned to hold in June 1975. The Americans were firm advocates of UK membership of the EEC. But they hesitated to speak out publicly. Instead Administration officials indulged in the tried method of a hint or two to favourite media to allow their concerns to seep out into the public domain. Harold Wilson took it all in good spirits and thoroughly enjoyed what I termed 'an old-fashioned love story'. It began 'with an engagement party on the lawns of the White House, some ritual bargaining behind closed doors, and a splendid razzle-dazzle banquet with reinforcements from Hollywood brought in to underline the standard clichés of Hands across the Oceans for all eternity to save the world from disaster'.

Ford's unsuccessful tussle with Congress over aid to the Thieu government in South Vietnam was a major defeat for him, but a victory for all who wanted finality to that war. The Paris agreement of 1973 had brought home the US troops but had not ended the fighting. Having followed the beginning of the Vietnam peace negotiations in Paris in 1968, I was now again writing a great deal about the debate surrounding the administration's policy of supporting the Thieu government and thus supporting the continuation of the fighting between the North and the South.

But at the end of April, when Saigon fell to the North's forces and the Americans were ingloriously forced to airlift their remaining personnel out of the city, I was not in Washington. I was in London after a three-week holiday that later turned out to have upended my life. Part of it had been spent with Ralf Dahrendorf in France. At the end of that trip we had decided to live together. During those heady spring days, I was convinced that we both believed in our fairy tale. A few months later I discovered that only one of us had really believed in it. The other turned into a fairy-tale denier and thought of himself as a 'monk'.

Ralf and I had kept in regular touch ever since our first meeting in Washington. I sent him chatty letters about Washington life. After he joined LSE letters I received from him told me something of his tussles with students and staff as he settled into the Directorship. I also learned about his preoccupation with the 1975 Reith Lectures, which he was due to give. The chosen theme was 'Justice, Not Bondage: The New Liberty'. He felt that writing the lectures allowed him to refine his thinking on the preservation of liberty and democracy in a turbulent, rapidly changing world. The principles he set out in the Reith Lectures provided the framework for all his later work, both in the books he wrote and in his political work after joining the Lib Dems in Britain. While he was still drafting the first of the three Reith Lectures, he told me that the experience was turning out to be very profound and termed it a life-and-death experience. He even added that he really meant that. His letters taught me much, but not enough, about his complex and often tortured mindset.

In the early months of 1975, Ralf made occasional visits to Washington and afterwards described one of them as a beautiful dream. As I try to reconstruct my feelings, I can't quite tell when I began to realise that I was falling in love. Ralf could not have been more different to Narendra, and yet I began to think I could find happiness with him. But I do know exactly where and when I abandoned any lingering doubts and felt certain that my future life was bound to Ralf. It was April 1975, when we were staying at the Colombe d'Or in St-Paul-de-Vence, the hotel famed for its wondrous art collection of Picasso, Matisse, Leger and so much more. The skies were grey. Ralf was half-preoccupied by the Reith Lectures – and half-preoccupied with our future. It had been his suggestion to spend a few days together in France. I accepted happily, and took three weeks' leave during the Easter period. At the end of the trip we had both agreed that I would leave Washington and return to London to live with him at the Anchorage, the house reserved for the LSE Director's residence.

Back in London before returning to Washington, I told Peter Preston, who had now become Editor, of this turn in my life, and Ralf even joined us briefly to support my decision. Peter left me in no doubt that he was dubious about the relationship and made me promise to give it more thought. He also warned that if I returned to London, he would only be able to offer me a desk job, writing occasional commentaries about Eastern Europe and the Cold War.

But I was in love and totally blindsided, wrongly convinced that Ralf was as free from reservations about our mutual feelings as I was. I understood – only dimly then – that Ralf's bonds to his wife went very deep and that concern for his three children would always have priority. But I only barely perceived his struggles with his mental devils. I brushed all that aside. I did the same when one of his close friends, a German journalist I had known for many years, warned me that I had only seen one side of Ralf and had failed to recognise an inborn instability that my friend loosely described as schizophrenic. And so I flew back to Washington and wrote to the Editor to confirm that I would give up my cherished post in mid-summer.

During my remaining time in Washington, I blissfully told all my friends of a promising life ahead as Ralf's partner. Talking far too loosely, I led many to believe that I would soon be marrying Ralf. When he came on a brief visit he was unpleasantly surprised to find that my friends were offering their congratulations. However, his long letters to me during this period were always full of promise for the future and often introspective, suggesting that my presence in his life would have a healing impact. In one of them he wrote of his confusion about the meaning of love, even when it came from me. He had always found it incredibly difficult to be with another person for 24 hours a day. Yet he found it relatively easy to be with me. Caring for someone was incredibly precious, and that was certainly what he felt for me. In the same letter, Ralf mapped out a timetable for our adjustment to joint life. Ralf proposed an initial four weeks' holiday either in the Black Forest or Davos, followed by a month's travel to familiar places in Europe. This would show us whether we would be able to keep our respective friends. Finally there would be a month in London without any formal obligations and giving us time to settle in. He thought there was every prospect that we would be living in London for a few years. However, he added that he was uncertain whether the larger part of our lives would be spent in the UK.

A few days later Ralf sent me a poem about John Keats he had written 12 years before and had never shown to anyone. He explained that he had decided to let me see it because I was the first person he had met in many years, or perhaps ever met, in whom he had profound and total confidence. If I ever betrayed it, there would be nothing left in or for his life. In the same letter he told me that his mother, who allegedly had a deep dislike for his wife Vera, had been happy to hear about me. Ralf thought it might keep her alive to know that something good and constructive had happened in his life. Straying once again into self-analysis, Ralf went on to say that he was often incredibly tense, unable to hold a glass or stand still, or to look somebody direct in their face. But tension was creative. After all, there were two great sources of power, volcanoes and electricity. Ralf described himself as of the latter type.

I came to London on 3 June on a brief stop-over before flying to Brussels to cover President Ford's visit to NATO headquarters in the city. Ralf had an important meeting and sent his driver to meet me at Heathrow. He brought me the key to the Anchorage, the LSE Director's residence, together with a note saying it was mine for keeps. Ralf and I had a happy and relaxed reunion before I joined the White House media on President Ford's European trip. Somehow a few of the journalists had caught wind of my affair with

Ralf and there were some pointed remarks about me in a couple of tabloids. I was very upset. I was uncertain whether Ralf knew of it, and nothing was said about it.

I made my goodbyes to the Washington posting at the end of July. The Anchorage was being renovated, so we had arranged to use my flat for the few days we would be in London before setting off for our holiday. But from the moment of our reunion, there was an unexpected tenseness between us and an awkwardness that I found hard to understand. Ralf wrote me one of his long letters full of warnings that he might not be able to cope with our lives together. He still wanted a future for us. But there was no guarantee he would not want to break away. He warned that he was going through one of his phases where he was unable to cope, adding that I should understand that much of what he did or said must be understood as pure survival strategy. It was a relief for him to know that I would be with him when his mind would again be able to turn in other directions.

Early in July 1975 we set off for a summer in Switzerland. Ralf had rented a large, comfortable chalet outside Davos. For the first few days all went well. We spent days walking, and in the evenings we talked or listened to music. Friends of his spent a couple of relaxed days with us. But suddenly the mood changed. Ralf declared that our tastes in food differed. I was buying the wrong food, and in restaurants I failed to follow his choice of dishes. If I stumbled over a stone during our walks, I was criticised for ineptness. It irritated him that I was painting my fingernails or colouring my hair . . . and so it went on with one triviality after the next. Then his two younger children arrived, and the atmosphere changed for the better. We played happy families and the children appeared to accept my presence.

That short phase came to an end when an angry Vera phoned and announced her imminent arrival to rescue her children from 'that dreadful woman'. Ralf's reaction was to tell me to pack my bags and leave. He wanted no scenes. Evi Wohlgemuth and her husband were staying in nearby Klosters. They rescued me. Vera never turned up, but Ralf did not want me back.

I was devastated, distraught. I simply could not believe I was being discarded. Evi did her best to comfort me. I wrote to Ralf begging him for us to work things out together. That was the wrong tone to take. Back came a missive from Ralf with a warning that he reacted very strongly against pressure and that he would always work out important things by himself. He would return to London alone to clear his mind and wanted no distractions. I lost hope but still could not bring myself to accept that Ralf's mindset was immovable.

Alena and Norman Lourie also happened to be staying in the area, and suggested it might be helpful to distance myself for a few days and join them on a trip to Israel. I agreed. But was not much distracted and was so unhappy that I began to have serious thoughts about suicide. Back in London, I saw a psychiatrist who strongly advised against further contact with Ralf. I ignored the advice, and pleaded to Ralf to come and see me. He did but only to talk about his own psychological problems and his struggles to deal with his demons. I still could not let go and sent him letters that demeaned me, pouring out my unhappiness and also my belief that I could help him to find stability in his life.

His reply came in the form of a revealing self-analysis that ended with the admission of a deep sense of guilt, indeed of sin. He had come to the conclusion that he neither wanted to nor could share his life with anyone. He believed that most of what he called his life energy went into his cerebral existence. What energy remained had to be devoted to his children as well as what he termed do-goodery and administrative work. He even inferred that he had developed a preference for the fleeting relationships of nightclubs because they were without consequence. He did not want to blame me for failing to recognise his true nature. After all, I had never had to deal with a creature, which he described as sick by normal standards, yet arrogant enough to justify as an expression of creative pressure leading to unbearable tension. He fully expected to continue with his erratic, tense existence and was emphatic that a stable, trusting relationship had no place on his horizon.

In a subsequent letter, written early in 1976, Ralf tried to convince me that he had hinted at impending disaster even while we were in St-Paul-de-Vence and were jointly deciding that I should return from Washington for us to live together. Now he claimed I had pushed him further and further away from his true self, and that he had been reluctant to be rude by pointing to my misconceptions. Apparently all those plans we made and all the loving letters he wrote had to be understood as a regrettable aberration. In a subsequent letter, the last I received, he declared that he had no need of a continuing relationship with me. We had already hurt each other more than was defensible. The monk, he wrote, would remain the monk. The finality of the message was unmistakable.

Had I really been deceiving myself, or had I been deceived? Or both? Had I been a victim of Ralf's deeply flawed mind or a victim of my own wishful thinking? Had I wilfully destroyed my career by leaving Washington? I was certain only of one fact: I was profoundly shattered and unhappy, and saw no good way forward. I was back to my suicidal thoughts.

I sat down in my kitchen and wrote a handful of farewell letters to friends. I also wrote, incoherently, to Ralf. Like the other letters, it was to be posted after my death. I told Ralf that I had

already realised in Davos that you could not and would not live with me. I had already then begun to wonder whether I could survive this rejection. Until now I thought I could. I put all thought of suicide out of my mind. But it has all come back and my despair is now far deeper. I simply don't see how anything can come right again. And I sit here and look around at all the things that my mother and I have collected through long years of work – and hope – I feel it is utterly wrong to think of giving up. And yet it doesn't have anything to do with right or wrong. It's simply my ability to go on living day in, day out deprived of love and of the opportunity to love; and now also deprived of the opportunity to find a substitute fulfilment through work.

So in a stupid way I have been asking myself whether I have

the courage to swallow pills and end it all. I don't want to bungle anything. If you get this letter you will know I haven't bungled.

Writing those suicide letters may have saved my life. They did not have to be posted. My mental wounds were slow to heal. Ralf, the monk, married twice more. The fears for my career turned out to be unfounded. The Cold War served as an unlikely saviour.

CHAPTER II

THE COLD WAR FALTERS

'Poland will never be the same again.' These words came from Mieczyslaw Rakowski, Editor of Poland's influential weekly magazine, *Polityka*, and future Prime Minister. It was a mellow June day in 1979, and together with a group of journalists, we were standing in the courtyard of the Archbishop's Palace in Cracow. Looking down from a balcony, Pope John Paul II, alias Karol Wojtyla, offered us his blessing and thanked us for having joined his eight-day homecoming pilgrimage to meet his flock in Poland. Earlier that day well over a million Poles had turned up for an open-air Mass. It had been the same wherever Poland's very own Pope had preached the Christian faith and in the process had thrown down the gauntlet to Marxism. The popular slogan doing its rounds said: 'The [Communist] Party is for the People. But the People are for the Pope.'

I have always thought back on Rakowski's pronouncement as a symbolic moment for me: it was an intuitive flash bringing me conviction that the Soviet empire was on a downward spiral of gradual collapse and implosion.

I was of course well aware that the crucial trigger for change had been an act of patient Western statesmanship: the 1975 Helsinki Final Act, better known as the Helsinki Declaration. The Soviet Union had been the driver pushing the West to embark on these CSCE negotiations, confident that the end result would be the West's formal recognition of the territorial integrity and inviolability of Europe's frontiers, and by inference the inviolability of the Communist bloc in Europe. The Russians had not anticipated the astuteness of Western diplomacy in driving a hard bargain to extract major concessions on human rights. One of the three 'baskets' of the Helsinki Declaration included a commitment to human rights, freedom of emigration, cultural exchanges and freedom of the press. The Declaration lacked enforcement provisions, and it was self-evident that Soviet compliance would be minuscule. Still, a chink of light had appeared. Some restrictions were lifted. East–West détente became more tangible, and dissidents became more hopeful and sometimes more daring. The genie was trying to break out of the bottle.

I had covered the early stages of the diplomatic marathon that led to the Final Act, but was absent for the celebratory climax. I was preparing for my heartbreak holiday in Davos with Ralf Dahrendorf and unable to join the throng in Helsinki on 1 August 1975, where a mega European summit, joined by US President Ford and Canada's Prime Minister, had convened to sign the Helsinki Final Act. They were united in proclaiming the launch of a new, more hopeful era. Did the Soviet leadership suspect that this new era might not go their way? Did the Western leaders calculate that the Helsinki Declaration had the potential to deal a fatal blow to the Soviet bloc?

The Helsinki Declaration and I became close companions for more than a decade. The *Guardian* 'gave' me Eastern Europe as a consolation prize when I found myself high and dry and tearful after the collapse of my relationship with Ralf. Appointed East European Correspondent, it was some consolation to discover that I would not after all be desk-bound in London, pontificating about a largely unfamiliar world, but would be expected to spend much of my time travelling around my extensive parish in East and Central Europe. In addition to the Communist bloc, Yugoslavia and Austria were included in my bailiwick.

How and where to start? My trusted United Nations provided an answer. I learned that the UN Industrial Development Organisation (UNIDO) was bringing a diverse group of ministers from developing countries to a week-long meeting hosted by the Bulgarian government in Sofia, keen to show off its Communist-style economic planning. I was allowed to join them. I wanted to know whether Bulgaria was fertile ground for the Helsinki Declaration and what life was like in the Soviet Union's most devoted and most loyal satellite. President Zhivkov, a cheerfully robust, jovial 64-year-old, clarified: his small country was an ally, not a satellite of Big Brother. 'We just happen to be two lungs working in one body,' he told us as he took his guests around his new home – an outsize People's Palace in acres of landscaped gardens replete with waterfalls and ornamental sculptures. All the furniture and fittings were made in Bulgaria, the President proudly pointed out, except for the showers of chandeliers that had been brought in from Austria. But soon, he said, Bulgaria would be making these too. We were regaled with endless statistics of Bulgaria's almost wholly state-owned economy and assured that they had a steady, reliable export market for all their products. Several years later, when I came back to Bulgaria with the Foreign Secretary, Sir Geoffrey Howe, Mr Zhivkov, without blinking an eyelid, stressed that the Soviet Union was a perfect outlet for Bulgaria's machine tools and other industrial products, because the Russians suffered from such shortages that they had little concern for quality control. Even the shoddiest goods would be welcome in Russia.

On my original visit to Bulgaria, I unwittingly struck gold. I asked my ever-helpful guide and interpreter whether there was any possibility of interviewing Andrei Lukanov, the Minister for External Trade. 'No problem,' was the answer. 'He is my husband.' But instead of taking me to his office, Lilly invited me to their house, the home of a senior member of the ruling clique. This was a rare, and on their part, daring gesture – inviting a foreigner, and worse, a journalist, into their inner sanctum was remarkable. It could not have gone unnoticed by the secret police. The Lukanovs must have felt very secure. They lived in a modest three-room apartment. They made me feel instantly at ease. Both were graduates of Moscow University but had liberal instincts coupled to their Communist convictions. I met a few of their friends, also high up in the Party ranks and also of a seemingly reformist bent – which was only articulated within the privacy of their small circle. Andrei had a steady rise in the Ministerial and Party ranks, but eventually turned and played a strong hand in toppling Todor Zhivkov in 1989. For a short spell, he became Prime Minister. He was assassinated under mysteriously murky circumstances in 1996.

Lilly became a friend who showed me a little of Bulgaria's placid countryside and – almost – made me like Bulgaria's heavy red wine. In spite of my influential friends, or rather because of Lilly, I narrowly avoided arrest as I was leaving Sofia. Lilly gave me a letter to her sister who was living in England and asked me to post it when I was back home. Clearly, she didn't want to risk the letter falling into the censor's hands. She also gave me a sheaf of typewritten pages full of official propaganda descriptions of the marvels and achievements of Communist Bulgaria. At the airport officials seized these papers. None could speak English but all were adamant that this was subversive literature. I must be a spy. I could not be allowed to leave the country. Finally English-speaking higher authority arrived, the true nature of my suspect papers was understood and I was declared free to go. Fortunately, nobody discovered that I was carrying a possibly subversive letter written by a senior Party member!

My verdict on Bulgaria as a candidate for Helsinki Declaration-inspired loosening of the Party's or the Kremlin's grip? Very low down in the pecking order. Bulgaria remained a solid member of the Soviet bloc. The same applied to the GDR – the German Democratic Republic. I say this even though the GDR used the Helsinki Declaration's Basket Three (freedom of speech and movement) language to offer accreditation and multiple entry visas to Western journalists. The offer was not available to journalists based in Bonn. At the time the *Guardian* did not have a permanent correspondent in West Germany. So I became a so-called beneficiary of the GDR's willingness to show itself off to Western journalists. Beneficiary in the sense of being able to come and go at will? Yes, though only to East Berlin. Beneficiary in the sense of escaping constant surveillance and able to talk freely with people? Almost never. The Party's stranglehold on people was tight. Intellectuals were more accessible. But dissidents among them stayed well below the horizon.

By signing the Helsinki Declaration the West German government in Bonn had accepted the concept of two sovereign states in one German nation. However, East Germans were conditioned to believe in the GDR as a German nation with its own identity and beneficial Communist political system. The Wall served as a fearsome reminder that any thought of reunification was out of bounds. The GDR's economy was heavily dependent on the Soviet Union and the presence of half a million Soviet troops was a constant reminder of Russia's might. Loyalty to Moscow was a given.

It was an anomaly that, to get to East Berlin, I had to fly to Tegel Airport in West Berlin. Then on to the GDR in one of the handful of taxis allowed to cross the Friedrichstrasse opening through the Wall. I had reached the GDR cage. My visa actually caged me into East Berlin. If I wanted to go anywhere else in the GDR, I was required to apply for a special permit. Western journalists were generally required to stay in the Hotel Metropole, just off the Friedrichstrasse, where the rooms were all suitably bugged, and you just had to take it for granted that every phone conversation had an invisible audience. During my travels in Europe, I had come to know a couple of well-informed GDR journalists. So when I came to Berlin I would phone them to set up a meeting. Invariably, the answer came back that they had to check diaries and would call back. The subliminal message was to tell me that they had to seek permission. Mostly the answer was yes.

The GDR treated the Federal Republic like any other foreign state; Bonn, for its part, until the GDR secured UN recognition, persisted in maintaining its dealings with the GDR on the basis of 'inner-German relations'. Logic would have dictated that the GDR leaders would object. Realism dictated otherwise. The 'inner German' concept allowed the GDR to maintain duty-free trade with the Federal Republic, and also gave it access to EEC markets.

A favourite contact in the GDR was Hans-Otto Bräutigam, Bonn's 'Permanent Representative' in East Berlin. Bräutigam told me – always argued, would be more accurate – that the character of German–Prussian culture had been far better preserved in the GDR than in the Federal Republic, and in his view this had given its people a specific identity. Thanks to its Communist regime, the country had not yet been tainted by Western consumerism and materialism. The influence of the Evangelical Church, with its puritanism, must not be underrated. East Germans were proud of their culture. But Bräutigam did not regard the GDR with rose-tinted glasses. He knew the rigidities and foolhardiness of the regime, their role as a massive Soviet military base, and their dependence on Soviet economic support. Dissidents had to be suppressed. Reunification was a prohibited concept. With the notorious Berlin Wall straddling the divide of Germany, the GDR could not afford to allow its people any greater freedoms. But the West could not be kept totally out of East German lives. They could see it on their TV sets. Many were in contact with relatives in the West, and some were lucky enough to receive gifts in the form of hard-currency marks that enabled them to buy such rarities as nylon tights or authentic Western jeans.

There was one place where East Berliners were allowed to laugh at some of the absurdities of their lives and their rulers. That was the Diestel Cabaret in East Berlin. Sketches made fun of shortages amid constant claims of plenitude, or of Party officials proclaiming patently fake truths. Surprisingly, Western journalists were allowed tickets to the performances, and I always made a point of going there. My impression was that the audience was composed of trusted Party members who regarded a stranger in their midst with deep suspicion. People sitting next to me watched me taking notes. Nobody ever said a word to me. Could I be a Party member sent to observe their reaction to the political jokes? Worse still, if I was a Westerner, to be seen talking with me might be dangerously suspect.

In October 1979, the GDR celebrated its 30th anniversary with a great deal of fanfare. Every available outdoor wall space had been plastered with posters proclaiming that the GDR was 'stable, recognised and respected' throughout the world and was 'living proof of the teachings of Marx, Engels and Lenin' and proof of 'the triumph of Marxism'.

With all this self-congratulation, I thought it might persuade my GDR minders to let me see something of the country beyond the confines of East Berlin. Yes, I could go to Weimar where the authorities would arrange for me to spend time with an ordinary East German family. I was allowed to stay at the famed Elephant

Hotel, which generations of writers and artists had frequented since Goethe's days. Though it was dilapidated and tainted by Hitler, who had also stayed at the Elephant, it felt so romantic to be in a place that had once been graced by Goethe. On a sunny October day, with trees turning all shades from green to rose-brown, and fallen leaves providing a patchy carpeting, it was genuinely moving to wander around the park where Goethe had mused and built his summer house.

But back to work: meet my Party-selected 'ordinary' happy GDR family, Dieter and Anneliese Bernhard and ten-year-old Henry. The instruction to meet with me had come out of the blue a day earlier, and they insisted that nobody had schooled them what to tell me. Dieter was a well-regarded mechanical engineer. Anneliese was a teacher. They told me that they saw no need to join the Communist Party but were well contented with the way the Party ran the country. Their story was textbook GDR litany.

'We are the product of the German Democratic Republic. We have grown up in this country. We live well and like our work. We identify with this nation and its achievements and we are proud of it.' Both of them routinely participated in group activities that were an inescapable part of life in the GDR. But they also said they preferred to concentrate on home and family. They had spent holidays in Hungary and Romania, but found the GDR to be the cheapest and the best. They considered that the Berlin Wall was fully justified. Dieter rationalised that before the Wall went up, West Germany had syphoned off East Germany's expensively trained doctors, while West Berliners came to the East to buy up its cheaper food. He traced the improvement of GDR living standards back to the erection of the Wall. Anneliese said that reunification was inconceivable to them. In West Germany, Neo-Nazis were allowed a platform. That was not the kind of freedom they wanted. The freedom that Dieter and Anneliese appreciated was freedom from unemployment and the freedom of social equality.

A dozen years later, after the fall of the Wall, I received an un-expected message:

I am Henry, the little boy you met way back in Weimar. I want you to know that my parents were told what to say to you, and to paint a picture of a contented family happy with the life the GDR could give them. Now at last I can tell you that they were under instruction to give you that carefully fashioned version of their contentment. Their true thoughts were very different. But there was no way they could have allowed themselves to speak more freely. The risk to their jobs and comfortable lifestyle would have been too great.

I had guessed as much.

My visits to East Berlin became rarer. But with more and more attention focusing on developments in Poland, it was important to keep an eye on the GDR's reactions to events in their biggest eastern neighbour. It was always an uneasy relationship. It became worse in the mid 70s, when the stirrings against Poland's Communist regime and the demands for reform became apparent. The GDR leadership became nervous that the Polish 'virus' could spread to the GDR. Historically deep-rooted prejudices against Poland re-emerged, even among some of the intellectuals I had come to know. Routinely people spoke about the *'Polnische Wirtschaft'* (Polish mess). Years of efforts to condition the Warsaw Pact countries to value their unity in the Socialist International had not been able to eradicate the mutual antagonism between East Germans and Poles. Religious differences between the Evangelical Church in the GDR and the Roman Catholic hierarchy in Poland added to the tensions.

The election of the outspoken Polish Pope created even more of a dilemma for the GDR regime. Events in Poland were an ever-present threat to stability in the GDR. Beneath the bland surface of daily life, long-silent reformers took strength from the example next door. Yet the GDR leader, Erich Honecker, remained set to resist reform in the GDR – as indeed he did until the day in 1989 when President Gorbachev appeared alongside him at the GDR's 40th anniversary celebration and declared that 'life punishes those who come too late'.

Poland was an early caller in search of reform, maybe even too early, given that the fight for freedom had to be carried out via two years of martial law. I already had a fair sense of Polish complexity when I began to visit Poland as the *Guardian*'s East European Correspondent – enough to think that Poland was almost bound to become a trailblazer to exploit the Helsinki Declaration's promise of a more open society. A few years earlier, I had been part of a group of journalists invited by the Polish authorities to learn about their country's alleged progress. That was when I met Mieczyslaw Rakowski and began a friendship with this controversial individual, who taught me much about the intricacies and contradictions of Polish society. He was a prime example: of peasant-class origin, yet he had become editor of a magazine unique behind the Iron Curtain for its frankness, sophistication and disregard of censorship. He was accepted by members of the Polish intelligentsia and despised by others. He had a cosmopolitan outlook, with friends that included Willy Brandt, but was distrusted by the Russians. Yet he was also an insider in the rigid Polish Communist Party and was the key government negotiator during the Gdansk strikes in 1980 that led to the formation of Solidarity. As Deputy Prime Minister he was a determined supporter of General Jaruzelski and always defended martial law as an essential measure to save Poland from a Soviet invasion. Yet as Prime Minister from 1989 to 1990 he presided over Poland's first multi-party elections and remained the Communist Party's chief just long enough to transform it into a Social Democratic party. He always divided opinion and was admired by some, and deeply distrusted by many. I was steadfast among the trusters.

'Paradox' should have been Poland's motto in the 1980s. The Communist Party was the official power. The Roman Catholic Church was the semi-official power. Both had learned to practise an uneasy co-existence – until Pope Wojtyla had appeared on the scene. The Polish intelligentsia acted as a mainly liberal phenomenon of considerable influence, and when they made common cause with the working class, they also became a powerful political force. The Polish diaspora, conservative and patriotic, with its large numbers and significant wealth, also made an impact on the domestic scene. For me, observing these elements gingerly cavorting around each other, sometimes coming together and gradually moving towards collision, was fascinating. From 1976 onwards, I began to make frequent visits to Poland. There was always much to write. For a classical music lover like me, there were also rare opportunities to hear performances by Sviatoslav Richter and other great Soviet artists. Those concerts provided an unusual bonus: you could always be sure of being able to buy caviar during the interval. The Russians brought it to earn themselves some hard currency, and the likes of me acquired a favourite delicacy at an affordable price.

A fixture in my Warsaw 'life' were evenings spent in the comfortable, spacious home of Jerzy and Mira Michalowski. He had been Polish Ambassador in London and in Washington, and during an anti-Semitic drive, was ousted as Director of the Polish Foreign Office. They were as much at home in the West as in Poland. They were friends with the Western diplomats and the foreign correspondents posted in Poland. They were friends with prominent members of the intelligentsia. They had a productive relationship with a peasant family who supplied meat and eggs and home-baked cakes – not to mention home-distilled *slivovitz*. The Michalowskis held open house at least once a week, sometimes even more often. Much of the talk was about reform and the limited ability of Soviet power to stifle the rumblings of rebellion. They gossiped with and about potential opposition leaders. Those gatherings were relaxed and always provided useful nuggets of information. But you could never be sure that something was really stirring or whether the fighting talk was just wishful thinking.

Then suddenly, on a mid-October day in 1978, wishful thinking acquired concrete substance from the most unexpected quarter. The election of 58-year-old Karol Wojtyla, Cardinal of Cracow, to become Pope John Paul II. It came as a complete surprise. It was the first time in 400 years that the Cardinals gathered in conclave had elected a non-Italian Pope (after eight rounds of voting). Austria's Cardinal Koenig had played a key role in promoting Wojtyla, who was widely known and well liked by Poland's overwhelmingly Catholic population. Further afield, Wojtyla was an unknown quantity. The news of his election reached me just as I was arriving on a visit to Vienna to prepare a special report on Austria. I counted among the ignorati and had to play rapid catch-up to learn enough about Wojtyla to introduce him to *Guardian* readers.

His background was as unusual as his election. Poland's senior prelates had mostly come from Poland's plentiful aristocracy. Wojtyla was born in 1920 in the small town of Wadowice. His father was a non-commissioned officer. Young Karol managed to be accepted by the Jagiellonian University in Cracow and continued his studies in Prague. The priesthood was not in his mind. He joined an avant-garde theatre group, wrote poetry and toyed with an actor's career. During the war, with Poland under German occupation, Wojtyla did forced labour first in a quarry and later in a chemical factory. It was during that time that he took up clandestine theological studies and, in 1944, went into hiding in the Archbishop's Palace in Cracow to complete his studies for the priesthood. He became a popular parish priest, but also made his name as an intellectual. By the unusually young age of 38, he was promoted to Bishop, and six years later, in 1964, he became Archbishop of Cracow. Three years later he secured a coveted place in the College of Cardinals.

As he rose in the Church he developed a reputation as a moderate, veering towards conservative in doctrine, and yet dedicated to both religious and intellectual freedom. The Church's role was to act as guardian of individual freedom. His record suggested that he saw himself as a diplomat who calculated that freedom in a Communist system was best advanced by a carefully handled policy of détente rather than by encouraging popular explosion and revolution. Even so, the Polish authorities were far from relaxed about the Polish Pope, and very wary when Wojtyla decided, just over six months after his election, to kiss his native soil and pay a week-long visit to his homeland. As the Vatican's plane swooped down to land at Warsaw's airport on a pleasant June day, bells pealed throughout the country from its multitudes of churches. Streets and houses were festooned with the flags of Poland and the Papacy. Across Poland's many divides, the Pope briefly shone as the people's king.

From my tenth-floor room in Warsaw's Hotel Forum, I had a perfect view of the city's outsize Victory Square as Poland's very own

Pope led a Mass for a quarter of a million or more Poles crowded into every nook and cranny of available space. Nuns stood shoulder to shoulder with rock bands; Communist Party faithfuls joined an explosion of pride, patriotism and religious fervour. The Pope, deeply moved, told the crowds that he 'wished to sing a hymn to Divine Providence which enables me to be here as a pilgrim'. For the next few days, I followed the pilgrim's progress through to its conclusion a week later in Cracow. It may sound trite to say that it was an unforgettable experience. I can still see in my mind's eye the happy crowds and shining faces that greeted the Pope at every stop, and I can still sense the Pope's growing crusading zeal. His pilgrimage was turning into a freedom march and a challenge to Communism. It was hard to know who was the most disturbed: the Polish leadership, the Kremlin or the Church's conservative hierarchy.

As I look back on it now, the most heart-wrenching 'event' – if that is the right word – was the Mass held at the abominable Auschwitz concentration camp. And the most joyous day was the Mass celebrated at Jasna Gora, the monastery that holds the Black Madonna and is one of the Polish Church's holiest shrines. The Jew and the refugee in me fought with my journalist's task during the Pope's visit to Auschwitz. My mind and my emotions were in turmoil. Moreover, I felt, probably unjustly, that the Pope had confected this into a Roman Catholic occasion and resented that few of the survivors invited to the service were Jewish. At least he turned his sermon into a ringing appeal for human rights and respect for individuals of every creed. An altar had been set up on what had been the railway platform where the Nazis' victims emerged from the cattle-truck trains that brought them, and from where they were marched to the gas chambers. The journalists were confined to follow the proceedings from the shallow ditches where the railway rails had once been laid, and the phones we used to send our stories had been set up in the concentration camp's watch tower. I was numb with grief, with sorrow – and with anger. It was sacrilege.

In religious terms, the Pope's visit to Jasna Gora was the high-water mark of his visit to Poland. The painting of the Black Madonna in the monastery is addressed as 'Holy Mother of God and Queen of

Poland and the Poles'. She is the subject of deep veneration. The monastery stands high up on a hill. Tall trees line the fields leading up to the summit. The scene resembled an amphitheatre closely packed with human beings of every age. Nuns buzzed around the Pope like teenage girls at a rap concert. Bishops flanked him. Children competed for an embrace from him. Folk songs intermingled with the liturgy. The Pope joined in with a raucous voice. Yes, there was the formality of an emotionally charged Mass and there was also the informality of a folk festival. On a more serious level, the Pope also had a private meeting with Poland's senior episcopate, where he stressed that the time was ripe for the Polish Church to take a more militant role in fighting for freedom and individual human rights.

The Polish leadership was obviously watching the Pope's trip super closely and with growing concern. All the more so as the international press had reported on it in great detail, making the outside world aware that right in the heart of the Warsaw bloc there were signs of incipient rebelliousness. Several hundred journalists had followed the Pope's visit for at least part of the time, and the Polish authorities decided to cut their losses by at least syphoning some money out of the foreign journalists. High fees had to be paid for accreditation and permission to follow the Pope around the country.

On the last full day of the trip, the Pope addressed what might have been his largest audience yet. At least a million Poles bestraddled the fields on the outskirts of Cracow as Pope John Paul II exhorted them to fight for the Church, and for liberty, to be true to their beliefs and to themselves. The Cracow Mass put a seal on the Pope's message that it was time for Poles to be on the offensive for their rights, their freedom and the independence of their country. The turn-out throughout his voyage had unquestionably demonstrated that the mass of Poles stood behind a militant Church. Stalin's question about how many battalions a Pope could command may have been less cynical than the Soviet leader had imagined.

No wonder my friend Mieczyslaw Rakowski whispered to me that day in the Cardinal's Palace in Cracow that elements of deep change had irrevocably been planted by this crusading priest. I persuaded him to write an article for the *Guardian* that turned only just short of acknowledging that Poland was a pluralistic nation. There were veiled hints that

> the Pope's visit has made the Communist Party review many problems. But from the point of view of the development of our [Marxist] doctrine and the practice of socialism this is not a negative element . . . Church–State relations constantly need new impulses . . . and new impulses mean in practice new forms of actions and cooperation.

By the time the Pope next came back to his native country in 1983, 'new forms of action' had indeed been found. *Solidarnosc*, the Solidarity movement led by Lech Walesa, had emerged, implanting itself as a decisive force for change. And although it had provoked the imposition of martial law, Poland was well on the way to genuine multi-party democracy.

If my experience with the Pope's trip was uplifting, my experience with President Ceausescu was surreal. I had first been in Romania in 1968 after the Warsaw Pact invasion of Czechoslovakia. I already knew that Romania shifted around in a world between fact and fiction. I had seen close-up Ceausescu's strategy of using an independent foreign policy to distance himself from Moscow and win friends in the West, while at the same time running a tight autocratic state and portraying himself as the Romanian people's very own God. Free speech was not available. Security was so tight that dissent was virtually impossible. The public mind was suffused with the Ceausescu myth.

In 1978, I was back in Bucharest. My unfortunate mission was to interview the President. This rendezvous had come about in a roundabout way. British Aerospace had been trying for many months to complete a deal to sell Romania a valuable fleet of BAC III aircraft, some of which were to be assembled in Romania. Known as slippery negotiators, the Romanians always seemed to be on the verge of signing and then baulking at the last moment. The contract was worth a large sum. British Aerospace and Rolls-Royce were seriously keen on the sale. As a diplomatic gesture, Prime Minister Callaghan invited Ceausescu for official talks in Downing Street. That was not nearly good enough. It had to be a state visit, with the Queen hosting the President and Elena, his wife, at Buckingham Palace. Callaghan allowed himself to be blackmailed – not just because of the aircraft contract but also because at the time, Ceausescu, with his assertions of Romania's independent foreign policy, was courted as the acceptable flavour of Communism. The West knew well enough that Romania had no serious intention, let alone possibility, of breaking out of the Warsaw Pact. But there was a school of thought – mistaken, to my mind – that gesture-diplomacy towards Romania had the potential to drive a wedge between Moscow and its satellites.

So the state visit invitation was issued. The date settled. That is where I became a small cog in the wheel of diplomacy. In advance of the visit, Romania's Great Leader was generously offering an interview to the representative of a Great British newspaper. It would take place in Bucharest and the condition was for said newspaper to publish the President's dulcet tones verbatim. Wisely, all the Great Newspapers declined this loaded gift – bar the *Guardian*, which chose to accept on my behalf. So off I went to Bucharest, curious to discover what would transpire. On arrival, I was met by three members of the Romanian Communist Party's Central Committee. I was informed that the interview would only take place if and when there was agreement on the questions I would put to the Holy of Holies President. Questions about Basket Three of the Helsinki Declaration – would definitely be out of bounds.

I had to transform myself into a negotiator. After three days of this game, there was an agreed text – and I now had a much better understanding of how real diplomats must feel when negotiating with the Communists. I was told the interview would take place the next day, and though it was a summery June day, protocol required me to wear a long-sleeved dress, tights and gloves. I was spared a hat. I was also told I would be allowed precisely three minutes of informal chat with the Conductor, yet another of Ceausescu's self-defined titles. The chat was to be conducted in French. Then the formal interview would begin. A tape recorder was out of bounds. But I could take notes. The

President would speak in Romanian. But there would be an English transcript.

Romania's Chief of Protocol was charged with taking me to the Presidential Palace and led me to an ornately decorated room of outsize proportions. Ceausescu, a compact-looking man of stocky build, looked almost lost in the wide-open spaces. I was greeted with a wooden smile. I am not usually lost for words. But it was a relief that my allotted period for so-called informality was blissfully brief. Now for the Great Interview. Each of us was escorted to armchairs not facing each other but placed parallel with a long, low table separating us. The President had a sheaf of prompting cards. My first question was innocuous: was he looking forward to his state visit? Ceausescu had to consult his notes. I had no idea what he said. He had an interpreter. But I had none. I asked my next question – his expectations for the state visit? Out comes prompting card number two. Again no interpretation for me. By now I felt the theatre had gone far enough. I decided to jumble my questions, and insert a new one that had not even been discussed during my 'negotiations'. The Great Leader looked disgruntled. His speech slowed down. He fumbled among his papers. His interpreter looked confused, worried. This was not going to script.

I had to wait two days before I received a so-called transcript, an indigestible officialise version of what may or may not have been said. One example: I had asked about Romania's discrimination against its minorities. Ceausescu's apparent reply: 'Romania is among the few countries which have solved the problems of their nationalities in a democratic humanist way.' I could hardly inflict this stuff on *Guardian* readers.

For me, there was one plus from the excursion to Bucharest. I was invited to lunch at Downing Street during the Ceausescu state visit and could observe Prime Minister Callaghan doing his level best to flatter his Romanian guests. He was obsequious, heaping praise on the President's 'wisdom and courage' in pursuing an independent foreign policy. It was a good sales pitch for the aircraft industry. After the Queen had pinned on him the Order of the Bath, President

Ceausescu allowed that elusive contract with British Aerospace to be signed.

It is unusual, to say the least, for the Queen to allow her opinions about state visitors to escape into the public domain. But after Ceausescu's state visit, it became known that it counted among the worst duties she had had to perform on behalf of the government. Under no circumstances would she pay a return visit to Romania. It must have given her considerable satisfaction when, 11 years later, after the Presidential couple had been dethroned and shot dead, Buckingham Palace was able to announce that Nicolae Ceausescu had been stripped of the Honour the Queen had conferred on him during the state visit.

A couple of months after that state visit, I was back in Romania. This time it was to cover a major diplomatic event. The Chinese Party Chairman, Hua Kuo-Feng, was making his first trip to Europe. Romania was his first stop and Yugoslavia would be his second. It was an early stage of China's opening to the world, and Hua's trip attracted major international interest and news coverage. Ceausescu was evidently determined to make sure that nothing went wrong during Hua's presence in Romania. But I only realised the lengths to which he had gone when I went to the mammoth spectacle that had been laid on for the Chinese guest. Everything seemed to be going like clockwork, including Ceausescu's welcome speech – and suddenly I realised that the singing and speaking was not quite in sync with the live performance. The whole event had been pre-recorded. The actors and singers were miming to the recording. I couldn't tell whether the President had pre-recorded his own speech or had the courage to speak live. I strongly suspect it was the former.

I had two more encounters with Ceausescu's world. I was among the journalists who went with the Foreign Secretary, Lord Carrington, on an official visit to Romania in 1980. The objective was to gain Romania's support at the United Nations to condemn the Soviet invasion of Afghanistan. Ceausescu, for all his independent foreign policy, was not prepared to fall in with the British ploy. For Carrington, that visit was an endurance test. The laid-back Foreign Secretary found it hard to endure the 'Lay God's' presence, and when we finally reached the sanctuary of the British Airways plane, all of us, including Peter Carrington, spent the flight back drinking ourselves into relief and merriment.

My last time in Romania was in the winter of 1985. Another official British visit. This time Sir Geoffrey Howe was Foreign Secretary. There was a severe power shortage. The Ambassador's residence, where Howe was staying, had no power, and meals on wheels had to be brought in by members of the Embassy who lived in more fortunate parts of the capital. The journalists were housed in a hotel that possessed a heated indoor pool, and where there was power. Diplomats from several countries flooded into the pool as a substitute for their own bathrooms, where only cold water was available. Geoffrey Howe reported icicles in the Foreign Ministry, even in the room where he met his Romanian counterpart. Next day, when we were allowed to accompany the Foreign Secretary to the opening of his meeting with Ceausescu, We were marched down long corridors past offices where we saw officials wearing heavy overcoats miserably hunched over desks bejewelled with more icicles. As we advanced, gradually it grew warmer until finally we encountered President Ceausescu in his lair – a vast over-heated comfort zone. Four years later, and it was the Ceausescu couple's turn to huddle in the cold and stare into the abyss that was ready for them.

I didn't just bury myself in work during those years when the waning Cold War served as my Dahrendorf escape hatch. Holidays were often spent in Provence staying with Paul-Marc Henry, the French diplomat who long ago, during my West Africa days, had alerted me that the French authorities suspected me as a British agent. He and his American wife had bought an old run-down farmhouse, La Seraphine, standing on its own small hilltop near Seguret, a picturesque village on a higher hilltop. La Seraphine had been transformed into a comfortable holiday home. Mary Henry wrote the story of *A Farmhouse in Provence*, a precursor to Peter Mayle's book *A Year in Provence*. Paul-Marc's poodle authored *Poodlestan*, about a dog's life observing the world of La Seraphine. It served as open house to an international cast of friends, to conviviality and great conversations. I was a familiar presence. It became my escapist home in France. My close companion was Leopold, a ginger-coloured half-Labrador, half-unknown-paternity dog whom I adored. He returned my affection. We took long walks in the surrounding woods and fields.

Nearby Vaison-la-Romaine is a small market town with a Roman amphitheatre, a Gothic cathedral, a popular farmers' market, an annual arts festival and . . . a small knitwear factory, the Usine de Laurent. Why mention this factory? Answer: because of its unique character. It made knitwear for St Laurent, for Givenchy, for Chanel and several other of the French couture houses. And its owner, Michel Paris, was a local. His parents had a village shop not far from La Seraphine, and his uncle was a master baker. Pierre Bergé, Yves St Laurent's partner, used to spend summers in the area and occasionally had an aperitif at the grocery owned by Michel's parents. Michel, as a boy, was taught by his grandmother to knit on her rickety home knitting machine. After he married, he made a couple of sweaters for his wife. She wore one of them at the arts festival in Vaison and was spotted by Juliette Greco, who proclaimed that this was 'couture quality'! Michel must show them in Paris.

Michel took up the challenge. He remembered Pierre Berge and presented himself and his sweaters at the door of the great couture house. Berge had not forgotten the teenager who used to bring him his glass of wine. As Michel told the story, Yves St Laurent appeared on the scene. It was an instant mutual admiration society, and Yves placed an impressive order for more designs. Michel scratched around for money to buy his first 'Rolls-Royce' factory-sized knitting machine, and good fortune remained with him. His manufacturing business, Michel Paris Mailles, was born, and soon the knitwear made in Vaison was sold under precious labels in Paris and Tokyo, London and New York and – lucky me – to the few cognoscenti who would be invited to the Usine de Laurent to buy samples or slightly faulty couture garments at very affordable prices. I still have the precious sweaters I bought so many years ago. I still wear them.

Holiday visits to Provence were always energising. So also, though in a very different way, were my trips to Belgrade. There was a sentimental attachment. In 1960, Yugoslavia had been my first direct contact with the Balkans and with a Communist (albeit unorthodox Communist) country. And of course it is the city where my *Guardian* career took off. But while Tito was alive and Belgrade remained the capital of Yugoslavia, and not just Serbia, it was a vibrant country with a charismatic leader who counted as a major figure on the world stage. Sentiment apart, Yugoslavia was an international player of consequence whose security and relationship with Moscow was always a cause for concern. After the rigidity of the Warsaw Pact countries, it was always a relief to be in a country that had escaped the Kremlin's diktat, decided its own 'self-management' form of Communism and its own external policies; and moreover, was relatively relaxed and open to the outside world. From time to time, there were events to be covered or invitations from the Yugoslav press services for study tours or special events. I eagerly took them up.

One year the Yugoslav authorities invited a small handful of British journalists to come to the island of Korcula for the wedding of one of Sir Fitzroy Maclean's sons. Sir Fitzroy was instrumental in bringing Tito out of the cold of battle to Winston Churchill's attention during the war. He was a hero figure in Yugoslavia and the only foreigner allowed to own a property in the country. Nobody had told him or the bridegroom that Yugoslav officials had invited us to the wedding! We were definitely not expected. But we were not turned away and were even asked to join the riotous wedding feast. All I remember of the day-turned-into-night is that we somehow found ourselves in a small boat, bobbing around in a fortunately becalmed sea and drunkenly waving and singing with the revellers on dry land. As I am still here, presumably we ended up back on the island and found somewhere to sleep.

From the mid 19th century onwards, powerful forces among Croats had promoted a merger between Croatia, the kingdom of Serbia, Bosnia and Herzegovina to set up a unitary state. In 1918 after the end of the First World War, Yugoslavia was recognised as a sovereign state under Serbia's monarch as head of state. It barely survived the inter-war period and was carved up between Hitler and Mussolini in 1941. Tito, a Serb, emerged as the Communist head of a partisan group. By 1944, he had built it up into an efficient army of almost a quarter of a million fighters, including women. Winston Churchill was persuaded to break with the monarchists, and instead support Tito and his partisans. By the end of the war, Tito was Marshal in command of Yugoslavia's forces, and after the war became the country's political head as President of Yugoslavia. The monarchy was exiled. In its place the country, always an uneasy mosaic of different cultures and ethnicities, was to be ruled by Tito and the League of Yugoslav Communists as a one-party 'self-managed' state. In 1948, Tito broke with Stalin and took Yugoslavia out of the Comintern. For the rest of his life, Tito was guided by twin security priorities: on the home front, overriding the interests of constituent nationalities and cementing Yugoslav nationhood; on the international front, securing a solid standing and reputation, and deterring the Soviet Union from intervention or forcing the country back into the Warsaw Pact fold. Born of necessity, Tito became a fervent advocate of East–West détente.

During the period when I was covering Yugoslavia and knew it best, I became convinced that most of its people saw themselves as Yugoslavs first and only then also as Serbs, or Croatians, or Macedonians and other nationalities. I was meeting a wide spectrum of people, from taxi drivers and the occasional farmer and factory worker to intellectuals, politicians, diplomats and resident journalists. Regularly, when I asked a Yugoslav about his or her nationality, the answer would be: 'Yugoslav.' I thought this sense of Yugoslav nationhood had taken sufficient root for the state and nation to survive beyond Tito's over-arching presence, which bound its nationalities together. I still believe I was right about the country, as it was then. But national unity was more superficial than I had realised. My optimism had been misplaced. I had been wrong, and so were many others who had become used to seeing Yugoslavia as an active and respected member of the international community.

Tito clung to the concept of collective leadership but was not grooming any single politician to succeed him as leader who could command sufficient authority to hold it all together. In January 1980, worries about Yugoslavia without Tito to cement the country suddenly became acute. He was 87 and seriously ill. By the end of February, he was reported to be close to death.

Tito's constitution was tough. The dying leader lingered on. In mid-April doctors again predicted that Tito could not last much longer. I returned to Belgrade for the death watch. As always, I stayed in the well-worn Hotel Moskva, a haunt of Belgrade's literati and much beloved by the regulars among foreign journalists. This time there were about half a dozen of us, all sending out regular reports and features about Tito and the future of his country without him. In the evenings, our little group met in the room of *Time* magazine's Marsh Clarke. Marsh was normally based in Moscow and had come with lashings of caviar. We had vodka and room service provided toast – and a merry time was had by all. I discovered a potential for caviar addiction. Sadly, it has had to remain unsatisfied.

One day we decided on a diversion from the Tito-watch. We hired transport to go to a village famed for its peasant artists who all specialised in naive painting. We went from simple house to simple house, and each of us made trophy buys. Some now hang in an apartment in New York; others in a house in Thailand. Mine is in my home in London. For all of us, it is a reminder of those days in Belgrade when somehow time stood still while we waited for the Yugoslav leader's death.

President Marshal Josep Broz Tito finally expired on 4 May 1980. Four days later, leaders from around the world set aside their differences to attend Tito's funeral. China's Premier, Hua Kuo-Feng, was among the first to arrive. Leonid Brezhnev came. President Carter stayed away but sent Vice-President Mondale. The Duke of Edinburgh was there together with Prime Minister Margaret Thatcher. The GDR leader Erich Honecker and the German Chancellor Helmut Schmidt found themselves face to face. The polyglot list of leaders went on and on, with 120 countries represented at the state funeral. Such a gathering could not just be about mourning. Tito's final gift to the world had been to provide a rare occasion to explore solutions to international tensions, with the Soviet intervention in Afghanistan high on the agenda. My bête noire, President Ceausescu, seemed to be the busiest of all, having taken it upon himself to find a way of securing at least a partial withdrawal of the Soviet Union from Afghanistan. Unsurprisingly, he failed.

Tito's state funeral was kept simple, heightening the tension. Belgrade was at a standstill. Its people stood silent, their emotions filling the atmosphere as his coffin, placed in a small red gun carriage, was taken through the streets to the grounds of his residence. His peacocks shrieked as the funeral procession reached his burial ground. His unpolished oak coffin was placed in a plain, white, rectangular marble tomb. The inscription only has his name in gold letters, and the date of his birth and death. Tito's designated successor at the head of the Yugoslav Communist Party, Stevan Doronsjki, gave the eulogy, declaring that Tito had been 'a symbol of humane socialism, freedom of thought, creativity, struggle for justice . . . and for a world without war'. Leonid Brezhnev was the first to walk past and salute the dead leader under his marble slab. The long line of leaders who followed him served to emphasise that this was a day of loss not just for the people of Yugoslavia, but also for the wider world.

Post-Tito, Yugoslavia lingered on for another decade before its fragmentation. But I now believe that the Tito funeral also deserves to count as the death knell and day of mourning for the Socialist Federal Republic of Yugoslavia.

CHAPTER 12

INTERLUDE WITH THE AGA KHAN

'My advice is: don't do it! K is like a lighthouse. At present, because he wants you to write the book, the beam is directed to you at full strength. But there will come a time when he changes his mind and the beam will move away.'

The speaker was Prince Sadruddin, uncle of the Aga Khan. This was in 1980. I had made friends with Sadruddin earlier when I was working in Geneva. Now I had come for advice on whether to accept a proposal from the Aga Khan to write his biography to mark his Silver Jubilee in 1982.

I ignored the advice. That turned out to be a mistake – or rather a 50:50 mistake. The beam did indeed move on when the book was about to be published. But even the Aga Khan couldn't take away the unique experience I had in working on it, gaining a close-up of the man behind the glamorous image of fabulous wealth, horse-racing and high society, and discovering a hard-working, earnest individual, deeply committed as the Imam of the Shia Muslim Ismaili Community. I would probably never have met this interesting and diverse Muslim group, who are so open to the outside world. I would have missed privileged journeys to China, to India and Pakistan, to East Africa, to Canada, and to Sardinia's Costa Smeralda. I would never have had the comfort of flying around the world first class or in the Aga Khan's private plane. I would never have been a temporary resident in the surroundings of a unique institution in Islam.

It all started in New York with my close friends, Fred and Jane

Rosen. They had formed a warm friendship with the Aga Khan. Fred's public relations firm had 'His Highness, Prince Karim Aga Khan' as one of its clients. The Aga Khan had a profound distrust of the media – and with good reason. One of Fred's important tasks was to keep the Aga Khan out of the gossip columns, and instead to focus on his positive image as head of the Ismaili Community and as a respected voice on Third World development issues. Fred was familiar with my work. So at one of their meetings Fred suggested to Karim an interview with the *Guardian* – to whit, me. He agreed. The *Guardian* naturally welcomed the idea, and I was mightily pleased with the opportunity to have an exclusive about 'the real Aga Khan'.

The interview took place at the Aga Khan's principal home at Aiglemont, near Chantilly, just outside Paris. Set in forested grounds, the complex also included very modern stables and a sober office building housing the secretariat of the Ismaili Community. I encountered a smiling, welcoming individual whose rounded face, receding hairline and solid, slightly overweight figure was familiar from many media photographs. Reticent at first, the Aga Khan visibly warmed up and became charm itself when he realised that I was genuinely interested in his development projects and also wanted to know more about his other initiatives to promote the security and well-being of the Ismaili Community.

I wrote up my interview. I described how the Ismailis, mainly of Asian origin, their faith on the liberal wing of Islam, were scattered around the globe in India, Pakistan, Africa, Canada and Europe as minorities in structured, self-reliant communities with the Aga Khan, their Imam, as their absolute religious authority and their respected guide. He had set up key institutions to promote economic and social development, and fiercely believed that Ismaili communities had to modernise and share their resources and know-how with the societies of the countries where they had made their home. His basic strategy was to convince the Ismailis that their social acceptance and security demanded close involvement in the development and well-being of the countries where they were settled.

The interview was well displayed in the *Guardian*. Fred Rosen sent a message: 'Well done, Kid.' I did not expect a follow-up. Two days later I returned to my persona as East European Correspondent and wrote an article about Yugoslavia after Tito. The Aga Khan, however, thought otherwise and decided to turn that famous searchlight in my direction. Evidently, I had made a good impression. On the strength of my interview, I was asked to write his biography, timed to be published for his Silver Jubilee in 1982. I was surprised, and of course I was flattered, but I was also uncertain whether I was the right person to tackle a book about a Muslim leader and his following. But the temptation was too great.

Peter Preston, the *Guardian*'s Editor, agreed to give me a sabbatical, and in truth, after five years of commuting between London and my various parishes in East and Central Europe, the prospect of putting the Cold War aside for a few months looked rather attractive. Decision taken, the literary agent Hilary Rubinstein took me on and painstakingly negotiated my contract. The Aga Khan reserved the right to select a publisher – and to have the final word on publication. If I had not accepted those conditions, the searchlight would have been turned off straight away. However, the Aga Khan made one concession: I was invited to the Costa Smeralda, his fiefdom in Sardinia. There, surrounded by his chief lawyer, Maitre Andre Ardoin, and senior aides as witnesses, His Highness Prince Karim Aga Khan delivered a firm assurance that he alone would be the final arbiter of the book.

I decided to trust his word and signed the contract. Another mistake – and this time a 100 per cent mistake. But I only discovered that more than a year later.

1981 became my 'Aga Khan year'. The publishers, William Collins, agreed to take on the book project after other prominent publishers apparently turned it down on the grounds of the Aga Khan's reservation of rights over the project. I was soon immersed in discovering the intriguing personality of 'His Highness', and in absorbing the diversity of his interests while also puzzling over the complexity of the relationship between him and the Ismaili Community. I became intrigued by what I saw as a distinct similarity between the structure of Jewish communities and how the Ismaili minorities organised themselves in their host countries.

I turned to basics: were there really 12 million of them, as was widely claimed? I soon suspected that the real number was much smaller. And what differentiated them from other Shia Muslims? The shorthand answer: the Aga Khan and his forebears believe they are in the direct line of descent from the prophet Mohammed. The long answer is that I had undertaken to include in the biography an account of the history and beliefs of the Ismailis. That was mistake number three – this time again a 50:50 mistake. On the plus side: the Aga Khan wrote on the draft chapter that 'This is some of the best I have ever read about our history.' On the minus side: this view was not shared by prominent members of the older generation of Ismailis.

My early work on the biography took in visits to Aiglemont to meet the Aga Khan's chief aides and, above all, for an initial series of talks with K – as his close friends often called him. I never actually addressed him as K, or even as Karim to his face, but did not follow Ismaili deference by calling him 'your Highness'. I always avoided addressing him directly by any name. The degree of familiarity was left undefined, but our meetings continued regularly over the months while I was working on the book. I normally stayed in Paris and was driven out to Aiglemont. Once, however, when I was invited to stay in the house, I was also asked to join the family to fly to London in their helicopter. They wanted to see a sold-out Nureyev ballet performance at the Palladium. I knew the impresario, Victor Hochhauser, and secured an invitation. When we arrived at the theatre, the Aga Khan family, and me as an attachment, were taken straight to the Royal Box. And that is how I came to spend an evening with not just one Highness but also with a second one: Princess Margaret.

Many of my conversations with the Aga Khan, especially the early ones, surprised me by the frankness of his account of a profoundly unhappy childhood. In later conversations, he was also very open, very undiplomatic about the frustrations of modernising Ismaili institutions, but far more reticent about his wealth and private life.

As a young man he was already firmly engaged in Islamic studies and it was self-evident that he was profoundly committed to his mission as the Imam of his Ismaili flock. But I always hesitated to follow through by pressing him to talk in greater depth about his religious faith.

I did not hesitate to try and draw him out on his wealth. But it hardly got me anywhere beyond firm assurances that the practice of *Zakhat* (personal tributes from his followers) belonged to distant history. However, I learned that Ismailis were expected to set aside a portion of their income for funding Ismaili Community projects. Karim debunked for me the fable of those famous ceremonies where his grandfather, Aga Khan III, had been weighed in silver, gold and platinum on his successive jubilees. Far from reinforcing his personal purse, the precious materials were borrowed for the occasion, and the Ismaili diaspora had to raise the equivalent value to invest in their own communities.

Karim was born in 1936 and his brother Amyn just over a year later. Their parents, Prince Aly Khan and their English mother, Princess Joan, were often absent. The two babies were moved around between Paris, Deauville and Gstaad. The boys spent the war in a somewhat dilapidated family house outside Nairobi, while their parents were based in Beirut – his father in the military, his mother working for the Red Cross. They rarely visited the children, and by the end of the war the marriage was on the brink of collapse. Back in Europe, Karim and Amyn were put into a pre-eminent boarding school, Le Rosey in Gstaad.

At first the two boys were so unhappy they tried to escape. But Karim said they turned back at the school gates because they didn't know where to go. In fact, the school came to be the one stable point in their young lives. It became home. During the school holidays, they were treated as nomads, bobbing between mother and father, sometimes in England, sometimes in the South of France or Normandy or Scotland . . . And all the time the boys saw their father portrayed in the media as a scandal-ridden wealthy playboy who eventually took Rita Hayworth as his second wife. Karim clearly felt the gossip ignored his family's, and specifically his father's, public achievements. He hated what he saw as distortions of his father's character and an invasion of privacy. It shaped Karim's profound distrust of the tabloids and his determination to keep them at arm's length.

In July 1957, Karim was still a few months from his 21st birthday when, on the death of his grandfather, he was suddenly pitched into the leadership of the Ismaili Community and was named hereditary Imam, 49th in descent from the prophet Mohammed. His grandfather, the heavy-set Aga Khan, often romanticised for those precious-stones weighings, had decided to jump a generation and select as his heir his grandson, 'a young man who will bring a new outlook on life to his office of Imam'. At the time, Karim was in his second year as a student at Harvard. Initially taking up engineering and architecture, he had switched to Islamic studies. He had become very close to his grandfather and had stayed with him during the old Aga Khan's last few weeks of life.

Even if Karim had been given an inkling of his inheritance, coming to terms with his new status was daunting. It was obvious to me that a lonely childhood and difficult adolescence had taught Karim a high degree of self-reliance. It had led him to be wary of others until he had tested their loyalty. All this, he told me, had helped him to face up to his essentially lonely responsibilities as Imam. One of his first decisions was to take as his aide Michael Curtis, a sturdy, experienced British newspaper man, who patently won the loyalty test with high honours and remained with Karim for the rest of his working life. Michael looked after me throughout the Aga Khan saga, and what a helpful difference that made!

But I digress. Loaded with my early insights into the Aga Khan's domains, I was ready for the field work – for on-site inspection. The first adventure was to join the Aga Khan, his English wife Sally and their three young children on a visit to Kenya, which was home to a significant number of Ismailis, including one of the Community's elder statesmen, Sir Eboo Pirbhai. The Aga Khan had not been in Kenya for several years. The religious highlight of the visit was the prayers led by the Aga Khan, their Hazar Imam, 'the one who holds Authority'. Thousands of believers, mostly of Asian origin, were there to receive his blessings at the Jamat Khana (the House of Prayer), as the Ismailis call their mosques, and they had come from all over East Africa. Portraits of the Aga Khan competed with precious carpets on the walls and sprays of sweetly scented flowers suspended from the ceilings. The women were in their most precious saris; the men were almost equally colourful and resplendent. Only Ismailis are allowed into the inner sanctum of the Jamat Khana, where the prayers are held. But even from the outside I caught something of the awe and respect they feel for their Imam – and of the power he holds in his person. It reminded me of the scenes and emotions I had witnessed during the Polish Pope's visit to Poland. But I felt that between the Aga Khan and his followers there was an extra element. I noticed during that Kenya trip that any cup from which he drank, and even the jeep he drove during a safari, instantly became treasured museum pieces, probably never to be used again.

Kenya was quite definitely not a leisure trip. Yes, it included a brief visit to the Masai Mara game reserve and a late-afternoon safari drive in search of elephants that also turned out to be a trip within sight of a lion's den, with mothers and cubs growling fiercely at our safely fortified jeeps. There was also an overnight stay at Treetops, where the Queen (then Princess Elizabeth) and Prince Philip had stayed when news reached her of her father's death. My high point of our Treetops sojourn was to watch the Aga Khan wrestle with a baboon who had decided to settle on his window ledge. Karim was humbled. The baboon won the day and arrogantly flounced off.

But even on these leisure jaunts, and certainly for most of the other days in Kenya and also large chunks of the night, I watched a workaholic, known as the Aga Khan, beavering away at his desk. As founder and owner of the *Nation*, one of Kenya's leading newspapers, he was a speaker at the annual meeting of the International Press Institute that was, coincidentally, being held in Nairobi. He used it to expound his theories about best-practice development policies. And then there were meetings of executives on Aga Khan projects who were flown in from Asia, Europe and East Africa. There were meetings on hospital projects and other planned developments in Kenya. There were other meetings about the major hospital and medical centre the Aga Khan was building in Karachi, and on and on with still more projects. There was always an audible sigh of relief when he pronounced: 'I am comfortable with this. I hope everybody else is also.'

We went down to the Kenya coast and stayed in the made-for-a-perfect-holiday Serena Beach Hotel, one of the several hotel properties owned by the Aga Khan's organisations. But apart from a brief transformation into Imam mode and prayers at the Jamat Khana in Mombasa, it was once again all work. Again invited to sit in on still more business and planning sessions, I ended up even more impressed by the ambitious mix of charitable and business ramifications of the Aga Khan's projects. A couple of times I had supper with Karim at the close of another long working day. Those meals served as an informal inquest on the day's achievements. They also left me with one trivial memory: the inordinate amount of salad that he could consume.

It is probably impossible to know for certain just how many Ismailis live in India and Pakistan. There is a wealthy layer. But they are generally poor and scattered in remote villages. The Aga Khan included me on one of his visits to Karachi. To India, however, I went on my own. Having their Imam's seal of approval opened doors everywhere and allowed me to meet both the Community leaders and simple villagers. I was spoiled with royal treatment and felt like a temporary princess. In both India and Pakistan, I saw the Aga Khan as a tightrope walker in diplomacy. Leading Ismailis were deeply conservative and hard to convince that modernisation rather than emigration was the answer to Ismaili poverty on the subcontinent.

In Pakistan, I witnessed Karim at his diplomatic best, working to ensure that his costly hospital and health reform project would be allowed to secure a firm footing. He was an unequivocal believer in private ownership. However, President Zia was in power and had made a firm rule of public ownership. I could see how Karim tried to steer clear of political judgement on Zia's autocratic tendencies and was emphatic that the Ismailis as an institution must remain apolitical. At the time it seemed to work. On a red-letter day, General Zia opened a nursing school, the first building of what would become 'The Aga Khan University of Health and Science'.

My personal highlight during that Pakistan trip was the discovery of Hunza, a place high up close to the Karakoram mountain range that borders on China. It is beyond doubt the most dramatic mountainscape I have ever seen. It is also the one area in the world where Ismailis are in the majority. Apricots had always been the subsistence crop in Hunza. But the Aga Khan introduced potatoes, which have become a successful export crop. I gorged myself on apricots in every form – fresh, dried, compote, kernels, jam, some form of fritters, and yes, also spirits – all of it guaranteed to give you long life! I went walking and talking. I crossed perilous rope bridges, gazed in awe at those indomitable, ragged mountain ranges. I was totally captive to the dramatic beauty.

Criss-crossing Canada was a very different adventure. Ismailis were scattered across the country. They provided a striking kaleidoscope of origin, education and occupation. Many had come as economic migrants from India and Pakistan and from East Africa. There was a sizeable number of refugees who had been expelled from Idi Amin's Uganda. Canada had made them welcome. I wanted to find out how this melting pot of Ismailis was settling down, and with the Aga Khan's support I set off from east to west to explore the Ismaili edition of Canada. It was fascinating and heart-warming. The vast country had become a kind of laboratory for Ismailis to integrate into contemporary society while remaining firmly anchored to their faith, their institutions and, of course, their Imam. I started off in Quebec and ended in Vancouver. On the way, I stopped off in Montreal, Toronto, Calgary and Edmonton. I talked almost exclusively with Ismailis, and many sat down with me to tell their tales of transiting from former lives to entirely different occupations – and preoccupations.

Meet Mr Shams Gilali. He had been a tailor in Kenya, moved to Uganda to run a bakery, left before he was driven out by Idi Amin and with a little capital went to Vancouver where he ran a small motel. Not good enough. Next move: Calgary, Canada's booming oil capital. The Gilali family had no experience of farming. So it was not entirely obvious why Mr Gilali decided to buy a small farm outside Calgary and turn himself, his grown-up children and his wife into egg producers. 'Our goal was to produce the largest eggs at the fastest rate and for the minimum amount of feedstuffs.' They lived crowded into a caravan for over a year before they could afford a house. But when I met the Gilalis, he was already employing a dozen workers, and his 'Sparks' eggs were being sold in Calgary supermarkets, hotels, hospitals and restaurants. The worn-out chickens were sold either as fowls to Saudi Arabia, or to a local catfood manufacturer. All members of the family remained closely linked to Calgary's Jamat Khana and the Aga Khan's portrait hung prominently on their walls. They had become Canadian citizens. But their Ismaili faith remained unimpaired.

Naturally, not every Ismaili in Canada had come with such an imaginative sense of enterprise. But broadly, I found that the pattern of enterprise was similar, even if the end product was far removed from battery-produced eggs. Most of the immigrants had been small-time traders, and only a few had come with serious money. In Quebec and Montreal, several of the Ismailis I met started off as shopkeepers. But their businesses were expanding and, encouraged by the Aga Khan's IPS business promotion arm, were taking up franchises or moving into small-scale industrial enterprises. Toronto had the largest concentration of Ismailis in Canada. It included about 70 doctors and many more professionals in other spheres of life. Quite a respectable number of them were women. What an advance that was on what I had seen of the Ismailis in Kenya and on the subcontinent, where professional women were virtually absent. Here in Canada, out of necessity and gradually also for personal satisfaction, the dominant trend among the Ismaili women was to opt for employment out of the house. In Toronto, a group of women had launched a Bureau of Economic Enterprise for Women, with branches spreading nationwide. The Ismaili women in Canada were on the march!

As I went further west, I found that in Edmonton, Ismailis of both sexes were occupying senior posts in the administration. And when I reached Vancouver, I met Ismailis who had started small and now were seriously wealthy property owners. One of their headaches was inadequate parking spaces for their limousines at the Vancouver Jamat Khana.

Now at the end of my Canada tour, I churned over my impressions with Uganda-born Zul Lalji, who headed Canada's Ismaili communities as President of their Federal Ismaili Council. I discovered an instant understanding with this prematurely white-haired, quietly spoken man. He drew an honest, convincing picture of the Ismaili experience in Canada: of the mistakes people had made and how they were learning from them; how they were spreading out in Canada and coming to feel that Canada was home. Intermarriage was becoming a problem. But it still only involved small numbers and the Aga Khan had not ruled against it. Maybe 'we will lose 5 per cent through intermarriage,' Zul Lalji conceded. 'But the thing that keeps us all together is the Jamat Khana, our religion. Believe it or not, people here are more religious than before. The children go to Canadian schools. But we bring them back into the Ismaili environment and religious education classes . . . my feeling is that religion will continue to hold us all and that we will keep our moral values.' I have often wondered whether his optimism was justified. Apologies to myself – I should have checked a decade or so later. But by this time it was my searchlight that had moved on and away . . .

My travels across Canada had given me a snapshot of a country at ease with itself and with doors open to an Ismaili immigrant community at various stages of adjustment. It was heart-warming and made me feel good about the world. Would the feeling persist when I joined the Aga Khan in China?

It was October 1981. Beijing was bathed in autumn sunshine. The city looked like a symphony of shades of grey, with men and women alike all dressed in grey tunics and grey baggy trousers. Just a few blobs of colour on little children. Bicycles reigned supreme. The city's wide streets were not much bothered by cars. China was still recovering from Mao's Cultural Revolution and only beginning to feel the impact of Deng Zhao Ping's economic transformation. Into this scene sweeps a large multinational, multi-gifted group of mostly men and only a few women also included, led by the Aga

Khan and his brother Amyn. They were an assortment of architects, historians, sociologists and economists from Europe and America, from Japan, Egypt and Turkey, and from China itself. Lacking any of their speciality qualifications, I too was part of the spectacle, and so also, to my great joy, were Jane and Fred Rosen.

The Aga Khan had brought this caravan of experts to spend two weeks in China to study 'The changing rural habitat' as part of the preparations for the biannual Aga Khan Award for Architecture. Their remit was to consider whether better housing and related amenities could stem the tide of people flooding into cities, while still preserving their cultural values. It reflected the Aga Khan's search for building bridges between Western know-how and Third World needs; between modern technology and age-old culture and experience; between isolated rural areas and the mushrooming metropolises. But for the Aga Khan, the trip to China also had a deeply emotional appeal, as he would be meeting long-inaccessible Muslims including some Ismailis when his group reached the north-western province of Sinkiang.

China had invited the Aga Khan, perhaps without too much knowledge about the Ismailis, but clearly under the impression that he belonged to the super-rich. They had arranged a VIP programme for him and allowed Chinese experts to join the Aga Khan's group for their entire itinerary. In Beijing, he was given a grand tour of the Forbidden City. His Chinese minders, anxious to keep him away from mere ordinary mortals, were startled when a tourist approached and shouted: 'Are you the Ali Khan from Turkey?' 'No, I am the Aga Khan.' 'So they call you Aga now. That's nothing to be ashamed of.' Words of comfort for His Highness. Words of praise followed at a grand banquet where he was feted by his Chinese ministerial host – and he had plenty of praise for Chinese hospitality in return – though he may still have ended up having to foot the banquet bill.

The serious business of the trip began with a two-day seminar in Beijing's drab Friendship Hotel, inevitably grey inside and out. I stayed there, and even the sheets were unappetisingly grey. It was fascinating to listen to the interplay between different cultures tackling lifestyle problems of rural communities in modern times.

The eminent author, Han Suyin, put the Aga Khan's initiative into its historical perspective and underlined the cross-fertilisation of knowledge between Chinese and Islamic cultures that had been carried through centuries along the Silk Route. 'The great Horses of Heaven' had been brought from Arabia to the rulers of the Tang dynasty; silk and paper had been brought out from China to Persia and Arabia. Benevolent millionaires from the Near East had brought their cooperation to the Tang rulers long ago. The hint was not lost on the Aga Khan.

The latter-day benevolent millionaire's caravan left Beijing behind and set off for the Silk Route, heading for Kashgar, an oasis city in Sinkiang Province, with its predominantly Muslim population. Magically, over ten days, the group never mislaid any of its members or their luggage. At all our overnight stops, everybody was adequately housed – though on a few occasions with rats as uninvited intruders. But why worry about the occasional inconvenience, set against the opportunity of a visit to the Quin Army vaults in Xian and meeting the 2,000-year-old terracotta soldiers? It was barely seven years since the vault had been accidentally discovered by peasants digging for a water-well. So far only a modest section of this historic find had been dug out. But the sight of the warriors in their tight formations, each face with its individual features, was both humbling and uplifting. It was indelibly imprinted in my memory.

Xian was the starting point of the Silk Route where the caravans would gather for their long trek across the Taklamakan Desert to Kashgar and beyond. Our group gathered for a cooler and quicker means of travel, catching planes first to Urumqi, the capital of Sinkiang Province, and then on to Kashgar. Urumqi had no claims to beauty during any of its history. A British missionary wrote in a book entitled *The Gobi Desert* that 'no one enjoys Urumqi. No one leaves the town with regret, and it is full of people who are there only because they cannot get permission to leave.' Our group had permission to use the city as a base for driving to Turfan, an oasis on the Silk Road famed for its melons, grapes and raisins. The Aga Khan, his brother Amyn, the distinguished academics and naturally also Hella the scribe, now all indulged in tourist shopping. Sackfuls of raisins were purchased, together with an assortment of fur hats, Chinese silk, even carpets. But there was serious business too. Turfan has many mud dwellings that were of interest to the group for its studies. They were also of interest to our clothes, which became dustier and muddier by the hour.

A clean-up in Urumqi, and finally on to legendary Kashgar, an ancient trading post on the Silk Road and the centre of Sinkiang's Uighur Muslim population. It is close to the borders of what was then Soviet Asia (Kyrgyzstan today). With the Taklamakan Desert on one side and the Himalayas on the other, it can also claim to be further away from the oceans than any other city! It has many an entry in the history books and has served trade in ideas, goods, travellers and explorers through the centuries. And now here was our scruffy, much-travelled, polyglot group scrambling out of the tightly packed plane, bulging with cameras, our faces a uniformly open book full of excitement and high expectation. I heard one of them solemnly proclaiming: 'We are making history – though it's hard to say what kind of history.' This was not just a facetious comment.

Kashgar was a tightly closed city in 1981 – as it is again today. But there was one significant difference: today the Chinese are suppressing and persecuting the Uighur Muslims. In 1981, the Muslims certainly appeared to be relatively free to maintain their lifestyle, go to the mosques and practise their religion. But the outside world knew little of this. Tourists, foreigners in general, even diplomats were all refused access. So it was quite an achievement that the Aga Khan and his 'troops' had been given a three-day dispensation to visit this latter-day 'Forbidden City'.

The town possessed no hotels fit for foreigners, and we were accommodated in a students' hostel – possibly not quite up to the Aga Khan's normal standards. But what Kashgar lacked in amenities, it certainly made up in providing a wealth of access to the city's numerous mosques and its Muslim population. In stark contrast to China's treatment of the Uighurs today, back in 1981 we saw mosques being restored after being badly defaced during the Cultural Revolution. Uighur shops and street traders were ubiquitous. The Chinese were far less in evidence. Our group was a seven-day wonder and attracted much attention. Market prices shot up. Prince Karim was in his element, walking in and out of houses, shops and mosques and identifying himself with the traditional Muslim greeting. He was a man whose face often reflected his changing moods, and it was obvious that this experience was bliss. A special entertainment was laid on for the visitors and Kashgar's prima ballerina, not the lithest of ladies, offered her somewhat unusual interpretation of *Swan Lake*. It was unclear whether the Uighurs knew anything about the Ismaili community, or indeed whether any of them actually believed themselves to be Ismailis. But for sure, they all understood that this Muslim who called himself the Aga Khan was a very wealthy man. Good things might come from his visit.

What a difference there was between the world of Kashgar and the world of the Costa Smeralda. Sardinia is the Aga Khan's playground or personal retreat – though he would argue, with some justification, that the Costa Smeralda is proof of his conviction that architecture can be blended into the natural landscape to create modern living spaces and serve as a model for successful tourism. The starting point for my own description would be 'Rich People's Paradise'. I was intrigued by the backstory that led Karim to develop this coastal beauty strip of Sardinia. It started when Karim was only 24 years old and had been Imam for just three years. His half-brother Patrick Guinness described to him an extraordinary land of granite mountains and velvety white beaches nestling between rocks etched into natural sculptures and jutting out into a clear sea of shimmering shades of emerald. The land was untamed and filled with shrubs and trees – eucalyptus and junipers, chestnuts and cork oaks, and carpets of wild flowers. Mosquito infested, the area had very few inhabitants. Sard people called it 'the Valley of Hell' and sensibly lived on higher, safer ground. Patrick Guinness had bought some of the coastal land. He urged the Aga Khan to follow suit. He did.

Karim was persuaded that tourism could be implanted and perhaps even light industry, such as a pottery, could be established without debasing the natural environment. His lawyer, Maitre Ardoin, and a small group of friends ended up acquiring 33 miles of unspoiled coastline with around 50 beaches. With its deadly mosquitoes, the land had little worth for the Sardinian owners. So it was cheap. The Sards did not know what the Aga Khan probably already knew through his connections: namely, that the World Bank had authorised a project for the eradication of the mosquito in the coastal strip that included the future Costa Smeralda!

The Costa Smeralda required massive investment. Where there had only been wilderness and a few rough tracks, roads had to be built; water, sewage, power and communications systems had to be installed. When I first came to the Costa Smeralda, it already had its own designer village, Porto Cervo, complete with luxury-label shops, café and hotel. An extensive marina had been developed, fit for top people's yachts, including Karim's. With well-known architects brought in, two splendid hotels had been built, together with 1,700 villas and apartments. All this development was rigidly controlled to ensure that it blended in with the spectacular natural setting. It was enticing to be indulging myself in the infinity pool of the Hotel Pitrizza, giving the impression of swimming straight into the emerald-blue sea below. But in a way, just as an infinity pool is designed to create an illusion, I felt that the whole of the Costa Smeralda was designed to create an illusion. This was not a setting for ordinary mortals. It was, and probably remains, an artificial construct: a holiday paradise for Top People.

I had to be in the real world to write the Aga Khan biography. Where best would inspiration come? In Austria, high up in the mountains in a small hostelry owned by Hans Seger, the Aga Khan's long-term ski instructor and close friend. I spent almost six weeks there, with Hans and his wife making sure I was well fed and watered, and with their young son typing out fair copies of my musings, fit to be sent to the Aga Khan for his inspection. Other parts of the book were written in London in between my travels. With the help of the Aga Khan's brother Amyn, revisions were made. The final draft was in the hands of the publishers.

Then the unexpected happened. The Aga Khan had decided to show the text to the senior Ismaili leaders. They did not like much of what they saw and returned the compliment by highlighting a daunting number of passages they claimed to be misleading or requiring correction. The subtext, as I interpreted it, seemed to be: the Imam had opened himself too much to me, an outsider.

Next move? Publication of my book was halted, never to be revived. I was given no explanation, no justification. Only Michael Curtis tried to console me. The Aga Khan remained silent. I was banished into outer space. Prince Sadruddin's prediction had been right: the searchlight had moved on and away.

CHAPTER 13

JIGSAW PIECES

GDANSK, 11 DECEMBER 1983

Hands folded, lips pursed in silent prayer, his eyes cast down and brimming with tears, Lech Walesa stood motionless in the small refectory of his parish church, St Brigidy's. He was listening to the broadcast of the Nobel Peace Prize award ceremony in Oslo. Eventually the tension was broken by the plop of champagne being opened. Just one bottle could be procured from Poznan, where they confect it, and Walesa raised his glass first to 'Victory for the ideals of Solidarity', and then to his wife Danuta, standing in for him in Oslo to receive the Nobel Peace Prize. I was in the small group able to toast this former Polish shipyard worker at the moment when he joined the illustrious line of men and women, Nobel Peace Prize alumnae, deemed to have made a significant contribution to the settlement of conflict.

Official Poland boycotted the award ceremony and we could only listen to it thanks to the Polish service of the Voice of America. There was no TV or Zoom to let us watch the proceedings. Walesa had not gone to Oslo himself, partly because he feared that the Polish authorities would see this as a way of ridding themselves of a troublemaker and bar his return. But he also stayed home as a gesture of solidarity for many of his Solidarnosc companions who were still in prison. The right place at this momentous moment in his life was to be in St Brigidy's Church at the side of his close friend and controversial adviser, Father Jankowski.

As he tried to picture the colourful ceremony in Oslo, Walesa looked at once sad that he was shut out from the event, yet at the same time proud that his wife was deputising for him. He listened carefully as she read out the shortish acceptance speech he had prepared, checking against his own copy, and looking a little grumpy when she occasionally departed from the text. After she had finished Walesa raised his glass and declared that he was falling in love with her all over again. When the Voice of America commentator described Danuta's curtsey to the King of Norway, he stood on one leg and tried to copycat her. It was not very elegant. Solemnity went by the wayside. We laughed.

As he relaxed we talked for a while about his future. He was in a mood to stress that far from being a firebrand, he saw himself as a realist who understood that 'we cannot achieve everything . . . I understand the limitations better and I will continue to fight and fight again for negotiations and compromise and for peaceful solutions.'

Go back in time to a hot August Sunday in 1980. I was at my desk in the *Guardian* office. Scanning Reuters reports from Poland about the increasingly militant strikes in the Gdansk shipyards, it was obvious that this was turning into a serious political challenge to Edward Gierek, Poland's Communist Party Chief. The name of Lech Walesa, the most prominent of the strike leaders, was beginning to resonate loudly outside Poland. I summed up the situation in a news story that became the 'splash', the lead story in the next day's *Guardian*. I was already familiar with Poland's political tensions, and the Walesa saga in all its manifestations became a fixture in the steady flow of my reporting about Poland. There was his role in starting the Solidarnosc movement, whose formation triggered the imposition of martial law. There was the story of Walesa's half-secret support from America's AFL-CIO trade union movement and especially from its leader, Lane Kirkland. Thanks to my friendship with him, I had an insight into the assistance the Americans provided. There was the story of the banning of Solidarity and Lech Walesa's imprisonment, accompanied by the ultimately successful efforts by Pope John Paul II to secure his release in time for the second papal visit to Poland in 1983, and the award of the Nobel Peace Prize. There was a second edition of Walesa's glory days, when in 1989 he helped to secure the round-table negotiations that led to Poland's first free elections, the establishment of a Solidarnosc-dominated government and Walesa's election as President of Poland.

In April 1991, President Lech Walesa and his wife came on a three-day state visit to Britain. He relished every moment, even the apparently sleepless nights at Windsor Castle. 'The bed there was so big, at first I couldn't find my wife,' he told me. He had lain awake, unable to sleep 'because of all the things I am seeing here'. Not a tall man, Walesa was now more rotund. His hallmark moustache had turned silver grey, and in honour of the Queen had been tamed to uncharacteristic neatness. But with characteristic bluntness he proclaimed that 'I am not a classic President'. The Queen, he observed, belonged to another species. She was the very model of a classic head of state. She was a 'mother figure to her people'. Poland, he declared, unfortunately lacked such a mother figure – though he seemed confident enough that he was an adequate substitute in his role as a robust paterfamilias.

During that state visit, everybody from the Queen downwards paid extravagant tribute to Walesa, as if he had singlehandedly set Eastern Europe free. Walesa relished the compliments. He issued no denials. But with a mindset that always fixated on a single goal, he challenged his British admirers to decide how much aid they were prepared to give to Poland in recognition of his achievements. His commonsense message was clear and simple: 'The European Community countries, the rich man's club, must reach out to Eastern Europe and close the wealth gap. Anything less would trigger mass migration to the West. We must think of Europe as an economic whole.'

In the 1980s, Walesa had bulldozed his way to help bring down Poland's Communist regime and make Poland a trailblazer to end Communist rule in Eastern Europe. In the 1990s, the bulldozer technique was less effective. His talents were not well-fashioned for

the Presidency. Walesa dismally failed to win a second term. The
hero's glow deserted him.

A footnote: his successor to the Presidency, Aleksander Kwas-
niewski, took me to the chapel attached to the President's residence.
It held a beautifully fashioned crèche with a Virgin Mother and a
baby Jesus, given to Walesa as a gift from Yasser Arafat.

WARSAW: 10 NOVEMBER 1982

In Moscow, the death had just been announced of the Soviet leader,
Leonid Brezhnev. In Warsaw, it was early evening. Inside a massive
government building I was being led along dimly lit corridors. My
walk ended in a small anteroom to General Jaruzelski's office. A tall
figure straight as a rod, wearing his trademark dark spectacles, held
out a welcoming hand to greet me, disarmed me with a surprise
bouquet of red roses and invited me to sit in a comfortable armchair.
General Jaruzelski lowered himself into the other. He was ready for
a rare interview, the first he had given to a British journalist and
apparently only the third he had given to a foreign journalist. Poland
was under martial law and subject to Western sanctions. There was
a widely held view that Jaruzelski had betrayed the Polish nation
by imposing martial law. I had an open mind and as I prepared
for my interview with the General, I wrote a pen portrait where I
asked whether he was 'patriot, puppet or pragmatist?' He insisted
that he had imposed martial law 'as the only way to prevent Soviet
invasion . . . and tried hard to convince the world that he had never
been less than a patriot'. He was an enigma.

Naturally, nobody had calculated that the Soviet leader would
choose to die on the day set for my face-to-face interview with
Jaruzelski. My immediate reaction was to assume that the General
would strike me out of his diary and prepare to fly to Moscow. I was
wrong. He decided to keep his word. It was even more striking that,
the following day, Poland's official Party newspaper, *Trybuna Ludu*,
gave priority to an account of Jaruzelski's meeting with me, and only
gave second place to Brezhnev's death. This couldn't have been done

by accident. It had to be interpreted as a small political gesture to demonstrate the General's frequent assertions of independence.

The meeting with Jaruzelski had been arranged partly thanks to my good friend Mieczyslaw Rakowski, who had become Deputy Prime Minister. Jerzy Urban, the voluble and highly efficient Polish government spokesman, also had a hand in it. I had submitted some questions – thank goodness, without a repetition of the Romanian experience where the scope of the questions had to be negotiated – and the date was fixed for the meeting with the General. It would be an informal conversation, not just stiletto answers to the questions I had submitted. For those I would be provided with written answers.

Lech Walesa was about to be released after 11 months of internment, and in my talk with the General he gave the first indication that he was prepared to cooperate with the Solidarnosc leader and that martial law would soon be lifted. I came away convinced that the General accepted the need for significant political reform. This view caused me endless trouble. Exiled Polish journalists attacked me ceaselessly for kowtowing to the enemy. Some British colleagues joined the chorus. My defence was always the same: a good journalist had to seek contact with all sides in the Polish crisis. I was not there just as a campaigner for Solidarnosc. It did me no good. The attacks continued. It was unpleasant.

Another footnote: several years after the Communist regime had become history, I was in Warsaw and visited Jerzy Urban, Jaruzelski's wily government spokesman, who had converted himself into a wealthy newspaper magnate. He was living in an elegant villa. His garage housed two Jaguars – the latest models, of course. On the wall facing the Jaguars there hung a gaudy portrait of Lenin, holding out his arms in a blessing.

PRAGUE: 9–11 APRIL 1985

The scene was the dimly lit Seven Angels tavern in Prague. A hearty meal had been consumed. Moderate amounts of beer had been served. It was a private function hosted by the Czechoslovak Foreign

Minister, Bohuslav Chnoupek. His guest of honour was the British Foreign Secretary, Sir Geoffrey Howe. The evening had already been quite long and seemed to be drawing to a close. But all of a sudden one of the British officials distributed sheets of paper with the texts of traditional Welsh songs. Sir Geoffrey invited the bemused guests to join him in some rousing singing. Some gave it a try. Mr Chnoupek did not look amused. We discovered that Sir Geoffrey had a hidden talent. But put mildly, the Czech hosts were nonplussed. The small group of British journalists travelling with the Foreign Secretary had an inkling there might be method to the madness. Indeed there was. Two British diplomats, members of the Foreign Secretary's group, suddenly turned up at our tavern smiling broadly. The sing-song came to an abrupt end. The dinner broke up. The farewell handshakes were perfunctory. One Foreign Minister recognised that he had been taken for a ride. The other looked happily relieved.

Returning to the British Embassy, Howe filled us in while walking back over Prague's famous Charles Bridge. Christopher Meyer and John Birch, the two diplomats who had so conspicuously made a belated appearance at the dinner, had been able to evade their minders and had held clandestine talks with leading members of Charter 77, the persecuted Czech dissident group battling for democracy and implementation of the human rights provisions of the Helsinki Declaration. Vaclav Havel was one of the movement's founders. Howe only knew that it was a case of 'mission successfully accomplished' when the two diplomats, as pre-arranged, arrived thumbs up at the Seven Angels.

Next day Howe gave a press conference where he publicly confirmed the surreptitious meeting with Charter 77 and made no bones about Britain's full support for the movement. Sir Geoffrey Howe was outspoken about the Czech regime's human rights violations and complained to President Husak about the treatment of Charter 77 leaders. All to no avail.

This had been the first visit by a British Foreign Secretary to Prague since the Warsaw Pact intervention in 1968. If the intention had been to ease relations, it failed. And since the principal aim had been to jog the Czech regime into greater respect for human rights, the kindest comment was that Howe's tactics had misfired.

COLOGNE: MAY 1985

It is twelve o'clock on a Sunday morning. I am in the studios of WDR, one of Germany's leading TV channels. Sitting around the horseshoe-shaped table with me are four other journalists, one from Germany, and the others from Russia, France and the US. Presiding over the group is Werner Höfer, who conceived the idea for an international media talk-show way back in 1953 and called it *Internationaler Frühschoppen* (literally: International Morning Pint), meaning that the participants could strengthen themselves with a tipple while arguing fiercely about the latest international crisis. No reason to think that such a programme going out live on a weekend morning could become a magic formula for fame.

But in 1953, with Germany still recovering from defeat, and deeply affected by the tensions of the Cold War, this hour-long experimental talk-show turned into a roaring – though initially controversial – success from the day of its launch. It was daring to include journalists from behind the Iron Curtain. Suddenly,West Germans caught a first-hand close-up whiff of the mindset and the views of people in the Communist camp. At the same time, viewers in the GDR with access to West German TV had a small spyhole into Western thinking. The programme became a Sunday morning fixture. It soon had a regular audience of ten million viewers.

Ignorant me was unaware of any of this when, one day around 1978 or 1979, I received a phone call inviting me to take part in a Sunday morning TV talk-show in Cologne. I had other plans, and said thanks, but no thanks. I mentioned the invitation to a German journalist. He threw up his hands in astonishment. 'One never says no to *Frühschoppen*. Cross fingers they will come back another time.' It was my good fortune that another call did indeed come and that those calls became quite a regularity. Suddenly, 'Frau Pick' became a well-known figure to those millions of Germans who watched the show. Wherever I was in the world, if there were Germans around, people would come up to me and say: 'Frau Pick? We so enjoy *Frühschoppen*!' I became quite addicted to those ego trips. It was the best PR anyone could have wished, and not only was it free, I was actually paid a fee for winning my moments of fame. I loved it!

THE KHYBER PASS, PAKISTAN: 4 APRIL 1986

It was a truly improbable scene. The war in Afghanistan was in its sixth year. The Foreign Secretary, Sir Geoffrey Howe, was on a week-long trip, first in India and now Pakistan. We found ourselves seated comfortably on a well-upholstered heavy velvet canopy placed on a ridge high up at the summit of the Khyber Pass, the dividing line between Pakistan and Afghanistan. I happened to be in this curious setting because I had become the *Guardian*'s Diplomatic Editor. This had opened up wider horizons, more travel, more diplomatic summitry. Here from our theatrical Khyber settee we had a bird's-eye view of the fighting in the far distance. I could also see that, war or no war, traffic continued between the two countries, with gaudily painted lorries from Afghanistan bearing exports that very likely included heroin. We listened politely as Lieutenant Colonel Mahboob Shah, an officer of the Khyber Rifles, who guarded the Pass, described the heavy toll the Afghanistan War had brought on the country and its neighbours. We had a view of fighting in the far distance. Sir Geoffrey put a few polite questions. It was all so matter-of-fact but decorous, until one of the Pathans thrust a rifle into the Foreign Secretary's hands. Fortunately, Howe's back was turned on Afghanistan and he could not be tempted to turn around to target the invisible enemy beyond.

The tension broke when we were taken to lunch with the Khyber Rifles at the nearby officers' mess. A slightly unusual guard of honour was waiting to welcome the British Foreign Secretary. Two of the soldiers were displaying a dead sheep, possibly destined to be our meal. The sight provoked a burst of laughter from the British journalists. The Pathans were mystified. But then, how could they know that Sir Geoffrey, not always considered to be the most spark-ling speaker in the House of Commons, had been dubbed a 'dead sheep' by some of his parliamentary colleagues?

MALTA: 2–3 DECEMBER 1989

'How do you like our coffee? It's really good coffee. It's Russian coffee.'

No, this was not a coffee salesman. This was a grinning Mikhail Gorbachev. And his question was directed at me and my *Guardian* colleague, Martin Walker. We were in the Volga Bar in the inner sanctum of the Russian cruise ship *Maxim Gorky*, anchored near Valetta, Malta's capital. Gorbachev's wife Raisa, striking in a red dress, joined us. Soon Foreign Minister Eduard Shevardnadze came up to chat, and Anatoly Dobrynin was not far behind. The Commander-in-Chief of Soviet naval forces was also hovering in the group. It was a somewhat surreal situation. We had not anticipated such high-level communion when we boarded the *Maxim Gorky* earlier as members of a press pool selected to be briefed on a summit meeting between Presidents Bush and Gorbachev due to take place on board that afternoon.

The weather outside was atrocious, with heavy winds and pelting rain. There were about a dozen of us and we were asked to wait in the unheated entrance lobby of the ship. We waited and waited, and nothing was happening. I was chatting with the *Daily Mail*'s Ann Leslie, and we both wished the tedium could at least be relieved with a decent cup of coffee. We spotted a Russian in naval uniform crossing the lobby and pounced on him. Could he find us a warm drink?

'Come with me,' was the swift answer spoken in English.

'Are we allowed to leave the lobby?' I asked.

'I am the Captain of the *Maxim Gorky*.'

No further questions necessary. So it was that a self-confident, dapper Captain Vitaly Grishin led us to the Volga Bar and its coffee machine inside the security area set up for Mikhail Gorbachev and his inner group.

At first it was empty. But when I saw Gorbachev and Shevardnadze appearing on the scene, talking intently and clearly frustrated,
I quickly rushed back to the entrance lobby to fetch Martin Walker,
a Russian speaker. We soon discovered the problem. President Bush
was marooned on the USS *Belknap*, unable to get off the Cruiser
and prevented by high winds from being taken to the comfortably
anchored Soviet liner. For almost two hours we remained star-
struck witnesses as the Soviet leaders initially urged Bush to brave
the waters, but ended up making a mockery of the situation and
postponing the meeting to the following day. At first the Russians
tried to convince the US Secret Service officers, who were already on
the *Maxim Gorky*, that President Bush should be persuaded to brave
the storm. They could send a large, safe vessel to pick him up! Then
the Secret Service confessed that the storm had crushed the *Belknap*'s
ladder and Bush literally had no way of getting off without jumping
into the heaving seas. Mr Gorbachev was bemused. 'Your navy is
unreliable? We have to teach them to repair things?'

But he quickly relaxed and bantered with us. His earlier meeting
with Bush had been fine, and if Bush could still not get to the Soviet
ship for dinner, 'then I am ready to swim over there myself.' Shevardnadze chipped in, chuckling that perhaps a submarine should
be used for the 500-metre crossing. Gorbachev had an even better
solution. They would add a new item to the summit agenda: 'The
first thing to do is to eliminate – destroy – those types of ship which
you cannot board in this kind of weather. We will have a secret
agenda in this way to disarm the [US] Sixth Fleet.'

At this point we discovered that the US Ambassador to the Soviet
Union, Jack Matlock, together with other senior US diplomats, had
been kept in an adjoining veranda and not invited at any time to
talk with the Soviet leaders. The only way to communicate with the
Belknap had been for one of them to go out on deck and brave a
60-mile-per-hour gale to use a crackling walkie talkie. Not the best
way to resolve an impasse. The American diplomats were on the
Maxim Gorky because, unlike their President, they had decided to
remain on the Soviet ship after the earlier morning meeting between

Bush and Gorbachev. Only Bush had made the mistake of going back to his own quarters on the Cruiser.

Time was up. Mr Bush would remain in self-isolation until next morning. The Russian leadership would be having dinner without American guests – and also without the three British journalists who had kept them company for a good part of the afternoon. We rejoined our colleagues and kept the triumphal out of our voices. We knew we had a good story to write, and we were not about to give it away to competitors!

At the close of the Malta summit, Mr Gorbachev declared that 'the Soviet Union no longer regards the United States as an enemy'. It confirmed his intention to bring a new, constructive approach to the relationship between the two superpowers. And yet the Malta summit has gone down in history as an indifferent event, possibly as a missed opportunity to advance arms limitation negotiations or to secure closer US–Soviet cooperation in managing change in Europe after the fall of the Berlin Wall. But at the very least, the two men came away from Malta liking each other – maybe even laughing at each other over their experiences in real-life stormy waters. It would be a useful reminder when they next found themselves in stormy diplomatic waters.

OTTAWA: 12–16 FEBRUARY 1990

NATO and Warsaw Pact Foreign Ministers, altogether 27 of them, had come to Ottawa to discuss the future map of East–West relations. The focus was on the momentous prospect of German reunification and the reduction of conventional forces in Europe. A star attraction was Eduard Shevardnadze, the Soviet Union's Foreign Minister. He had already made his mark as an affable, accessible and well-briefed Minister, a welcome contrast to 'grim Grom', his predecessor Andrei Gromyko. Nattily dressed and with his shock of white hair and expressive brown eyes, he was well known for his courtesy and hallmark smile. But here in Ottawa he also revealed himself as a skilled negotiator and surprised his colleagues with the concessions he was able to bring to the table. He demonstrated that the Soviet Union recognised the inevitability of German reunification, and no longer insisted on neutrality for a unified Germany. This opened the way to agreement on a 'Two plus Four' framework to negotiate the German reunification process. The intense work in Ottawa also produced a formula to ensure that Germany's NATO membership could continue after reunification. The Russians calculated that it would take a long time, possibly years, to finalise agreement on reunification. That was wishful thinking. Seven months later, on 12 September 1990, the Treaty on the Final Settlement with Respect to Germany, also known as the Two Plus Four Treaty, was signed.

I had first met Shevardnadze in Helsinki in 1986. His whole political career had been spent in his native Georgia, and Gorbachev had only a little earlier plucked him away and surprised the Politburo by naming him Foreign Minister. More recently I had seen him during that curious afternoon on the *Maxim Gorky* in Malta. Now in Ottawa as a seasoned Minister, would he be willing to give me an interview? But there was no response. The ministerial meeting ended. I was staying on to spend the weekend with my friends, the British High Commissioner, Brian Fall and his wife. We were having a pre-dinner drink when a message came that 'Shevvy' would see me and that a car was on its way to fetch me. I spent the rest of the evening with Shevardnadze and his interpreter, Pavel Palazhchenko, whose brain worked so fast that the translation barely slowed down the conversation.

During the Cold War, formality had been the hallmark of most of my interviews with Communist leaders. There was none of that now during this evening with Shevvy. The talk was informal and wide-ranging. I learned about his time as Communist Party Chief in Georgia, and how, as he claimed, he had fought corruption there. He had no experience of foreign policy when his friend Mikhail Gorbachev nevertheless brought him to Moscow soon after becoming President and persuaded him to replace Andrei Gromyko as Foreign Minister. Shevvy stressed how close Gorbachev and he were in their foreign policy views. In handling relations with the West, 'We don't waste time on unnecessary things. If we can agree, that's fine. If we can't, then we postpone the discussion. But we no longer try to deceive each other. We are really establishing a new network of foreign policy relations.'

'I am not worried about depicting Western politicians as friends, even if domestic critics in the Soviet Union don't like it,' he said. 'Yes, some of our critics say that Gorbachev and I have gone too far, and that it is a bad sign when some of our class enemies are applauding us. But such people are out of step.' With a big smile lighting up his face, Shevvy declared: 'I am proud of having good relations with practically all my foreign colleagues.'

The talk turned to Germany. He agreed that German reunification was inevitable. But he was far from enthused by the prospect. He recognised that it was unrealistic for a united Germany to adopt a status of neutrality, but also stressed that Russia was not yet reconciled to NATO membership for the new Germany. The Russians had a pet project to build a new 'European security home' where East and West happily co-existed and reserved a special place for a united Germany. That always was a Gorbachev pipe dream. Did he really believe in it?

Years after my Ottawa session with Shevvy, Pavel Palazhchenko wrote his version of it in *My Years with Gorbachev and Shevardnadze: The Memoir of a Soviet Interpreter*:*

After the exhausting Ottawa marathon . . . Shevardnadze gave an extensive interview to Hella Pick . . . who had been asking for a meeting with him for a long time. She was for some reason in disfavour with the Soviet embassy in London, disliked and distrusted by Ambassador Leonid Zamyatin personally and some members of his staff. But Shevardnadze respected Pick for her professionalism and her balanced view of the issues. He talked to her frankly without trying to hide that it was not an easy time for him.

* Penn State University Press (1977), p.176.

On the German issue, Shevardnadze had to tread a cautious line, but whereas just a couple of weeks before, at the party plenum in Moscow, he spoke of the potential dangers inherent in unification, he was now saying that no artifical obstacles should be put in the way of the German people's unity. Still, he insisted on what he called 'a smooth process' that would make the transition less painful politically for the Soviet Union and economically and socially for the Germans themselves.

'Do you think this process should take some time?' I asked.

'Yes,' Shevardnadze responded.

'How long?' I asked.

'Well, maybe a few years,' came the reply.

I believe that at the time he really thought it should be a process extended to several years and that everyone would be better off for it.

Shevvy was a realist. Once the 'Two plus Four' negotiations got underway, he realised that reunification in slow motion could not be achieved. Better concentrate on protecting Soviet interests in the final settlement and accept the inevitable now rather than later.

ZIMBABWE: 18–21 OCTOBER 1991

Victoria Falls is a sightseers' paradise. John Major and his wife Norma were admiring the rushing waters and sounds of the Zambezi in full flow, plunging down with enormous force to the Devil's Pool below. Major had been Prime Minister for almost a year. Once again it was time for CHOGM – the biannual summit of Commonwealth leaders – and it was Zimbabwe's turn to host the week-long meeting in Harare. During a two-day break, the British participants had taken off for Victoria Falls with a few journalists in tow. During the few months when John Major was Foreign Secretary, I had covered his press conferences but had never managed any direct contact or conversation with him. So now, here in Victoria Falls, was my chance. I walked up to him, introduced myself and foolishly added, 'I hope we will see a lot of each other.' There came a curt, clipped answer: 'I don't think so.' End of conversation. Fortunately, it was not a permanent veto.

But it took quite a while for the ice to break. There was good reason for his dismissiveness at Victoria Falls. After Mrs Thatcher's resignation in 1990, the *Guardian* ran a series of articles to assess the pros and cons of the three candidates competing for the Conservative Party leadership. The three were John Major, Michael Heseltine and Douglas Hurd. The day before the John Major assessment was due, it was discovered that nobody had been commissioned to question his suitability to serve as Prime Minister. The lot fell on my colleague Alex Brummer, who would judge Major's work as Chancellor of the Exchequer, and on me, who would look at his performance as Foreign Secretary. Between the two of us, we were expected to explain his shortcomings.

I described John Major 'as a diligent worker who commandeered senior officials to give him a crash course on foreign affairs, and whose most important decision was to delegate work to junior ministers'. I suggested he had been weak enough to allow Mrs Thatcher to humiliate him at the recent Kuala Lumpur Commonwealth summit, and argued that so far he had shown little initiative or independence of mind. I concluded that John Major had yet to demonstrate a sense of broad vision to steer Britain's place in Europe and the world. I am genuinely ashamed that I wrote any of this. It was intolerant. It was pretentious and unfair to judge John Major's abilities on the basis of his brief Foreign Office tenure. Having become a firm admirer of his political courage, I am well aware that my hasty judgement back then was foolish and unfair. I should not have agreed to write about his fitness – or rather unfitness – for high office. Thinking back on that episode, John Major at Victoria Falls should have advised me to take a plunge into the cascading waters of the Zambezi.

THE UNITED NATIONS: 6 OCTOBER 1992

Surveying the UN scene from his 38th floor, the UN's Secretary-General Boutros Boutros-Ghali claimed he was well satisfied that a majority of the body's 179-strong membership had woken up to the fact that new thinking and new commitment were essential to match the UN's daunting range of responsibilities. He was cautiously optimistic that his 'Agenda for Peace', a comprehensive set of proposals to improve the UN's capacity for peacekeeping had provided a realistic blueprint for reform.

Boutros-Ghali had been in office for just over nine months, and I had come to interview him about his experience in the new job. A man of compact build, formally courteous in manner, what marked Boutros out was an expressive face that easily conveyed warmth but was just as adept in expressing cynicism. It was a rare exception that Boutros had agreed to be interviewed. He was not a natural with the media and preferred to keep them at arm's length. He probably surprised himself that he was actually enjoying talking with me about the Agenda for Peace. He decided to trust me, and in later conversations he opened up about his running battles with the US administration.

Boutros-Ghali had been one of six Africans put forward to succeed the previous UN Secretary-General, Xavier Perez de Cuellar. His credentials were impressive. As an Egyptian, he belonged both to Africa and the Middle East. He was a distinguished international lawyer. As a member of a high-ranking Christian Coptic family and married to a Jewish wife, he had succeeded in carving out for himself an influential role in a predominantly Muslim country. The UN Security Council, which appoints the Secretary-General, accepted that Boutros ticked many boxes, though nobody accused him of charisma. Only the French championed him. His age – officially 69, but thought to have been three or four years older – told against him.

As I came to discover, Boutros felt – and indeed was – embattled almost from the beginning. The task was enormous. The Security Council showered the UN with peacekeeping tasks without providing the means. There was a moment of optimism when the Security Council gave him the mandate to explore ways of improving the UN's peacekeeping operations. This led to the Agenda for Peace. It was an ambitious design for a revamped UN complete with peacemakers and peacekeepers and an organisational structure capable of responding to humanitarian challenges. The Boutros-Ghali plan could have transformed the world body into a much more credible agent for the settlement of international disputes. But only a few bare elements of his proposals have been implemented. Hypocrisy is always common currency at the UN.

Boutros, for the rest of his term, soldiered on in the face of constant sniping from President Clinton and Secretary of State Madeleine Albright. They made sure he would not win a second term as UN Secretary-General.

SARAJEVO, MOGADISHU AND ADDIS ABABA: 31 DECEMBER 1992 – 6 JANUARY 1993

New Year's Eve in war-torn ex-Yugoslavia. Festive mood was in short supply. I had started the day in peaceful, placid Geneva. It ended in Sarajevo, a bitter war zone. I was one of four journalists who had been invited to join the UN Secretary-General, Boutros Boutros-Ghali, on a week-long tour of flash-points in the Balkans and Somalia. It was primarily intended to boost the morale of UN personnel. But Boutros also planned to have a stab at peacemaking in Somalia by bringing the warring factions together at a meeting in Addis Ababa. It turned into quite an adventure.

Boutros-Ghali cut an incongruous figure in Sarajevo, wearing a fur-collared ski jacket over his flak jacket as UN soldiers brandishing machine guns rushed us down Sniper Alley to meet Vice-President Ejup Ganic. 'Life here is slowly going down. Life in Sarajevo means death,' Ganic told us. He blamed the UN for failing to broker peace. A crowd outside screamed at Boutros: 'Assassin, murderer.' Ganic insisted that Boutros face the crowd. Boutros was not made for this kind of confrontation. Lamely he called for patience and for trust in the UN. He made it worse by telling them that people in countries like Cambodia and Afghanistan suffered far more. Sarajevo should count its blessings to have a UN peacekeeper presence. How insensitive! I was shocked by his lack of understanding for Sarajevo's plight.

It was another world to move on from Sarajevo to the Somali capital Mogadishu. The civil war there involved even more factions than the break-up of Yugoslavia, and the small UN peacekeeping force there was even more helpless. Boutros had told us his main reason for venturing to Mogadishu was to boost the morale of the UN peacekeepers. As it turned out, his booster talents, if he had them at all, could not be put to the test. Quite the opposite. When we landed, Boutros, tightly surrounded by security forces, was immediately whisked off to inspect a food-aid operation, while the rest of us set off for the UN compound to wait for him. No military escorts for us lesser beings. As we approached the gates of the compound, an ugly mob, sent there by one of the Somali factions, met us with a hail of heavy stones to denounce the UN's presence. They obviously thought that Boutros was with us. The UN guards just about managed to get us inside the compound. But the crowds outside only grew bigger and angrier. The UN flag was torn down and replaced with a Somali flag. 'Boutros-Ghali is responsible for death and starvation,' shouted the crowd. We were besieged.

Inside the compound, a table had been set for lunch with the Secretary-General. Norwegian members of the UN guards had flown in an outsize salmon and a plentiful supply of shrimps. They had planned a feast. With the Secretary-General still absent, we decided to eat and be merry – for a while. But the stone pelting was getting heavier and more accurate, and we were told to move to greater safety in the upper reaches of the house. One of us grew seriously fearful and had to be calmed. No attempt was made to bring Boutros to the compound. He was taken to the airport and flown to Addis Ababa. So much for his morale-boosting mission in Mogadishu.

American forces formed the bulk of the UN deployment in Somalia. An American rescue mission was mounted to extricate us, but only after the situation had eased outside the compound and calls had been made to the State Department. Our rescue was somewhat farcical. With a flurry, a back gate to the compound was opened. Amid clouds of dust, six US military vehicles carrying GIs drove in. As we rushed out to get on board, a handful of women and children in the street smiled and waved. The mob was gone. There was no ambush, no stones, no protestors. We flew to Addis Ababa to rejoin the UN Secretary-General.

Another day. Another anti-Boutros demonstration, each more violent than the previous one. In Addis Ababa, one demonstrator was killed and at least 20 were badly wounded when police intervened with totally unjustified violence. The demonstrators were students leading a protest march over Boutros-Ghali's declared intention to visit Eritrea. They wanted to register their resentment over a UN decision to send observers to an independence referendum scheduled for early in the new year. I witnessed the brutality. Boutros did not. He was holed up with the leaders of the warring Somali factions, pleading with them to overcome their enmities and negotiate a peaceful settlement. It ended with a tentative agreement to prepare for a Conference of Reconciliation in the late spring. Boutros decided to interpret that as progress and expressed optimism. Ethiopia's President Zenawi thought otherwise. He told the Somalis: 'There is no lack of agreements among you that are not torn up before the ink was dry.' And of course, so it was again this time. Somalia has still not found the secret of peace.

LONDON: 30 APRIL 1996

I didn't quite make it to four decades. But after thirty-five years of roaming around the world, my *Guardian* career was finally at an end. I had covered so many events, written about so many people and learned so much. But I never tired of it and fortunately never lost my curiosity.

In this chapter, I have recalled a handful of outstanding memories. There could have been many, many more. So when it was all over, when I knew I would not be creating any more *Guardian* memories, I felt bereft. I was at an age where most people would accept retirement. I could not. I had my energy and a clear mind. I had not lost ambition. Luck was on my side. My long-standing friend, George Weidenfeld, another person who refused to recognise the concept of retirement, came to the rescue. A new career lay ahead.

CHAPTER 14

GAP YEARS – BACK TO MY ROOTS

The *Heldenplatz* in Vienna is the parade ground outside Vienna's Imperial Palace, the Hofburg. In 1938, a jubilant crowd of many thousands of Austrians had shouted themselves hoarse to welcome Adolf Hitler as he proclaimed his takeover of their country. Move on, past the Second World War, past Austrian complicity in the Holocaust, past Austria's controversial claim to be Hitler's first victim, and arrive in April 1995, the 50th anniversary of Austria's post-war Republic. Once again the *Heldenplatz* is filled to capacity. There is a fierce April downpour. On the majestic balcony, on the same spot where Hitler once stood, there is an elderly man slowly hauling himself up to his full height. An umbrella shields his semi-bald head and neatly trimmed moustache. In a strong and steady voice this man tells the crowd of his Utopian vision of a world 'without dictators and without ideologies' and dominated by a commitment to human rights and civil liberties. The youngish crowd responds with long and thunderous applause.

The speaker is Simon Wiesenthal, Nazi hunter by dedication and commitment, a man who survived the concentration camps and the death marches and then spent his life seeking to bring Nazi war criminals to justice and sealing the Holocaust into the conscience of the world. Even in his wildest dreams he had never imagined he would be standing in this historic place and receiving such a warmhearted ovation. It is extraordinary testimony to his dogged work carried out against heavy odds and often against fierce opprobrium.

Naturally, it made him happy. But he also felt it was his due; it was his vindication after the abuse he had suffered in post-war Austria.

Switch back a handful of months and over to Poland – to be precise, to Birkenau, the crematorium extension of Auschwitz concentration camp. It is October 1994. Under a pure blue sky sparkling with innocence, Simon Wiesenthal, supporting his imposing stature with a lightly held cane and bearing a modest wreath of purple chrysanthemums, was walking slowly towards a handful of slabs, a monument to millions killed in this infamous place. He had been here before – almost exactly 50 years ago. Only then he had been inside a railway cattle truck, sandwiched so tightly he scarcely knew who was alive or dead. The four crematoria were working to full capacity, gassing tens of thousands each day. After three days in the stationary cattle trucks, an Auschwitz manager ordered the train to move on to a concentration camp that would have the available capacity to undertake the killing. Wiesenthal ended up in Mauthausen, Austria's edition of Auschwitz – and survived.

Now, on this October day in 1994, he rested for a while on a rickety chair and reminded the crowd around him that he was one of the last witnesses. 'While I remain alive I can serve as an eyewitness for the young. It is more effective than any amount of reading about those terrible events. My whole life's meaning is to ensure that the murderers of tomorrow, who may not yet even be born, must know that they will have no peace.'

Wiesenthal returned to the theme later that day in the richly furnished Aula of the Jagellionian University. The rector, Aleksander Koj, was leading a solemn procession of the University academics, all of them robed in black-and-red gowns with a cape of ermine, to escort Simon Wiesenthal to his place of honour to receive an honorary doctorate. It was the first time in its more than 600-year history that a Jew had received such a distinction. Even now it had taken three years of debate among the University's senior academics – and the decision had still not been unanimous – to give Wiesenthal this doctorate.

Wiesenthal's visit to Poland, the first since his infamous Auschwitz sojourn, had begun in Warsaw. Poland's post-war Communist regime had accused Wiesenthal of a mix of betrayals, alleging that he had collaborated with the Gestapo; alternatively that he had allowed himself to become a Western tool and that his Vienna office was an umbrella for an anti-Communist alliance. But now in 1994, the Communist regime was gone. Lech Walesa was President, and Wiesenthal was treated as an honoured son of Poland. Walesa, shorter and rounder, almost had to stand on his toes to reach up to Simon Wiesenthal to pin on him Poland's highest honour, the *Polonia Restituta*. Hero to hero, the two men embraced. Wiesenthal drew himself up taller still: he was proud; he was happy. Once vilified, he was as close as any Jew could come – which is obviously not very close – to being sanctified in the country of his birth.

I witnessed these extraordinary scenes in Poland and in Vienna because I was writing his biography, a project that went back to a day in 1993 soon after Alan Rusbridger, the *Guardian*'s Editor, had told me that my time was up. I had been Diplomatic Editor for over ten years. A successor, younger and well qualified, was already lined up. Alan offered to promote me downwards – impressive title, part-time ill-defined work – to become 'Associate Foreign Editor'. It would involve writing some editorials and the occasional feature. Unwilling to separate myself completely from the paper, I accepted half-heartedly and fell into a mood of deep gloom. Had I become a reject?

Before I could work myself into a real depression, good fortune intervened. My old friend George Weidenfeld came calling. As a publisher, he had concluded it was high time to have a biography of Simon Wiesenthal, the prominent Nazi hunter who was based in Vienna. Would I be interested in writing it? Yes, I certainly would be interested.

A great many biographers wait until their subject is no longer around to check up or question the authenticity of the author's product. I had already been bloodied with my abortive book on the Aga Khan. I wanted no repeat of that experience. Wiesenthal must undertake to give up all control over the book and its content. George Weidenfeld supported me by writing a letter explaining to Wiesenthal that he would be allowed to see the finished typescript,

correct facts and offer comments, but crucially would have to accept
that my views and interpretation were ultimately my own. George
added that he felt very happy about the 'prospect of this collaboration because Hella is not only someone whose integrity and ability
I esteem, but someone who approaches this task with enthusiasm
and great admiration for your life's work'. Unsolicited praise always
feels good.

Before long I had acquired a wonderfully supportive agent, Mike
Shaw at Curtis Brown, had signed a contract with Weidenfeld &
Nicolson, had been to Vienna to meet Simon Wiesenthal and had
embarked on a new working life that eventually led to a second
career. But at the outset, I did not anticipate the extent to which the
book project would propel me to confront both my culture and my
responsibilities as a Jew. In turn, this also forced me to ask whether
reconciliation with my Austrian roots was justified. I had been a
frequent visitor to Austria since the end of the war. When I started
covering European affairs back in 1975, Austria was part of my parish,
and I went there both to cover international meetings and also to
write about national politics. I already knew the Austrian Chancellor
Bruno Kreisky, who even offered to restore my Austrian nationality
several years before that option was opened to all Austrian refugees.
I had also come to know other leading politicians, including Heinz
Fischer, later to become Austria's President. Hannes Androsch, who
was Kreisky's Minister of Finance when I first interviewed him,
became a treasured lifelong friend.

But those working visits were always fairly brief, and I felt more
of a passer-by than a native. Now, with the Wiesenthal biography,
I was spending longer periods in Vienna. I was able to rent a flat
and had a growing circle of friends. I felt very much 'at home'. As a
Kindertransport child, I had been torn away from Austria. And yet
here I was, happily reconnecting without rancour. Was I at risk of
turning a blind eye to the country's 20th-century history?

Obviously my priority now was to gain Simon Wiesenthal's confidence and trust, to learn the intimate story of his background, of
his survival, and to understand the mindset that had turned him
into one of a small band of Nazi hunters. What had led him to

become a messenger dedicated to bringing Nazi criminals to justice, not as an act of revenge and as a means of exposing the horrors of the Holocaust and as a warning to future generations?

Wiesenthal was brought up as an orthodox Jew who emerged from the concentration camps as a secular Jew but remained closely tied to his Jewish culture and lived the rest of his life haunted within a Holocaust capsule. He was never comfortable with the Austrians and after the war had only made his home in Vienna the better to expose Austria's Nazi perpetrators. He told John le Carré that 'if you are studying the disease you have to live in the swamp'. He had an Austrian passport. But he never really set down roots in the country.

I felt challenged: could I be a responsible and aware Jew, and yet grasp at the opportunity to reconnect with my Austrian roots? How could I reconcile these two identities? Could they be reconciled? It was not the first time I had been confronted by this dilemma. But it had never been posed in these extremes – and the more time I spent with Wiesenthal, the more it lurked in the background of my effort to understand him and learn the story of a singular life dramatically shaped by his suffering during the Holocaust.

Wiesenthal and his wife lived in a small suburban garden flat. He owned a battered car, and every morning drove himself to his equally modest office in the garment district of Vienna's inner city. It was on the second floor of an anonymous block of flats and identified itself with a small plaque: *Documentationszentrum*. A permanently bored policeman kept guard in the dimly lit corridor. Anyone who expected to find hard-working sleuths assisting Wiesenthal with his work would have been rapidly disabused. His staff consisted of two devoted secretaries who could always lay their hands on any document buried in boxes next to a plethora of books that lined the three shabbily furnished rooms of Wiesenthal's office. He spent much of his day sitting behind a massive desk piled high with papers and books. As I discovered early on, there was a daily ritual to perform before he went to his own room. He would sit himself down opposite his PA, Rosemary Austraat, take charge of the day's mail and open letters with great care. Almost every day, a few $5 or $10 notes or small sums in other currencies would come tumbling out, accompanied by short notes, often from young people, to express support for Wiesenthal's work. I was taken aback when I learned that these minuscule donations were an important source of income.

Listening to Simon Wiesenthal was enthralling. He had a computer-like memory. But there was nothing machine-like in his vivid, dramatic telling of his life and of his mission. Highly emotional, his words often came tumbling out, accompanied by tears. The pain of the Holocaust was never quite absent. He continued to live it for the six decades after his liberation from Mauthausen concentration camp. The recall of certain events never ceased to move him, and to the end of his days he believed that only a miracle allowed him to survive the concentration camps. A second miracle brought about his wife Cylla's survival and their reunion. But it was by no means all tears. Wiesenthal also had a remarkable store of anecdotes and a warm sense of humour. Laughter was a regular counterpoint to sorrow. And even if most of the day's work was hooked to remembrance of the Holocaust, there were regular phone calls from the reclusive Cylla, reminding him to buy bread or some other essentials on his way home. There was also a long ongoing saga about a faulty boiler and his endeavours to get it repaired.

Wiesenthal had various versions of the incidents that triggered his conviction that the leading executioners of the Holocaust must be tried in a court of law where their crimes could be exposed and used as a warning to future generations. The Nuremberg trials had only done part of the work. He never for a moment questioned his mission to expose the perpetrators. First and foremost, that meant finding Adolf Eichmann, principal author of the Final Solution.

At the beginning I did not realise the extent of the bitter controversy that swirled around his claim to have located Eichmann in Argentina five years before Israel's Mossad became convinced he was there and organised his capture to bring him to trial in Israel. Whether or not Wiesenthal romanticised aspects of his role in the Eichmann story, there was ample evidence that he was fixated on the search for Eichmann well before others. Wiesenthal's search for Eichmann became the foundation of his fame. He was convinced that Eichmann had survived and set out to find him from the moment he settled in Vienna. He mistakenly located Eichmann in Linz in Austria, but correctly located Eichmann's wife in Altaussee, a village in Austria's Salzkammergut, which has become one of my favourite holiday haunts. I have skirted around Veronica Eichmann's former abode. Wiesenthal claimed that he was able to thwart her attempt in 1947 to secure a judicial declaration of her husband's death. He always asserted that had she succeeded, it would almost certainly have ended the hunt for Eichmann. Some of his detractors insisted that story was an invention.

It was an interesting challenge to piece together Simon Wiesenthal's story from his birth in Buczacz to his life in Vienna at the age of 84, when I first met him. His own account was obviously the key. But naturally I talked to many people who had crossed his life, including some who questioned certain aspects of the story he told. Wiesenthal always aroused strong feelings in those who knew him or even only knew of him. They divided roughly into admirers or detractors. I came across some people who used his fame to further projects of their own, and I spoke with academics who tried to assess the significance of Wiesenthal's actions. All had very decided views about him.

The admiration society was led by two eminent figures, Germany's ex-President Richard von Weizsäcker and Chancellor Helmut Kohl. Both gave me generously of their time when I asked to speak with them about Wiesenthal, and both described him as a figure of outstanding importance in the post-war period. Von Weizsäcker, a notable intellectual who brought great distinction to the German Presidency, spoke of Wiesenthal as a kindred spirit. A study in contrasts, the two men had only met fleetingly. Wiesenthal was a little in awe of the German leader. There was no need. Weizsäcker told me that he had learned more about the Holocaust from the way Wiesenthal mined his own memories to wrestle with the past and to challenge established ethical concepts of guilt and forgiveness, than from academic studies about the nature of evil.

Chancellor Helmut Kohl's warm personal friendship with Simon Wiesenthal surprised me. One was a statesman preoccupied with German reunification and world affairs. The other had a tunnel mind focused on the Holocaust and a determination to bring the perpetrators to face justice in a court of law. In the process, Wiesenthal had defined a moral compass that attracted Kohl. The Chancellor told me that Wiesenthal enabled him to gain a deeper, better understanding of the Holocaust: 'The chemistry between us worked from the beginning.' There were numerous phone calls and occasional meetings, always out of the public gaze. The two men often met around Easter-time in some hideaway for a couple of days. It was by no means all serious talk. There was gossip, and there were anecdotes and laughter – and as both possessed healthy appetites, there was plenty of good food. Kohl told me that he saw his friend as 'a great man of passion and for justice. He is an historic figure.' In the United States, Wiesenthal was honoured with a Congressional Gold Medal and a reception at the White House.

In 1986, Wiesenthal was a contender for the Nobel Peace Prize. Elie Wiesel won it. But Wiesenthal was not just admired from a few heights of power. There was a large public in Europe and America who saw Wiesenthal as a Don Quixote, battling through life for his beliefs. His passion and his emotional nature had gifted him with excellent communication skills. With few resources, publicity was essential to support his mission. He had an open door for favourite media. Leading journalists in Europe and America sat at his feet, publicised his mission, and wrote about the Nazis he was hunting down. Frederick Forsyth described to me how he turned up one day with a rough outline for a new thriller. Before long, the two men were sitting together sketching out a plot involving the hunt for Eduard Roschmann, the 'Butcher of Riga', who was one of Wiesenthal's targets. This collaboration led to Forsyth's novel *The Odessa File* in which Wiesenthal figures. The subsequent film actually helped to track down Roschmann. A popular TV series about Wiesenthal's exploits, in which Ben Kingsley plays the Nazi hunter, gained him even greater recognition. Wiesenthal became a popular lecturer in America. His books, including the controversial account of his role in tracking down Adolf Eichmann, earned him still more fame – and in some quarters notoriety.

Rabbi Marvin Hier, an astute New Yorker, spotted an opportunity.

He would probably dispute this, but I class him among those who tried to exploit Simon Wiesenthal's fame, at least partly to promote projects of their own. Based in Los Angeles, Hier had a perfectly laudable plan to establish a Holocaust centre in this racially mixed city with a large number of Jews amongst its residents. Given Simon Wiesenthal's popularity in America, Hier reasoned – correctly – that fund-raising would be much easier if his project could be named 'Simon Wiesenthal Center'. So he took off to Vienna to negotiate what effectively was a licence of the Wiesenthal name. Wiesenthal was dubious, but knowing him, I suspect he was finally persuaded after a promise of a Hollywood dinner with Elizabeth Taylor and other well-known stars.

The Center has flourished and has established itself as a leading institution in the fight against anti-Semitism and for the defence of human rights. Its Museum of Tolerance is a remarkable institution dedicated to the education of future generations. But it also sits on the right wing of US politics and is intolerant of anyone who does not share its views. Rabbi Hier and his colleagues flattered and used Wiesenthal when it suited them and were dismissive of him when he did not fall in line with their views, and especially with their campaign against Kurt Waldheim as an alleged war criminal. Wiesenthal was always reluctant to speak critically of Hier. For my part, I was surprised, to put it mildly, by the Simon Wiesenthal Center's lack of generosity to their patron. Hier had seen for himself that Wiesenthal was reduced to a shoe-string operation. Yet the sums Wiesenthal received from Los Angeles amounted to little more than his telephone bills.

Coming to know Simon Wiesenthal also meant coming to recognise his fault-lines. I was determined to avoid judgement until I was ready to finish the biography. But I was taken aback by the fierce animosity he attracted in several influential quarters. 'You have to concede Wiesenthal is a charlatan,' I was told when I came to New York to meet senior executives of the World Jewish Congress. When I protested that I was still researching and keeping an open mind, doors were firmly closed to me. Wiesenthal and the World Jewish Congress had clashed on many issues, most notably over the hunt for

Eichmann and the allegations of war crimes against Kurt Waldheim. Early in the search for Eichmann, the WJC's eminent leader, Nahum Goldman, ignored Wiesenthal's claim to have some evidence of the Nazi criminal's whereabouts. But beneath it all there was a clash of cultures. The WJC, with its high-profile leadership, its bureaucracy and international outreach, would never have been able to make common cause with a determined loner like Simon Wiesenthal. But did that justify their efforts to undermine his reputation? I do not think so.

The enemies list grew when I discovered how certain Israelis involved in Eichmann's capture were forensically trying to destroy Wiesenthal's reputation. With the help of Eric Silver, my former *Guardian* colleague who was now living in Israel, I had access to an unpublished version of Eichmann's eventual capture, written by the head of the Mossad mission. One of the account's aims was to destroy Wiesenthal's credibility to smithereens.

Another unpleasant surprise was to discover the rivalry between the handful of Nazi hunters. Cooperation between them was not part of their vocabulary. Wiesenthal and Beate Klarsfeld competed against each other in the search for Josef Mengele and were sharply critical of each other's methods. Wiesenthal and Tuviah Friedmann clashed over their respective roles in tracking Eichmann. Efraim Zuroff wrote with derision about Wiesenthal and the other 'private' Nazi hunters, claiming they muddied the waters in needless competition to hunt down the Nazi perpetrators.

But among Wiesenthal's detractors none was as vicious, or wounded Wiesenthal as much, as the Austrian Chancellor Bruno Kreisky and his allegation that Wiesenthal had been a Nazi agent during the war. The trigger had been Kreisky's flirtation in 1975 with Friedrich Peter, leader of Austria's far-right FPO party, as a potential coalition partner. Wiesenthal produced an explosive dossier to prove that Peter had been a member of an extermination unit of the SS. Kreisky countered with a declaration that he had proof of Wiesenthal's collaboration with the Gestapo. It was 'a matter of justice that someone like him [Wiesenthal] is not allowed to assume moral authority in such a matter – Peter's past history – because he has none'.

Kreisky based his allegations on the discredited anti-Wiesenthal campaign in Communist Poland and the GDR. But Kreisky was unstoppable. When he developed a blind spot for someone, reason became an alien concept. Wiesenthal set out to sue the Chancellor for slander but eventually withdrew. That failed to silence Kreisky. Willy Brandt also tried to convince Kreisky that warfare against Wiesenthal was doing him no good. I remember a convivial evening with members of the Socialist International at Kreisky's favourite *Heuriger* (tavern), where Brandt was using his charms to talk some sense into his good friend Bruno. It again fell on deaf ears. In 1986, Wiesenthal sued again. This time it reached the courts. Kreisky, now in retirement, was given a heavy fine – symbolic only, as it did not actually have to be paid. He expressed some regrets but still did not withdraw his allegations against Wiesenthal. A few months later, Kreisky died. When Wiesenthal spoke about his experience with Kreisky, his eyes produced a fountain's play of tears.

I turned to academics, students of the Holocaust, to help me assess Wiesenthal's contribution to the studies and understanding of the Holocaust. Here too there were mixed views, sometimes very passionate. But after three years, as I came to the end phase of the book, I had to make up my own mind. I had spent a great deal of time with Wiesenthal and had grown to like him. I certainly respected him. But from the outset I had been determined to keep a certain distance. I wanted to preserve objectivity in judging Wiesenthal's achievements.

I had no hesitation in pointing to Wiesenthal's weaknesses or to discrepancies in the stories he told about his life. After all, memory plays tricks. Wiesenthal also had a vivid imagination. But I never doubted his integrity. I recognised him as a Jew who gave his all to create a memory bank of the Holocaust's ravages, in the conviction that this would act as a forewarning to future generations. His greatest achievement was to convince political leaders and public opinion alike to confront the facts of the Holocaust as a way of cleansing the moral fabric of our societies. In practical terms, I was also optimistic that Wiesenthal's legacy would help to strengthen the International Court of Justice. Such optimism was misplaced. I was wrong. But of course, Donald Trump was not yet on the scene.

Overall, I concluded that Wiesenthal, for all his shortcomings, had been an exemplar and deserved to be seen not just as a Jewish hero, but as a hero of our epoch.

I would not have expected Simon Wiesenthal to be a bridge to a prince of the Church who became my personal hero and caring friend. Yet without Wiesenthal I would not have found myself in a relaxing, comfortably furnished living room with Cardinal Franz Koenig, former Archbishop of Vienna, cheerfully exclaiming: 'You have to choose between two women.' The choice was between his secretary and me. The choice was between a collection of the Cardinal's theological writings edited by his secretary, or a book of autobiographical reminiscences, with a role for me to assist the Cardinal with research and writing. The secretary won this contest. The more worldly memoir was left unwritten. But even if I lost a somewhat unusual opportunity for a joint venture with a prince of the Church, I had the good fortune of coming to know this remarkable prelate.

Though he is surely unaware of it, I owed that meeting with Cardinal Koenig to the popular Mayor of Vienna, Michael Häupl. He hosted a big reception in the City Hall to mark the publication of the German translation of the Wiesenthal biography. Wiesenthal was the guest of honour. But Cardinal Koenig was among the many notables who also turned up. Wiesenthal was in his element, beaming happily, and fortunately for me, emphasising his satisfaction with the biography. I was introduced to the Cardinal. He congratulated me and we exchanged just a few words. That could have been the end of a brief acquaintance. Instead I received an invitation to tea at the convent where he was cared for by a group of nuns. A welcoming, elderly nun took me up the lift to the bright sixth-floor flat. An imposing presence in a plain black cassock, the 80-year-old Cardinal instantly disarmed me with a warm smile and kind words. From that day onwards, I visited the Cardinal on each occasion I was in Vienna. Our conversations ranged far and wide, from politics to philosophy. He had a singularly open, liberal mind with wide-ranging interests and friends well beyond the Church. It fascinated me.

So I readily agreed when George Weidenfeld dreamed up the idea of a Cardinal Koenig memoir and suggested that I should act as editorial aide. Cardinal Koenig is credited with a decisive role in the election of Pope John Paul II. George had long known the Cardinal and wrote to him that future generations would want to read 'the story of a towering figure and bridge-builder between religions, cultures, nations, individuals and again notably between Eastern and Western Europe'. Cardinal Koenig debated long and hard whether to go ahead. In the end, the pressure from his aides in Vienna's Church establishment must have been too strong. There would be no memoir.

Not long after Cardinal Koenig's death in March 2004, on a warm June day, a little procession was winding its way past a garden along a narrow path to the entrance of a small ground-floor flat in one of Vienna's suburbs. It was led by the British Ambassador, John Macgregor, and most importantly, followed by the Embassy's butler, Antonio, weighed down with bottles of champagne. They were on their way to celebrate Simon Wiesenthal's award of an honorary knighthood.

The decision to honour Wiesenthal had been announced three months earlier. British Honours lists are drawn up in mysterious backwaters. But in this case it had plainly been the work of the Ambassador and the Minister for Europe, Denis McShane. The award was in recognition of 'a lifetime of Service to Humanity'. The knighthood took its place with Poland's *Polonia Restituta* as an honour way above all the other awards that came Wiesenthal's way.

Wiesenthal was now 95 years old. In the last couple of months, his health had deteriorated and he had become too frail to leave his home. His wife had died. He received the Ambassador, his substantial figure folded into a heavy, red, plush armchair, and he remained sitting while John Macgregor pinned the medal on his lapel and handed over the citation. He was now a 'Knight Commander of the British Empire'. Had he been a British citizen, he would have become Sir Simon Wiesenthal. But to be an 'Honourable' Knight was more than enough to satisfy him. His words of thanks were inevitably laced with tears. But the champagne was sipped dry-eyed, undiluted. It was a profoundly poignant scene.

It was the last time I saw Wiesenthal. He died just over a year later. I offered the tapes of my conversations with him to the Simon Wiesenthal Center in Los Angeles. I had no response. I have given the tapes to the Holocaust section of the Imperial War Museum.

While I was still finishing the Wiesenthal biography, I had been offered a welcome diversion – or better put, a reversion – to the Cold War. Jeremy Isaacs, the great documentary film director of *The World at War*, was making a 24-part history of the Cold War. I was asked to write the script for the period between 1977 and 1981, when the delicate beginnings of détente went into troubling freeze. Unhelpful developments included martial law in Poland, the acceleration of the US–Soviet arms race and the Soviet invasion of Afghanistan. The events were familiar to me. Condensing a multi-faceted story into a few hundred words that had to be aligned with the available picture material was a novel test of my ability with words. The experience of working as part of a closely knit team was a welcome change from the solitude of book-writing. New bonds were forged. I loved it all. It was a happy interlude. Cate Haste, my producer had become a close friend whose loss in 2021 I continue to mourn.

Austrian officialdom labels Austrians living abroad as *Auslands Oesterreicher* (Austrians living abroad). I rank as a member of that tribe. Just conceivably, there were other minor matters – such as having just written a well-received Wiesenthal biography, and also having acquired some recognition in Austria as a journalist. But at any rate, in 1987, when I had barely had time to consider 'what next?', one of Austria's leading publishers suggested a book about Austria's post-war image in the outside world. I was tempted. It would extend my working life by at least two more years. It would give me more opportunities to test my relationship with Austria. It would only earn me a pittance and barely cover my expenses. But with any luck, a British publisher might be interested. In short – I said 'Yes.'

During the years spent with Simon Wiesenthal, my focus had

been primarily on Austria's pre-war lurch to right-wing extremism and the Nazis, and on Austrians as willing executioners of Hitler's orders. Now I had the opportunity to look at the wider picture of Austria's post-war behaviour as a small country geographically wedged between East and West. I would have to analyse how Austria had survived and eventually even thrived without being drawn into the Cold War. Crucially, it would allow me to search for answers to Austria's reluctance to recognise its war crimes and deal with anti-Semitism and restitution issues. Post-war Austria had developed into a stable democracy. So how come a far-right movement, the Freedom Party, was emerging as a major political force in Austria? I wanted to explore why Austrians had long insisted that their country had to be seen as Hitler's victim and not as a willing perpetrator. For decades Austrians had lived with a lie, and the outside world had remained indifferent until the mid 1980s, when Kurt Waldheim was elected Austria's President.

My answer to the conundrum was best summed up in the title of the English edition of my book, *Guilty Victim*. Austria had a claim to victimhood. But the scales were overwhelmingly on its guilt. Until Waldheim's election forced them to confront reality, the Australian public had only tiptoed around the challenge. The Austrian public had long preferred to remain in denial. Finally, it was the widespread outrage over Kurt Waldenhim's presidential election that forced the country – still only half-heartedly – to confront the true history of its role in the Nazi era. Characteristically, the title (not selected by me) of the German version of my book was far more neutral: *Und welche Rolle spielt Oesterreich?* (*What Role Does Austria Play?*).

Austria's claim to victimhood was not a self-invention. It originated with the 1943 Moscow Declaration by the wartime Allies – the Soviet Union, the US and Britain – which committed them to the re-establishment of a free and independent Austria. The document describes Hitler's annexation of Austria in 1938 as an 'occupation' and names Austria as Hitler's 'first victim'. But (a crucial 'but') the Moscow Declaration also said that Austria 'must be reminded that it carries responsibility for its participation in the war on Hitler's side'. The reminder remained a dead letter. The Allies made no attempt to follow up. The Austrians conveniently forgot the inconvenient part of the Moscow Declaration.

Austria was under four-power occupation for ten years. The 1955 State Treaty to establish Austria's independence again described Austria as Hitler's 'first victim', and, after a last-minute intervention from the Austrian Foreign Minister, Leopold Figl, the reference to Austria's responsibility for its war-time record was dropped from the Treaty text. The signatories – the US, the Soviet Union, the UK and France – raised no objections. Austria had secured international complaisance to live a lie. It is hardly surprising that the Austrians cultivated the perception of their country as Hitler's victim. It helped to graft a new identity onto their society. It also served to establish Austria's bona fides on the international scene – not least in 1972, when the UN Security Council elected Kurt Waldheim as the UN's Secretary-General, and even re-elected him for a second term.

In the book, I explored the impact of the Cold War on Austria's efforts to establish a credible, internationally respected identity in the post-war era. I divided the period into roughly three phases. The first phase was the ten-year four-power occupation when Austria served as a kind of incubus for the Cold War and the West competed with the Soviet Union for long-term influence in the strategically well-placed country. NATO membership was mooted but not considered realistic. The eventual solution, accepted by both sides of the East–West divide, was for Austria to declare itself a neutral state.

The second phase lasted 30 years, during which Austria established itself as a successful democracy with a flourishing economy and a sound welfare system. Though the country continued to have a plentiful number of titled families, most of them had lost their fortunes and influence, and the country had become a remarkably egalitarian society. For more than a decade, Bruno Kreisky, Chancellor and leader of the SPÖ, the Austrian Socialist Party, dominated the political scene and also pursued an activist, often controversial foreign policy. Vienna became a popular hub for diplomacy, for the UN and other international organisations, for business, for culture, for tourism – and for international plotting and espionage. Austria was persuaded that it could afford to be dismissive of pressure from Jewish organisations to focus on reparations for Austrian victims of the Holocaust. Austrians were persuaded that the country's international image was secure enough to allow them to minimise, even ignore, charges of anti-Semitism.

The third phase began in 1986 with the controversial election of Kurt Waldheim as President. He was the catalyst to force Austria to confront its *Identitätskrise* (identity crisis) This finally broke down the dam that had been built to dissemble Austria's invidious role in the Holocaust. Large segments of international public opinion had come to believe that Waldheim was guilty, at worst with personal responsibility for war crimes, and at best as an obedient officer who had turned a blind eye and complied with orders to commit atrocities in the Balkans. None of this had stopped Austrians from electing him to the highest office in the land. The Austrian Chancellor, Franz Vranitzki, knew he had to act in order for Austria's good name to be restored. Victimhood had to be minimised, if not shed altogether. Acknowledgement of guilt had to be publicly stated. Reparations had to be speeded up. History teaching had to be radically corrected.

The German version of my book was printed just before the election in 2000 that brought Jörg Haider's far-right neo-Nazi party into government as a minority partner. The English version, published a few months later, allowed me to update the book and to question whether Austria was, after all, capable of healing itself.

I never met Haider. But researching the book, I talked with all the leading politicians and many figures in Austria's world of culture, media and academia. Hugo Portisch, the pre-eminent commentator and historian of post-war Austria, gave me invaluable access to some of his confidential research material. My favourite priest, Cardinal Koenig, was always available for guidance. I gained a deep familiarity with the Austrian scene and enjoyed it. How could I reconcile it with all the evidence I had gathered about Austria's long, drawn-out failure to address its complicity with Nazi Germany, its anti-Semitism, and its long-delayed decision to address the problems of restitution and reparations? My cowardly answer can be summed up in one word: escapism.

Prince Charles might have been one form of escapism. But it did not work – and it was Jörg Haider's fault that I failed to bond with Prince Charles. An odd assertion? Yes. But true. Shortly after publication of the book on Austria, my German publisher, Rowohlt, proposed a book about the role of monarchy in the context of European integration and of globalisation. How would monarchies adapt to a changing concept of national sovereignty? Prince Charles would have to be a central figure in the book. I was intrigued by the concept.

I went to Buckingham Palace to consult with Robin Janvrin, then the Queen's Assistant Private Secretary. We already knew each other, and his advice was to discuss the project with Mark Bolland, Prince Charles's Private Secretary. So off I went to my second palace, St James's. I was not turned away. Prince Charles must have been intrigued. He would cooperate, subject to some crucial red lights: he could not be quoted. Nor could any views be attributed to him or the monarchy. And his name or views could not be used for publicity purposes. To my surprise, Rowohlt agreed to these stringent conditions, and a draft contract was sent to my agent Mike Shaw.

St James's Palace gave me the green light to talk with the Prince's Trust and some of Prince Charles's other charitable institutions. I received invitations to get a whiff of Royal duties by joining some of his public engagements. It was a useful lesson in social distancing. Then Mark Bolland came up with a great idea: Prince Charles was due to pay an official visit to Austria. With my Austrian background, it would make sense to join him on the flight to Vienna. We could have an informal discussion about my book project. He could judge whether my ideas interested him enough to encourage me to take them further. It would be a test. Could he trust me? Could we bond?

Unforeseen circumstances then became a factor. Austria held a general election in October 1989, just ahead of the Prince's scheduled trip. Jörg Haider won enough seats for his far-right Freedom Party to become the junior member of Austria's new coalition government. In protest, the EU slammed a sanctions regime against Austria. Prince

Charles had to cancel the visit to Austria. The bonding opportunity was lost. No alternative was proposed.

I was disappointed but not very surprised. In fact, I was quite relieved. A few weeks' experience in the outer reaches of the monarchy had convinced me that Prince Charles had surrounded himself with first-class brains and was involving himself in progressive projects with a special focus on young people. But the culture and the deference that surrounded the monarchy would have stifled my writing, and very likely stifled my free spirits.

There was all-round agreement to abandon the monarchy book project.

So what now? Once again George Weidenfeld came to the rescue – and this time the rescue lasted a couple of decades.

CHAPTER 15

LIFE WITH GEORGE

It is the year 2009. A September sun is setting over Lake Geneva. The skies are darkening and there is a glimmer of an emerging moon. An elegant crowd in evening attire is on a terrace, sipping champagne, busy chatting. A sudden burst of fireworks takes everyone by happy surprise. With the wonder of light and colour and patterns in the sky, for a short while, everyone reverts to childhood and its joys; including the 90-year-old whose birthday is being celebrated.

An architect-designed marquee is not an everyday party venue. The unique marquee, complete with a terrace and a superb view of Lac Leman and the Alps, was designed by the pre-eminent architect Norman Foster as a birthday present for one of his closest friends. It is in the grounds of the Fosters' Chateau Vincy above a small lakeside village not far from Geneva. Inside the marquee is an elongated, sculptured table wending its way across the space in the shape of a snake. It is covered with a specially woven seamless tablecloth. The fireworks over, 233 guests drawn from the worlds of the arts, of politics, of academia, publishing and the media, are now seated at the table ready to enjoy a feast concocted by a Michelin three-star chef. They have come from all corners of the globe. It is a jaw-dropping list of names. What they have in common is friendship with George Weidenfeld. It is the life – and ongoing life – of a renaissance man, a cosmopolitan citizen of the world, that is being celebrated. The short speeches are perceptive, humorous, admiring, loving. George responds, vigorous in mind, youthful in spirit and deeply moved by it all. He might be 90, but there is absolutely no intention to slow down. Retirement is a non-starter.

It certainly meant a great deal to me to share in this celebration and feel at home in George Weidenfeld's cosmopolitan circle that included several of my long-time friends, but also a whole cluster of new people who had come into my life thanks to working with George.

Almost exactly eight years had passed since I'd begun work with George. Those years had brought a new dimension and a new career to my life. George was intent on building bridges across national divides. I became part of the small group that worked with him to translate those ideas into projects that brought together a wide range of influential personalities to address major issues – political, economic, strategic, cultural – confronting Western society. The work was stimulating, energising and absorbing. I felt rejuvenated. For the next seven years until a handful of hours before his death, George remained an integral part of my existence.

Austria created a strong bond between George and me. Crucially, though each of us had made our lives in Britain, there was always that niggling question mark over being wholly accepted. Was it because we were Jews, or was it simply that we were not British-born and almost by definition outsiders? At the same time, each of us was ambivalent about our relationship with Austria. Our backgrounds were not so dissimilar, though I had been too young in the 1930s to experience close-up the rise of the Nazis and the growing wave of anti-Semitism. Each of us had come to Britain alone as refugees; neither of us had lost our parents in the Holocaust; and neither of us viewed Austria and its people as so deeply ridden with guilt and anti-Semitism that reconciliation was impossible. Each of us enjoyed spending time in Austria. Each of us had good non-Jewish Austrian friends. We both loved opera, and though we were never there at the same time, we were both regulars at the annual Salzburg Festival.

When my work with George began in 2001, my main task was to help with the organisation of his Club of Three conferences that brought together senior opinion-makers from Britain, France and

Germany to search for improved cooperation on issues of vital interest to Europe.

The workload with George built up rapidly. 9/11 had triggered a new idea. The remit of the Club of Three should be widened. The proposal was for a second troika, this one composed of the Club of Three countries joined with the US and Russia to address the major strategic obstacles to closer cooperation between them and to consider wider global issues. We hoped such a troika would evolve into a continuing process for Americans, Europeans and Russians to identify common problems and challenges, and become 'a network for confidence-building and friendship'.

The initiative became known as *Ameurus* – America, Europe, Russia. Michael Maclay, already in charge of the Club of Three, now also took on responsibility for *Ameurus*. The more detailed preparatory work and the written summaries of the discussions were delegated to the *Ameurus* Co-ordinator. That person happened to be me. When I look back on those early days of *Ameurus*, I marvel at our achievements. There was some mysterious alchemy at work. Somehow we managed to organise four high-level meetings within one year, 2003, spread between the US, the UK, Russia and Germany. The focus of the discussions was on strategic, political and economic issues, on security and conflict management. We were engaged in a 'search for a new international order'. We maintained that pace during the following three years.

To my delight, in its second year *Ameurus* widened its horizons and reached out into the arts with the first of a series of annual conferences. They became my *Ameurus* highlight. I was responsible for much of the organisation and certainly gained a much deeper understanding of the cultural, political and financial challenges faced by the arts, even in the pre-Covid age. Our arts conferences brought together a virtual who's who of museum directors and gallery owners, collectors, arts administrators and Ministers of Culture. We roamed across a wide landscape of issues, including the financing of the arts, restitution of art seized by the Nazis, the role of the great public museums and cultural identity. They also opened a pathway to a series of projects with China that allowed me to make several memorable visits to the country and glean a modicum of understanding of Chinese culture and contemporary politics.

The involvement with China had come about thanks to our *Ameurus* arts conference in 2008. As an experiment we invited two members of China's arts establishment to join as observers. They were so impressed that they invited us to stage the next arts conference in Beijing. By then Weidenfeld's small team had acquired formal status as the Institute for Strategic Dialogue (ISD) with George at its head and Sasha Havlicek as its dynamic CEO. Michael Maclay remained as Senior Adviser, and I had acquired a new title: 'Director of Arts and Culture Programmes'.

George was initially half-hearted about the proposal. China was one destination too far away for him to contemplate. But I was enthusiastic about a return to China after that long-ago trip in my Aga Khan age. ISD decided to take up the invitation. We had little difficulty in recruiting an eminent group of Western and Russian participants. I was invited to Beijing half-way through the preparatory period to meet our Chinese partners and work out the logistics of our conference. I began to fathom the difficulties of reaching mutual understanding. But on this occasion, as a friendship gesture, I was offered a three-day visit to Shanghai. I stayed in the French Concession in a hotel that once served as a guest-house for the Chinese Communist Party leadership. Outside my room was a plaque saying: 'Mao Tse-tung'. Inside, the furnishings had been kept just as they were in Mao's days. I slept in what was said to be his bed. I used the huge bathtub which he had used. I made notes sitting at his desk. Unforgivably, I took no photos.

Our conference, early in October, had a curious preface. On the eve of the meeting, our sponsor hosted the conference dinner in the ballroom of his sprawling headquarters. Most of our *Ameurus* contingent had arrived that day and were jet-lagged. A small orchestra greeted us by playing a Mozart serenade. There was an elaborate menu of French cuisine. Mouth-watering wines were advertised. The first course of foie gras and related delicacies was served. And then? A pause for entertainment. Suddenly, our sponsor joined by a musician embarked on a series of karaoke songs. It went on and on. There was no sign of the waiters and no sign of food or drink. When the performance finally ended a good hour later, the Chinese guests started to leave. The visitors were hungry but no food arrived. Our sponsor was seen to depart. The rest of us followed. Next day we learned that the waiters had been hired only for a specific number of hours. The host's extended stage event had not been built into the timetable. So they simply left when the time was up. An example of Communist rebellion?

The arts conference was headlined: 'The Arts in the Global Society: Museums and Collectors in a Turbulent World – A Dialogue between East and West'. It was a rousing success. In fact, the Chinese authorities were so impressed that they came up with an totally unexpected proposal.

ISD was approached by the Beijing Bureau of Culture to help organise an annual Prize in Chinese Contemporary Art. It would be modelled on the Tate Gallery's Turner Prize. I was bitten by the China bug and persuaded ISD to take up the challenge. It was a bad decision.

The project came to grief, but only after we had worked on it for over a year and the Chinese side had defaulted on ISD's fee. It was a tough lesson on the uncertainties of working with the Chinese.

But it was not the end of ISD's or my involvement with China. The most satisfying period lay ahead. In November 2010, the Club of Three held its annual plenary in Berlin with 'Europe and China' as its main theme. I scored a brilliant dividend from that meeting. It was decided that ISD would set up an annual Europe–China Media Exchange – (ECME). Over the next five years. I had a key role in handling the European end of this project.

The concept was ambitious. In alternate years, ISD had to recruit a dozen European journalists to spend a week in a Chinese 'second tier' city to work with Chinese journalists and to collect material for feature articles or broadcasts. In the other year, a small group of Chinese journalists came to London to meet with leading news organisations and then go on to Berlin for a round-table discussion with European journalists.

Running ECME was work-intensive. I worked on it almost full-time. It was challenging and I loved the experience. We brought Chinese journalists to Europe on three 'Inside Europe' trips and there were two exchange trips to China.

Chengdu in 2011 was my initiation into the project. Our group consisted of a dozen European journalists, including my former *Guardian* colleagues Paul Webster and Linda Christmas, as well as the *Economist's* Anne McElvoy. Together with the Chinese media participants, we went to factories and schools and housing projects. We met start-up young capitalists and older ones who had already made it to high fortunes. We went back to Europe foolishly optimistic that a meaningful media bridge could be established.

Two years later, in 2013, ECME made a second expedition to China. This time we were in Nanjing. Xi Jinping's mega anti-corruption drive was already in full swing. We had brought some gifts for our Chinese contacts and had a handsome book about London for the Mayor of Nanjing. It could not be delivered. He was arrested on corruption charges on the day of our arrival. Nanjing's Communist Party Chief, Yang Weize, decided to give a press conference for our group. Yes, there was corruption, he conceded. But 'absolutely it must and will be stamped out. It is against the law, and those who violate it must be punished.' Nanjing's Mayor fell into that category. End of story? Not quite: a few months later, Mr Yang himself was arrested on corruption charges.

Nanjing made an impact on me that no other experience in China could have. Our programme included a visit to the Memorial Museum of the Nanjing 1937 massacres perpetrated by the Japanese. The tomb-like, mostly darkened underground museum, with its photographs and videos of the mindless massacre of hundreds of thousands of Chinese, left me as numb as I was when I visited Auschwitz.

Nanjing turned out to be the last of our ECME excursions to China, and probably also the last of my visits to the country. By 2015, we found ourselves at a dead end. Repeated attempts to find a host city failed. The Chinese journalists we had nurtured disappeared from our radar. ECME, one of my favourite projects, was closed down.

Throughout the ECME years, I managed to keep my hand in with the Club of Three and other ISD activities. But increasingly I was also spending more time with George to discuss his unending ideas for bridge-building. My visits to his flat on London's Embankment became more and more frequent. He enjoyed reminiscing. But he remained full of ideas for a future which he knew he would not live to see.

George died peacefully late in January 2016. He had been busy working at home and had only been in London's Lister Hospital for a week. I had just returned from a holiday in Thailand and dashed to the hospital. His wife Annabelle, his daughter Laura, his granddaughter Clara and one of the grandsons were all there. George was sleeping and we chatted quietly. When George woke, he asked for ice cream. He only spoke a little. But when he noticed me, he suddenly reverted to his mother tongue murmuring in German about Vienna. It was a farewell. He died later that evening. I was told that almost to the end his publishing antennae remained live: he suggested that a book should be commissioned about the Lister Hospital, its history and its excellence . . .

CHAPTER 16

HAS THE JOURNEY BEEN
WORTHWHILE?

1939: a *Kindertransport* refugee designated as an 'Enemy Alien'. 2000: Commander of the British Empire. 2018: first an Honorary Doctorate from Sussex University and then the accolade of a new identity as a BBC podcast destined to remain for all eternity on a distant desert island. These are markers in a colourful life and a long career that offered a role model for women in journalism. It has been quite a journey.

But look below the surface of success. Describing my life, how far should I undress myself? How deeply can I expose my mindset and my experiences? How open should I be, can I be? How far am I capable of confronting myself with me? Having used this memoir to tackle some of these challenges, do I know myself any better now? Has it been a catharsis? Answer: yes, and a partial no. Yes, I have gained a better perspective on the big events and influences in my life. I have a clearer understanding of my contribution to the advance of women in the media. My journalism was done in the pre-#MeToo era. But I have faced up to my regrettable failure to involve myself directly in organised campaigning for equal opportunity. I have been able to remind myself of the opportunities I have had to meet and find friendship among an amazing cast of significant men and women. I have reconstructed in my mind so much of the travel I have always enjoyed.

Here comes the partial no: with so much positive in the memory bank, the fundamentals, the root causes of my insecurities have not been banished. When I first outlined this book, I suggested my entire life had been punctuated by insecurities from which no amount of success or achievement had helped me to escape. I had been caged within invisible walls.

Now that I have re-lived my progression from birth in Austria to lockdown in Covid-19 London, I see more clearly that this has also been about escapism by way of compensating for my inability to break down those invisible barriers to freedom from insecurity. Escapism has been my way of dealing with unresolved questions of exile and identity, with vulnerability and self-doubt. Much of the time my escapism has taken the form of a drive for independence and self-sufficiency, a curiosity about world affairs and a passion for hard work, and a drive for self-sufficiency and independence. A love of music and enjoyment of travel have almost always helped to lift my spirits. I have no siblings and only a couple of distant cousins. I have a loving godson and am supremely fortunate to have close friends. Friendship has given me courage and saved me from loneliness.

Much of this book has been written during a period when the 'normality' of the social order and the lifestyle I had always known was transformed by the pandemic. But I began this work in the 'old' world in the spring of 2019. I had to clear a satisfyingly busy diary to concentrate on the memoir, but I still made time for a short trip to see friends in New York, and to spend part of August in the Dordogne with my ever-hospitable friend Pauline Neville-Jones, and the remainder in Austria, taking in the Salzburg Festival and feasting on opera, concerts and too much good Austrian cooking. On 11 November, Armistice Day, the writing and the gallivanting came to an abrupt halt. Arriving for dinner at a friend's house, I lost my balance, falling backwards down a steep street-to-basement staircase and managing to break a few ribs, my pelvis – and my neck. For two or three days, I hovered between life and death. During my more lucid moments, I was fixated on this memoir. I absolutely wanted to finish it. So I had to survive – but only if I survived whole in mind and body. If I risked becoming damaged goods, I begged to be allowed to go.

I was saved by a great surgeon who successfully operated on my fractured neck. It took almost four weeks in hospital and three further weeks in a rehab learning to be steady again on my own two feet. During that long period, there were two factors that helped me to regain strength and my spirits: there was the steady flow of caring friends who kept in constant touch and came to see me again and again; and there was my impatience to return to the book project.

My powers of concentration took time to return. But gradually I tried to sort out the highlights and low points of my life and my relationships and tried to grapple with my identity problems. I finally returned home on New Year's Day 2020. After being institutionalised for such a long period, suddenly to be home alone was discomforting and felt – oh yes, my favourite word – insecure. My escapism mechanism was put into overdrive and soon helped to restore me. Within a month, I made myself busy again with fund-raising for the Sussex University Weidenfeld Institute of Jewish Studies and was able to go to the Holocaust Day events at Sussex University. My social life was beginning to look good again. Friends who knew about this book project were cautiously asking when I would resume writing. The answer was easy. I had resumed. I was working hard, recovering long-forgotten memories and dipping deeply into my past. My self-confidence was restored. I was back to making travel plans for the months ahead. It was an interlude that lasted a bare two months before the pandemic struck.

The government's delay in ordering lockdown allowed the Jewish Book Week to go ahead early in March. I chaired one of the discussions. It was about two books that had exposed Switzerland's infamous support for Hitler, the Nazis and their stolen gold. There were large crowds milling around Kings Place. There were no facemasks, no sanitisers, no hand-washing, no visible precautions and very likely there was a mass of invisible coronavirus. It was my last outing in a large, non-socially distanced crowd of people.

Lockdown brought me isolation, discovery of helpful neighbours and Zoom. But it also offered me uninterrupted time to write. While others double- and triple-cleaned their homes, sorted out and tidied their belongings, learned to make bread and searched for artisan flour, I was hunched over my computer – unkind to my back and the healing screws in my neck – and was writing. Daily walks around the roadscapes of Primrose Hill and Belsize Park fuelled my thinking about the work in progress and the structuring of each chapter. The walks did wonders when I hit black spots or was suffering from a writing block. Computer access to the *Guardian* archive was invaluable. I could call up any of the many thousands of articles I had written for the paper and bring back to life experiences I only dimly remembered. It was a tremendous morale-booster to rediscover the enormous range of subjects I had tackled, the travelling I had done, the people I had interviewed, the friends I had made. I kept on asking myself how I could have done all that and still had a social life and holidays – but I did. I understood much better how my form of escapism – my work ethic – had kept the demons at bay for much of the time.

The intense work commitment continued in the aftermath of the *Guardian* career – two published books and a private family memoir of my friend Alena Lourie were written in the space of four years. There was no slowing down during the Weidenfeld years of work that followed. It was tougher – not because of any loss of energy, but because I had lost Evi Wohlgemuth, my closest friend, the sounding board for my thoughts and actions; also my Scrabble partner, a game that absorbed us both. Losing her to cancer was the bitterest of blows. Our backgrounds were very similar. She too was Austrian by birth. She too had come to Britain as a refugee and her parents had been able to emigrate. Our adult lives diverged. Evi married a German refugee and had a son. She had aunts and uncles, nieces and cousins scattered around the world. As part of a close-knit extended family, she knew the meaning of stability and had far fewer problems in dealing with identity issues. She was foremost European, partly American (where she lived with her parents as a teenager and went to university), British because it was in the UK where she and her husband made their life, Austrian because it was her homeland. Like me, she was not a practising Jew. Being a Jew was simply an open and welcome fact of life.

Evi was one of the friends who came with me to Buckingham Palace on a sunny day in 2000 when I received my CBE. The investiture is such a unique British ceremony, and during those moments when I made my prescribed, though clumsy, curtsey to Prince Charles – he replaced the Queen that day – my British identity felt very secure. After all, I was now part of a British group of men and women who had been recognised for their contribution to British society. But there was further symbolism to that day: the German Ambassador, Hans von Ploetz, and his wife, hosted a celebration lunch at his Residence. That lunch conferred a European dimension to my CBE. The British and the European identity complemented each other. Perhaps my self-doubt could take a pause.

Now, I feel that those events at the turn of the century seem like another age. At the time, though the UK had its entrenched opponents of EU membership, Brexit had not yet decisively reared its ugly head. For me, it was all change on the day that David Cameron called the referendum on the European Union. I am not writing that now with hindsight: I really had an immediate sense of foreboding that the referendum campaign would go badly for the Europe faithful, for the likes of me who believed that for Britain to leave the EU was self-destructive. The Remain campaign tried to speak to reason and economic interest, but never to the heart; it never really addressed the issue of European identity, or of Britain's cultural and not merely economic interdependence with continental Europe. The Leave campaign was preaching a mix of nationalism, patriotism and populism that worried me to the core. Johnson's grotesque bus and all his shenanigans saddened as well as angered me, most of all because I could see that people responded to his anti-Europe message and not just to his clowning. No amount of polling convinced me that the Remainers could end up winning the referendum.

Sadly, my gut feeling turned out to be right. David Cameron bowed out. The Brexiteers moved in. The new constellation triggered my alienation. I found it increasingly difficult to identify with a nation that consented to divorce itself from Europe and allowed itself to believe in a concept of sovereignty and independence that was out of step with 21st-century reality. Apparently British singularity would suffice to turn the country into a global power. Patriotism on an edifice of illusion. The pandemic and lockdown further deepened my sense of alienation. The Johnson–Gove–Cummings team brought a steely, doctrinaire determination to complete Brexit, irrespective of damage. The government's decision to make the definitive break with Brussels at the end of 2020 in the midst of the pandemic and profound economic crisis was bad enough. But for the bulk of British people to accept that without protest, and indeed to welcome the prospect of this new, 'independent, sovereign state', seemed even worse. I cannot identify with this mindset.

Lockdown provided the opportunity to reflect ever more deeply about my bundle of identities, my self-worth and my self-doubts. If self-distancing has become the signature tune of lockdown, self-distancing from Britishness has become my personal heartache. The net result? I no longer know where I really belong. My bundle of identities no longer has tangible priorities. Yes, I realise that identities can enrich each other and help one to understand each identity more clearly. And yet, if I question my British identity, can I give my Austrian identity pride of place? Not really: there will always be reservations about Austria's actions during the Nazi era. The European identity is foremost a cultural concept. The Jewish identity sits in the background but does not give me the anchor that my British identity provided for many decades. Where does this leave me with my insecurities? They have not gone away. I am still in my invisible cage. But that cage is now floating in a world undergoing profound change. I have no way of knowing what will happen to that cage, or the person within, in the post-pandemic world.

Even with all the barriers of the imagination and the uncertainties ahead, the scanning of my life has humbled me to recognise how much I have to celebrate. It is not the life I yearned for. And yet for all the stress and strain, the unhappinesses and the losses, I do know that great good luck has been on my side. There is excellent cause for thankfulness – even for celebration!

INDEX